The Life and Times of Congressman John Quincy Adams

The Life and Times of Congressman John Quincy Adams

LEONARD L. RICHARDS

New York   Oxford
OXFORD UNIVERSITY PRESS
1986

Oxford University Press

Oxford   New York   Toronto
Delhi   Bombay   Calcutta   Madras   Karachi
Petaling Jaya   Singapore   Hong Kong   Tokyo
Nairobi   Dar es Salaam   Cape Town
Melbourne   Auckland

and associated companies in
Beirut   Berlin   Ibadan   Nicosia

Published by Oxford University Press, Inc.,
200 Madison Avenue, New York, New York 10016

Oxford is the registered trademark of Oxford University Press

Library of Congress Cataloging-in-Publication Data

Richards, Leonard L.
The life and times of Congressman John Quincy Adams.

Includes index.
1. Adams, John Quincy, 1767–1848. 2. Presidents—
United States—Biography. 3. Legislators—United States—
Biography. I. Title.
E377.R53   1986   973.5'5'0924 [B]   85-30968
ISBN 0-19-504026-0

Printing (last digit): 9 8 7 6 5 4 3 2 1

Printed in the United States of America

For
Dan, Katie, Heather, and Matt

Preface

This is not a standard biography. It covers only the last years of John Quincy Adams's life, and it is by no means a complete exposition of those years. Instead of telling the story of his congressional career in all its detail, I have concentrated on certain controversial questions, selecting the data and arranging the narrative accordingly. Why, for example, did Adams run for Congress in the first place? Why was he at odds with both the Boston elite and the southern elite? Was he really as unique as his family claimed? Or was he a typical Antimason, a typical Whig, a typical New Englander in tune with his district? How did his actions and beliefs differ from those of others?

Throughout, I have tried to put Adams in historical context. He has often been portrayed as a lone eagle flying slightly off course, both by biographers who have hailed him as the most eloquent, the most honorable, and the bravest man in Congress, and by critics who have dismissed him as self-righteous troublemaker and one of the nastiest politicians of his day. Yet by himself Adams would have had little impact on the world about him. No matter how eloquent and honorable he was, or how contentious and nasty, he was still dependent on the support of a majority of his constituents and many of his fellow Congressmen, on the thousands of ordinary men and women who rallied to his cause or sought his help, and even on erstwhile enemies who seemingly had a talent for saying the wrong thing at the wrong time.

One of my chief concerns, therefore, has been to specify how many allies and opponents he had, who they were, what motivated them, and how they encouraged or limited his actions and beliefs. In doing so, I drew heavily on the research of others. I also spent many hours analyzing votes in Congress and scrutinizing election returns, studying various pressure groups in his district and state, playing one variable off against another and looking for patterns, compiling all sorts of lists and tables, assembling some worthwhile data as well as an embarrassing amount of useless information, trying to understand the world in which Adams lived and worked. The statistics have often crept into the narrative, but I hope not obstrusively.

There are bound to be complaints about the selection of illustrative material, the omission of some incidents in Adams's experience and the lengthy discussion of others. Much more could be said about Adams the family man, Adams the money-manager, Adams the legislator, Adams the politician. The curious reader can find further details in such excellent books as Samuel Flagg Bemis's two-volume biography of Adams and Paul Nagel's history of the family and its problems. But the reader should realize that despite the thousands of words written by Adams and about him, no one has discovered the formula that will fully explain his life. He remains in many ways an enigma.

I had help in writing this book. I owe a very large debt to many archivists and librarians, especially those at the University of Massachusetts, who repeatedly pointed me in the right direction. I am also in debt to my colleagues at the University of Massachusetts, particularly to Hugh Bell for critiquing the entire manuscript and Bruce Laurie for prompting me to revise the second chapter. Portions of several other chapters, which appeared earlier in a different form, benefited from the sound advice of Lewis Perry and Michael Fellman. Special thanks are also due to my daughter Heather, who checked the footnotes, and to Sheldon Meyer and Melissa Spielman of Oxford University Press, who made numerous suggestions for improving the manuscript and saved me from several careless errors. I alone, of course, am responsible for any errors that remain.

Leonard L. Richards

Amherst, Massachusetts
March 1986

Contents

The Life and Times
of Congressman
John Quincy Adams

CHAPTER I

The Road to Seat No. 203

John Quincy Adams was unique. Most ex-Presidents slip into oblivion after leaving the White House. Adams, after a short retirement, ran for Congress and became the Representative of the Plymouth district of Massachusetts. Arriving early and taking Seat No. 203, he was sworn in on December 5, 1831. He served in the House for the next seventeen years, until his death in 1848.[1]

Adams was sixty-four when he began his freshman year in the House of Representatives. He was a small man, about five foot seven, with a slight pot belly, a round face, and a bald head surrounded by a crown of white hair and white sideburns. His eyes bothered him: they were always red and watery, but he went without glasses and would do so the remainder of his life. He was also bothered at times by a nagging cough, and twinges of rheumatism and lumbago. Yet despite these ailments he had the stamina of many men half his age. Historians are fond of telling the story of how Adams as President skinny-dipped in the Potomac. What they often neglect to point out is that the old man swam against the tide for over ninety minutes at a stretch. In retirement at Quincy, long swims fatigued him, but he still swam regularly one-half mile, down and back between Daniel Greenleaf's upper and lower wharves. His time was sixteen minutes.[2]

Adams, as one Congressman noted, probably had more experience "than the rest of us combined." His career began in 1781, when as a fourteen-year-old he served as secretary to

Francis Dana, Minister to Russia. Since then he had been successively Minister to the Netherlands, Emissary to England, Minister to Prussia, State Senator, United States Senator, Minister to Russia, chairman of the American Peace Commission that negotiated the end of the War of 1812, Minister to England, Secretary of State, and President of the United States. He had witnessed first-hand the Battle of Bunker Hill, the fall of the Dutch Republic, and Napoleon's invasion of Russia. He had known all the heroes of the American Revolution—Washington, Jefferson, Franklin, Sam Adams, Lafayette. He had seen most of the leading figures of Europe—Napoleon, Czar Alexander, Talleyrand, Queen Louise of Prussia, Madame de Staël, Jerome Bonaparte, the Duke of Wellington.

Because of this long service, his seventeen years in the House came to be known as his "second career." Re-elected eight times, he was first regarded as an oddity in the House, then a fixture. Without question he was a vital force during his "second career," causing Southerners to denounce him as "the madman from Massachusetts," and Yankees to hail him as "the conscience of New England" and "Old Man Eloquent." But friends and foes alike generally agreed that eloquence was not his primary characteristic. They thought of him mainly as a tough, irascible, abrasive old man. One admirer, the philosopher Ralph Waldo Emerson, summed up the feelings of many when he pointed out that Adams was not really "a literary gentleman," as his public image would have it, but a "bruiser" who loved a good fight. "He is an old roué," said Emerson, "who cannot live on slops, but must have sulphuric acid in his tea."[3]

Why did the "old roué" agree to serve in the House in the first place? That is a difficult question to answer. Adams's own explanation was patriotic duty: the people of Plymouth had called him to serve. But even his family regarded that explanation as pure humbug.

And Adams, it should be noted, was a master at hiding his true feelings. His face seldom revealed a thing. Usually stern and solemn, it was a perfect poker face, which his youngest son Charles called the "Iron mask." Now and then, Charles thought he could see through it, and behind the frosty exterior he sometimes detected a hot-blooded and often impulsive man. But Charles had few illusions: he knew his father was a hard man to understand. "He is the only man, I ever saw, whose feelings I could not penetrate almost always, but I can study his countenance for ever and very seldom can I find any sure guide by which to move."[4] Adams's wife Louisa had even less understanding of him: she spent twenty-five years with her husband before she discovered his great passion for the theater.

Historians have often taken comfort in the notion that the "Iron mask" came off whenever Adams sat down with his diary. Adams wrote constantly—four, five, or six hours a day. He acquired the habit of diary keeping from his father, and he left a record of what he did each day, whom he talked with, where he went, what the weather was like, whom he hated, what he thought of various measures, what he read, and so on. The edited version of the diary, which totals twelve thick volumes, has long been a gold mine for historians studying the first half of the nineteenth century. The unedited version, which totals nineteen reels of microfilm, is even richer. The diary is so detailed and includes so many tidbits that after a while even the most cautious scholar starts to believe that "it is all here." But that is wishful thinking. In fact, while Adams revealed a great deal in his diary, he also left a lot unsaid. He had a gift of reticence as well as eloquence.

The diary in fact can be downright misleading. If you study the diary—the way it was kept, its careful order—you naturally conclude that Adams was a neat and meticulous man. Indeed, many historians have pictured him as such: it squares nicely with his reputation as "a stiff-backed New Englander," "a prim and proper Puritan," an "early riser" and the like. But then, if you accidentally pick up a reminiscence of his granddaughter, who learned to read in his study, this whole picture comes unraveled. The granddaughter remembered a kindly old man who lived in clutter, who swiped his wife's best Waterford dishes to keep the acorns and plum pits he was observing, whose desk was always a mess, who ate apples and pears as he worked and then threw them on the mantel or the floor to rot.

There are some matters, moreover, that Adams deliberately

kept out of his diary. He knew that it would become a historical record, that future historians would spend thousands of hours studying it, and there is little doubt that he screened out political secrets, particularly those that might injure his own reputation, as well as painful family problems. Everything, he once cautioned his oldest son George, "is not to be told, even of that which may most affect the peace and happiness of the Writer. There is much in the life of every individual which for his own comfort and that of others should be forgotten."[5]

In his diary Adams recorded very little about his decision to run for Congress. Still, it is clear that he had to give the matter much thought, simply because the rest of his family was vehemently opposed to it. His twenty-three-year-old son Charles nagged him constantly about accepting the nomination. It was a dishonor for a man of his stature to accept such a lowly job. It was a disservice to the family's good name. His time would be much better spent writing about his father, John Adams, the second President.[6]

Adams's wife Louisa was even more incensed. She made it clear to Adams and everyone else in the family that she hated the "Bull Bait" of Washington politics and that she had suffered more than her fair share of "mortification and agony." "There are some very silly plans going on here," she wrote her son John, "and God only knows in what they will end, but I fear not at all to my taste." Once it became clear that Adams would serve, she refused to go with him to Washington, even though she was a southern woman who hated New England winters and sponging Yankee in-laws. Her "nervous system" was "too shaken by long suffering" to plunge again "into the very focus of political machination." She could not stand to live again in "a house which will become the focus of intrigue" and bring back memories of "former sufferings."[7] Louisa was so adamant that Adams, at one point, had his son John put the family's two Washington houses up for sale. But in the end she relented, grudgingly, but only for financial reasons. "I have no right," she told her son, "to encumber the family with expenses."[8]

There is no evidence that Adams relented even for a moment to such pressure. On the contrary, he turned a deaf ear to his family's pleadings and set upon a course of action that brought him back into the "Bull Bait" of Washington politics. Returning as a freshman Congressman, he went knowing that he would "experience slights, mortifications—insults—loss of reputation."[9] Why did the defeated President take this path? There are no easy answers to this question, and the road to Seat No. 203 is tortuous. But perhaps his long-suffering wife Louisa, who spent more than fifty years trying to understand him, had the answer. She concluded that the life of a retired gentleman tending his garden, working on his father's papers, and following literary pursuits would kill him. He had an "insatiable passion" for political office and political strife, and could not "bring his mind to the calm of retirement . . . without risking a total extinction of life."[10]

Louisa Adams was not the only one who thought that her husband still lusted for political office. Many Massachusetts politicians had the same hunch, and it was they who took the first steps to coax him out of retirement. In fact, he was no sooner an ex-President than plans were hatched to elect him to the United States Senate. Nothing came of these plans, and hence he was still available when the incumbent Representative of the Plymouth district, Joseph Richardson, was forced to retire. Congressman Richardson was a Unitarian minister, and he was in trouble with his Hingham congregation. They wanted him out of Washington and back in the pulpit. They begrudged his serving in the present Congress, much less running for a third term, and thus he decided to quit politics. On September 6, 1830, the Boston *Courier* suggested that the Republicans in the district "would do well" to run Adams in Richardson's place. The ex-President dismissed the suggestion as an oblique attack, an attempt to embarrass him, since the editor, Joseph Tucker Buckingham, was one of his old Boston enemies.

But twelve days after the *Courier* notice, Richardson and John B. Davis, the editor of the Boston *Patriot*, paid Adams a visit at Quincy. They told him that the National Republicans could not maintain a firm hold on the district unless they ran Adams himself. Otherwise a dozen candidates would enter the contest, split the vote, and cause political chaos. Election would follow election until someone finally won the absolute majority re-

quired by Massachusetts law. Or, even worse, one of Adams's
old Federalist enemies might sneak in and grab the prize. Adams, according to his diary, assured his two visitors that he
thought it no disgrace for an ex-President to serve in Congress,
but he would not consent to be their candidate and would not
promise to serve if elected. He intimated that his decision depended on his health, whether there was anyone else in the
field who agreed with him on national politics, and the "degree
of opposition" to his election.

The local politicians concluded that he would serve "if hand-
somely chosen," and went to work to make certain that the
endorsement was overwhelming. Within weeks three conventions unanimously nominated Adams, and the district's two
newspapers enthusiastically supported his nomination. They
were lavish in their praise, making much of their need and the
nation's for a man of his talents in Washington, and of the
example he would be setting for the whole world. By accepting
a seat in the lower house, so the argument went, the former
President "would confer peculiar lustre upon his character
as an AMERICAN PATRIOT AND REPUBLICAN CITIZEN;
and afford a practical illustration of the beautiful theory of
our free institutions." The strategy worked, and within a
month Adams announced that he did not know "of any
sound principle" for withholding his service if the voters demanded it. On November 1, 1830, the voters elected him by
a landslide.[11]

Adams was overjoyed. Previously, he had never done well
in popular elections. He had been elected to the state senate
in April 1802. But later in the same year, when he ran for
Congress, he lost by forty-nine votes. In 1824, when he ran for
President in a four-man race, he placed second to Andrew
Jackson, but since none of the four candidates had a majority
of the electoral votes the election went to the House of Representatives, where Henry Clay gave his support to Adams and
made him President. Then, after four dismal years as a minority
President, he ran against Jackson again in 1828 and lost by
139,000 votes. Now he was a winner by a three-to-one majority.
"My election as President of the United States," he noted in
his diary, "was not half so gratifying to my inmost soul. No

election or appointment conferred upon me ever gave me so much pleasure."[12]

The margin of victory was not the only thing that was gratifying to his inmost soul. The chance to go back to Washington satisfied a number of needs, including the need for revenge, or something closely akin to it.

Never a good loser, Adams was particularly bitter about his defeat at the hands of Andrew Jackson in 1828. He was painfully aware that the only other President to be denied a second term was his father, who had lost to Thomas Jefferson in 1800. The four Virginia Presidents—Washington, Jefferson, Madison, and Monroe—had won re-election easily and retired gracefully after eight years in office. Why was it that the Virginia planters succeeded in getting re-elected, while the two Adamses failed miserably? Why did the ignominy of defeat befall only them?

Naturally, Adams refused to accept the notion that both he and his father were unworthy of a second term, or the obverse side of the coin which held that the four Virginians were unusually talented and deserving. Instead, he blamed the defeat and its stigma mainly on southern slavemasters and their northern sycophants. Behind the public issues, in his view, lay the hidden issue of slavery. The planters dominated the nation's politics, and they were determined to have only men like Jefferson and Jackson in the White House, men whose estates were exactly like their own, men who owned hundreds of slaves and therefore could be trusted completely on the slavery question.[13]

Until recently, twentieth-century historians paid little heed to the acerbic loser. For many years liberal historians gave Adams low marks as a political analyst, or simply dismissed his observations as those of a cantankerous old man, while they sang the praises of Jeffersonian and Jacksonian Democracy. The slavery question seldom entered the discussion, and the only serious debate for decades was over the origin of the democratic impulse.[14] Now, however, it is clear that Adams had a much better case than historians once acknowledged.[15] True, he was a cantankerous old man, sour and uncharitable, more than a bit paranoid, and he never gave the opposition their due. But he spotted a basic fact in the election returns that many historians long ignored, and his case can be documented with relative ease. Indeed, the fact that looms largest in both the election of 1800 and that of 1828 was the sectional appeal of the candidates, with New England backing the two Adamses, and the South championing Jefferson and Jackson.

The South, more than any other section, cost John Adams the election of 1800. The older Adams swept New England and carried the North as a whole by a margin of 56 electoral votes to 20. But in the South he won only 9 electoral votes to Jefferson's 53. Losing by only 8 electoral votes nationwide, the Adams forces blamed not only the South but also the "three-fifths clause" of the Constitution, which augmented the power of slave owners by counting three-fifths of their slaves in determining the number of House seats and electoral votes each state had. One New England Federalist bitterly lamented that the "federal ratio" gave the southern planter with fifty slaves as much power in national politics as thirty-one northern free men. Another calculated that "the black representation from the SLAVE COUNTRY amounted to 15: so that *the negroes turned the majority, and actually put in the President!*"[16]

John Quincy Adams, after his father's defeat, joined the Jeffersonian Republicans and ably served three Virginia Presidents. Still, like his father, he never had much luck in the South. He won the election of 1824 when the slaveholding states split their votes among three slaveowning candidates—Andrew Jackson, Henry Clay, and William Crawford—and the election ended up in the House of Representatives. Thereafter, Southerners of all stripes joined forces with the Jacksonians, partly because the favorite of many, William Crawford of Georgia, had suffered a debilitating stroke before the 1824 election, and Jackson was idolized throughout the South as an Indian fighter and the hero of the Battle of New Orleans. Also, Adams's policies helped push many Southerners, including the Old Republicans of Virginia, into the Jackson camp.

The Old Republicans, who claimed to be purer Jeffersonians than the great Jefferson himself, were strong in the worn-out tidewater country of eastern Virginia and North Carolina. As a rule they had no sympathy for Jackson. Jefferson himself regarded Jackson as "a dangerous man" and "most unfit" for the Presidency. But they were fully committed to old principles such as states' rights and strict construction of the Constitution, and they had canonized the Virginia and Kentucky resolutions of 1798 which clamored against national power. From the birth of the nation they had contributed more than their share of men and ideas, and they often thought of the national government as their private preserve. Their principles, however, had taken a beating after the War of 1812, with the establishment of the Second National Bank, the Supreme Court decisions of John Marshall, the full-scale debate over slavery during the Missouri crisis, and the defeat of William Crawford in 1824. Then came John Quincy Adams. They were stunned when they heard of his program. Not one of them, Martin Van Buren later commented, failed to see "the most latitudinarian doctrines," the most flagrant violations of the "Old Republican" faith.[17]

The Adams administration violated Old Republican dogma in virtually every way possible. In his first year in office, Adams laid out a program of national planning that took for its time the broadest view of constitutional powers. None of the specific proposals was new, and by modern standards the entire program seems rather commonplace—but at the time it made Henry Clay's "American System" of a protective tariff, national bank, and internal improvements seem modest by comparison. "The great object of the institution of civil government," said Adams, "is the improvement of the condition of those . . . over whom it is established." Accordingly, he called for the construction of a national system of roads and canals, a national university, a naval academy, exploration of western territories at federal expense, a uniform standard of weights and measures, a more effective patent law to encourage inventors, and an astronomical observatory. But what about the Constitution? Did *not* the Constitution limit severely the powers of the federal government? No, said Adams. There was more than enough constitutional authority to carry out his program. Indeed, if the federal government failed to exercise its power in behalf of the public good, that would be "treachery of the most sacred trust."[18]

Quickly Thomas Ritchie, the leading voice of the Old Republicans, sounded the alarm in the Richmond *Enquirer*. "Are we," he sneered, "really reading a state paper—or a school boy's thesis?"[19] Soon Jefferson issued dire warnings about the revival of Federalism, and John Randolph warned that if the government acquired "such vast powers" it would soon be meddling with slavery. Instead of backing off, the Adams administration pushed for the construction of a national system of roads and canals. The government bought nearly two million dollars of stock in four major canal-building companies, including one million dollars in the Chesapeake and Ohio Canal Company, and spent nearly as much on internal improvements in four years as had been spent in the previous twenty-four. In addition, the administration encouraged state projects through enticing land grants, including a large one to Illinois for building a canal from Lake Michigan to the Illinois River, and several to Ohio and Indiana for building both roads and canals. For the first time, to the absolute disgust of the Old Republicans, the country had a President who had no doubts about the government's constitutional right to build a vast system of roads and canals.

If the Old Republicans found the Adams program for canals and roads an abomination, they regarded his position on the protective tariff as even more heinous. The protective tariff was not only a manifestation of the nationalist policy they abhorred, and unconstitutional to boot, but it also cost them money. It simply meant higher prices for southern consumers. Why should iron masters in Pennsylvania and mill owners in Adams's New England get high tariffs to keep out English goods? Why should hemp growers in Clay's Kentucky get tariff protection against Russian competition? And why, thundered John Randolph of Virginia, should "poor men and slaveholders" bear the duty "on coarse woolens and linens, and blankets, upon salt and all the necessaries of life?"[20] It was not just unconstitutional, but highway robbery. On this issue the Old Republicans had the full support of cotton planters throughout the South, including many in the Southwest who were at odds with them over roads and canals. Yet to their horror, the drive for a high protective tariff, which the Jacksonians exploited to bring discredit to Adams, culminated in the tariff of 1828, the despised Tariff of Abominations.

Their hatred of the tariff in many respects coincided with the loathing that Jackson men elsewhere had toward the Adams administration's Indian policy. Men in Georgia, Alabama, and Mississippi were far more concerned with getting the millions of acres still belonging to the great tribes of the South than they were in getting a lower tariff. They hailed Jackson as their hero because he was a great Indian fighter, the man who slaughtered eight hundred Creeks at Horseshoe Bend and then quickly followed up his victory by driving harsh terms at the peace table, forcing the southern tribes to give up half of their ancestral lands, including one-fifth of the state of Georgia and three-fifths of Alabama. They were less doctrinaire than the Old Republicans, less concerned about the evils of an energetic national government, but they vehemently opposed the energy the Adams administration was showing in behalf of the Creek nation.

In 1802 Georgia had ceded its western land claims to the United States in return for the promise that the United States would extinguish Indian title to lands within Georgia. The federal government, in the eyes of most Georgians, had dallied for twenty-three years before getting the Creeks to sign the Treaty of Indian Springs in 1825. Then Adams, after learning that only eight of forty-six Creek towns had agreed to the treaty and that federal negotiators had acted more like Georgians than Washington representatives, ordered Georgia to stop the sale of Creek lands until a fairer treaty was drawn up. The Governor of Georgia threatened civil war if Adams dared halt the sale, and other Southerners howled about the dangerous interference of the federal government in the internal affairs of sovereign states. Like the tariff issue, the dispute was a crisis between states' rights and national power and caused Southerners of all stripes to wonder about the intentions of the Adams administration.[21]

What troubled Southerners most was Adams's position on slavery. He had voted with the South in 1804 against the Hillhouse amendments, which had been designed to curtail the growth of slavery in the Territory of Louisiana, and he had said very little publicly during the crisis over the admission of Missouri as a slave state in 1819. But the Missouri crisis had demonstrated vividly that there was a hotbed of resentment in the North against the South, especially against the South's domination of the national government and against the three-fifths rule which augmented the power of slave owners. Would Adams capitalize on this resentment? He was after all a minority President, and he desperately needed more northern support. Expecting the worst, many Old Republicans predicted he would raise a clamor against slavery and southern domination, thus pitting North against South, to hold onto his office. A few even pictured him inciting slave rebellions to put down southern power.[22]

Always watching and waiting, many southern Senators pounced on Adams when he proposed in late 1825 that the United States send two delegates to the Panama Congress of newly independent Latin American republics, a gesture that he hoped would signal hemispheric solidarity and block Spain's ambitions of regaining its lost colonies in the New World. Even limited participation, bellowed Senator Robert Hayne of South Carolina, was an outrage. The United States should never be involved in any conference that might discuss slavery or the African slave trade, and least of all the question of the independence of Haiti. As always the mere mention of Haiti, the black republic that was founded after a successful slave rebellion, sent chills of terror through the white South, raising the specter of millions of bloodthirsty slaves slaughtering their masters. The Jacksonians, looking for ways to discredit Adams, seized upon the proposed Panama mission and milked it for all it was worth, dragging out debate for three full months. Ultimately the Senate confirmed the two nominees, but the meeting at Panama never amounted to much, and the United States was never represented, as one delegate died enroute and the other was only halfway there when the meeting adjourned. Still, in the minds of many frightened Southerners, the Panama Mission remained an unwarranted and dangerous attempt to attack slavery indirectly.

Thus Adams's policies, in conjunction with the deep-seated fears of many Southerners, contributed to the growth of Jacksonian opposition in the South. Even Old Republicans who regarded Jackson as dangerous and unfit to be President rallied to his cause in 1828. So while Jackson got trounced in New England, Adams's home ground, and broke even in the North as a whole with 50.3 percent of the vote, he carried the slave states with a whopping 72.6 percent. In the deep South especially Adams had no chance at all on election day, making a respectable showing only in Louisiana, where sugar planters wanted tariff protection. Elsewhere Jackson won by a landslide, capturing Virginia with 69 percent of the vote; North Carolina with 73 percent; Alabama and Mississippi with over 80 percent; Tennessee with 95 percent; and Georgia, where Indian haters were after Adams's scalp, with virtually 100 percent. Furthermore, thanks to the mechanics of the electoral college and the three-fifths rule, Jackson's 200,000 southern supporters provided him with far more help, man for man, than some 400,000 Northerners: 105 electoral votes as compared with 73.

Hence Adams read the returns as a defeat for democracy and a victory for the South. In his judgment, the slave states had not only stood in the way of everything he held dear, but also ruined his political career. As he later put it: "When I came to the Presidency the principle of internal improvements was swelling the tide of public prosperity, till the Sable Genius of the South saw the signs of his own inevitable downfall in the unparalleled progress of the general welfare of the North, and fell to cursing the tariff, and internal improvement, and raised the standard of free trade, nullification, and state rights. I fell and with me fell . . . the system of internal improvements by means of national energies. The great object of my life therefore . . . has failed."[23]

Along with the bitterness of defeat, and the desire to get even, Adams was tormented by a far more painful memory when he made his decision to re-enter the "Bull Bait" of Washington politics—the apparent suicide of his oldest son, which occurred shortly after he vacated the White House in April 1829.

The Adams household was a tense one. John Quincy's marriage to Louisa Catherine Johnston, even though it endured for more than fifty years, was shaky from the start. Although no word of complaint is to be found in his diary, the writings of Louisa indicate that she was a very unhappy wife. She began two autobiographies, one when she was First Lady in 1825, and the other in 1840 when she was a Congressman's wife. The two accounts are so gloomy, so painful to read, that historians have often assumed that they were written during periods of exceptional stress. But even if there were brighter days in her life, the fact remains that by 1825 she had come to regret her marriage and sat down to write the history of its failure for the illumination of her three sons.[24]

She thought her life was ruined within two weeks of her marriage, when her father went bankrupt and blasted all hopes of a £5,000 dowry. She was convinced that Adams thought her family had tricked him into marrying a penniless daughter, and that he held it against her all their married life, even though he never said a word. She also brooded about the fact that Adams had loved another woman, Mary Frazier, whom his mother discouraged him from marrying, much more than he would ever care for her. And she was certain that none of her Yankee in-laws accepted her, except for the "old gentleman" John Adams. The others regarded her as a "nobody," too weak and flighty to be the wife of a man of John Quincy's talents. She even went so far as to tell her youngest son, when he became engaged, "that as it regards women the Adams family are one and all peculiarly harsh and severe in their characters. There seems to exist no sympathy, no tenderness for the weakness of the sex. . . ."[25] In fact, she used her own frail health, morbid moods, and hysterical fainting fits to control the men in her family.

It is hard to say what Adams thought but he undoubtedly knew that his wife was miserable, and that his marriage came far short of the standard set by his parents, who not only had a deep love for one another but also shared a common New England background and generally agreed on how their children should be raised. He even acknowledged in his diary that there were trials in his marriage and "differences of sentiment, of tastes, and of opinion in regard to domestic economy, and to the education of children."[26]

In fact, Adams had married a woman who was virtually an exact opposite of his mother. Louisa's father was a Marylander who distrusted Yankees, and her mother was English. She had been raised in Europe, in luxury, where she never "dreamt of anything beyond the hour."[27] Sickly and delicate, she lacked the mental toughness, the resourcefulness, the strict standards of thrift, and the zest for life that made her mother-in-law, Abigail Adams, the measure of womanly excellence in New England. She was also at odds with the Adams family over how children should be raised. She tended to be indulgent and easy-going, and she thought long absences from one's children were terribly wrong. The Adams upbringing included separations of many years and constant prodding of the youngsters to excel. It had produced striking achievement in the case of John Quincy Adams, but also noteworthy failure in the lives of both of his younger brothers, Charles, who had died a wastrel and drunkard at age thirty, and Thomas, who also drank too much, deserted his wife and six children periodically, and disgraced the family name.

Despite the examples of Charles and Thomas, John Quincy tried to raise his own children in the same way his parents had raised him. If anything, he carried the Adams style of child-rearing several steps further than they did, for while his parents granted him plenty of freedom when he was a young man studying law in Newburyport and starting a practice in Boston, he tried to control his sons' lives long after they reached maturity. Indeed, his ambition for his sons as future statesmen knew no bounds. He bailed them out of various scrapes and escapades, while nagging them constantly about their shortcomings, bombarding them with lectures and letters on the evils of riotous living and the virtues of staying sober, getting up before dawn, keeping a diary, being punctual, persevering, working hard, having a reading program, going to church, and the like. Only through such a regimen, he said repeatedly, would they be worthy to carry on the family name.

Not one of his three sons came close to meeting his stringent demands. The child who later achieved the most fame was the youngest, Charles Francis, who spent less time away from his parents than did his brothers and from whom the least was expected. But even Charles was a disappointment to his demanding father.

The tragic figure was the eldest son, who was named after

George Washington and was expected to be the dynastic heir. He was a sensitive youth, who from the day he was born craved affection and became dejected when criticized or treated with indifference. When he was eight his parents left him and his brother John, two years younger, in the care of aunts and uncles while they went on a four-year diplomatic mission to Russia. George did not see his parents again until he was twelve, when his father became Minister to England. During the intervening years he came to love the outdoors and reading Sir Walter Scott, discovered Shakespeare, and developed a taste for tales of crime, horror, depravity, and supernatural power. Under his father's tutelage in England he prepared for Harvard, while developing a passion for drama and poetry. He was talented, and despite numerous drinking sprees did rather well for several years, winning the Boylston Prize at Harvard over Ralph Waldo Emerson, studying law in Daniel Webster's office, giving the Fourth of July Oration at Quincy, winning election to the state legislature. But he never quite measured up this father's expectations, and the pressure on him to succeed was immense. He once wrote a friend, when he was a freshman at Harvard, about a dream he had about a girl. Suddenly, in the midst of the dream his father's face, stern and forbidding, appeared behind the girl, saying: "Remember George, who you are, what you are doing!"[28]

It is hard to say when George's life began to fall apart, but his troubles became very noticeable when he was in his twenties and his father was President. George was unlucky in love, becoming engaged to one cousin who eventually decided to marry his brother John, being turned down by another cousin, and in general falling flat on his face with the eligible young women of Boston. Already a heavy drinker, he caroused more and more, and his law office eventually became known as a center of drunkenness and fornication. His father had given him all the family's legal business in Boston, and he fouled up the financial accounts, was late with statements, and then neglected the accounts entirely. He grew more and more sloppy about his own affairs, squandering money, borrowing money "for books," falling hopelessly into debt. He suffered a breakdown, both physical and mental, and his mother had to rush to Boston to nurse him. He turned down the opportunity to run for Congress and eventually gave up his seat in the state legislature, indicating at times that his views differed sharply with his father's and claiming that his father's position made it difficult for him to stay in politics. He became something of a recluse, living like a "drunken pig," unable to even pay his board. He took up with a chambermaid, got her pregnant, and in a note addressed to his youngest brother made arrangements for her care in the event he should soon die.

Through all this, old family friends told Adams that George should be relieved of all cares and responsibilities. Characteristically, John Quincy paid off George's debts and tried to get closer to his son, while reminding him of the achievements of his grandfather and admonishing him to work harder, get up earlier, keep a diary, be temperate, and in general develop the self-discipline that was the hallmark of an Adams.[29]

Then in April 1829, after vacating the White House, Adams sent for George to help manage the trip back to Massachusetts. Run-down, broke, with a host of creditors and an illegitimate child to worry about, George dreaded the thought of facing his parents. As the day of his departure from Boston approached, he started to lose touch with reality, imagining that birds were speaking to him or that someone was breaking into his room. He made his way to Providence, where he boarded the *Benjamin Franklin*, a luxury steamboat bound for New York. He was all right during the day, but that night he began to act strangely, imagining that the ship's engines were talking to him, accusing various passengers of spreading rumors against him, demanding that the ship's captain stop the boat and let him off. In the wee hours of the night, he had a long talk with a Jacksonian enthusiast from Boston on his way to Washington to get a job. Ten minutes later he jumped or fell overboard and drowned somewhere off Long Island, where his body later washed ashore.[30]

The news reached Washington on May 2, 1829. At first, the shattered parents came closer together than ever before. Adams, usually harsh in his outward manner, became a tender husband always at Louisa's side, reading to her from the Book of Common Prayer, various novels, and travelogues, trying to distract her from her grief. Louisa, as usual in situations of emotional stress, became ill and took to bed, but she prayed fervently for her husband in this time of sorrow. Alone, Adams poured out his grief during long walks in the woods, and to save himself from utter despondency tried to bury himself in work. But deep down Adams blamed himself for what happened to George, and so did his wife. To her dying day she blamed George's death on the insatiable ambitions of the Adams family, and particularly those of her husband. She knew that it only added to her husband's misery to reproach him for pushing George too hard, for demanding from George exertions that were "foreign to his nature." But in moments of distress she found herself doing it nevertheless, and then begging him not to believe everything she said.[31]

Thus the death of "poor George" weighed heavily on Adams's mind when he made his decision to run for Congress. His youngest son destroyed most of George's papers to save the family from further grief, but he could not eliminate the debts or the illegitimate child, and various legal problems dragged on for several years, including one incident that led to a nasty court case.[32] What effect did all this have on Adams's decision? Did the former President have an inner need to humiliate himself by accepting the lowly position of a freshman Congressman? Was he, in part, intentionally punishing himself to make amends for what happened to his oldest son? Or was he merely seeking solace in work? Unfortunately, we cannot know. We can only add to the list of questions and speculate about what drove this man of many secrets.

Just as the impact of George's death is a matter of speculation, so too is the question of Adams's need for money. It has been argued, from time to time, that one motive for Adams's acceptance of a seat in Congress was that he "hardly knew where to turn to raise a dollar."[33] He thus welcomed the pay of a Congressman, which was eight dollars a day for each session of Congress plus forty cents a mile traveling allowance.

Actually, Adams was a very rich man by the standards of the day. When he died in 1848 he left an estate in the neighborhood of $250,000, which was six times as much as his father had left twenty-two years earlier. Indeed, at the time of his death, Adams had about $58,000 in personal property, which was much more than his father had in real estate and personal property combined. Of this, probably $40,000 generated income. The remainder of the estate was real estate, which for the most part also generated income.[34] Adams and Louisa therefore should have had more than enough to live in high style—and no need at all for a Congressman's pay.

The trouble was that in 1830 Adams's finances were in shambles, and he worried constantly about becoming another impoverished ex-President. He knew that most of his predecessors in the White House had ended up living off in-laws or heavily in debt, and with their example always in mind he tended to focus on the gloomy side of his finances. Where was he going to get the necessary cash to pay his taxes? How was he going to keep his creditors at bay? To make matters worse, he was often in the dark about the true state of his finances, partly because he was not an astute financial manager himself, and partly because he often turned his affairs over to others who were even more inept than he. His son George, for example, left his Massachusetts accounts in such a mess that it took nearly three years to straighten them out. And George was not the only incompetent steward whom Adams chose to manage his money.

Most of Adams's money was safely invested in real estate in Quincy, Boston, and Washington, in mortgages and government bonds, in United States Bank shares, and in the stock of various bridge, turnpike, and insurance companies.[35] But he also made dubious investments, including one that proved to be a monstrous headache. It began in 1823 when a Washington bank was about to foreclose on his wife's cousin, who owned some grist and flour mills in the District of Columbia called the Columbian Mills. The cousin appealed to Adams for help, and without knowing much about the property or anything about the business Adams bought him out. The cousin was kept on as manager, proved to be incompetent, and was replaced by Adams's second son, John, who worked himself to the bone and succeeded in getting the business barely solvent. The mills, Adams noted in his diary, preyed on his spirits like "gangrene," and he pictured himself becoming a typical ex-President, hopelessly in debt and one step ahead of the sheriff, like Jefferson and Monroe.[36]

The pay of a Congressman, however, was hardly enough to

keep Adams ahead of the sheriff. He owed about $40,000 when
he decided to run for Congress. He was heavily in debt not
only to the creditors of Columbian Mills but also to the beneficiaries of his father's estate. He also had to pay about $1,000
to settle George's debts.[37] He needed much more, therefore,
than eight dollars a day and forty cents a mile. What he needed
most was competent stewards, and he was lucky that his youngest son, Charles Francis, proved to the financial genius of the
family. Young Charles took over the Massachusetts accounts
after George's death, straightened out the mess that George
had left, collected the rents and handled his father's business
with efficiency and dispatch. Still, Adams had trouble with the
Columbian Mills. When his son John died in 1834 he replaced
him with his Quincy secretary, who had worked under John's
direction but was incapable of running the mills on his own,
and once again the mills became a constant financial drain.
Eventually Adams turned to his brother-in-law, who as luck
would have it proved to be a competent steward like Charles.
In the meantime, however, Adams found himself in the embarrassing position of repeatedly having to borrow money from
his old friend and former valet, Antoine Guista, to meet current
expenses and pay interest on his debts.

Adams's financial troubles thus continued well into his
congressional years. It was not until the 1840s, in fact, that his
financial worries subsided, and he finally paid off Guista and
his other creditors.[38] So if he thought that a Congressman's pay
would solve his problems, he was jumping at straws or made
a colossal miscalculation. His son Charles, who always had a
sharp eye for the dollar, thought Adams was impulsive and
perhaps even a simpleton when it came to his financial affairs.
Still, it is hard to believe that he miscalculated his finances to
the point that he thought he could pay off a $40,000 debt with
the help of an eight-dollar-a-day salary, which was trivial compared with his income from rental properties. He was never
that much of a simpleton. So while his decision to return to
Washington as a lowly Congressman will never be stripped
entirely of its mystery, it seems safe to conclude that his need
for work and political combat was far more decisive than his
need for money.

* * *

Once he was back in Washington politics, Adams liked to picture himself as representing the entire nation, but in fact he represented fifty thousand people who lived just south of Boston on the historic land the Pilgrims settled in the 1620s. Called the "Old Colony" by many, his district included a mixture of old fishing villages, small ports, several mining villages, numerous agricultural settlements, and a growing number of factory towns. It differed from the major industrial centers of New England, namely, Fall River and Lowell, in that it was not heavily dependent on either child labor or female labor. Outside the home, the typical worker was a male who usually had several ways to make a living: he was often part farmer, part fisherman, part artisan—and if any of his props failed he fell back upon another. But such facts do not show up in the statistics: when the 1830 census takers asked for occupations, they would not allow a man to list himself as a jack-of-many-trades; he had to choose between one and another. Under these circumstances, roughly 10 percent of Adams's constituents chose fishing, 40 percent farming, and 40 percent manufacturing. The numbers varied sharply, of course, from town to town, and so did the landscape. In half the towns in Adams's district the traditional high points of the skyline—the church steeples and the mastheads—still predominated. In the other half they had already been overshadowed by the factory.[39]

But it would be a mistake to make too much of such divisions: nearly everyone knew that the future of the entire region depended on the new industrial order. And in the early years, nearly everyone voted for Adams. Between 1830 and 1836 he won four elections by landslide margins, capturing between 71 and 87 percent of the vote. In 1838, after two-party politics finally made its way into New England, the opposition began to cut into his victory margin, reducing it to 52 percent in 1842. But that was the high point for the opposition, and in the next two elections his margin of victory widened, reaching 63 percent in his last election in 1846.[40]

There were some unusual aspects to this success story. For one thing, unlike most Congressmen of his day who served for many terms, Adams always had opposition on election day.

He never had the luxury of running unopposed, and he usually had to run against two or three candidates. One reason was that Massachusetts law required that the victor have an absolute majority, and it was thought to be good politics to run several local favorites to keep the front runner from getting the required 50 percent plus one vote, even if it meant the seat would remain vacant. Noteworthy, too, was the fact that all the great historical events of the early 1830s—such as Jacksonian Democracy and the Bank War—had no visible effect on the electorate. If anything, the celebrated actions that Old Hickory took as President simply drove more voters into the Adams camp.

Jackson, it should be noted, was weak not only in Adams's district but throughout the Bay State. His appeal was negligible, and his party had a rather narrow base and never caught up with the opposition during Adams's lifetime. Not only did Jackson finish dead last in a three-man race in 1832, but his party in the 1830s and 1840s never won a presidential contest in Massachusetts and won only two gubernatorial elections in twenty tries. Usually the Jacksonians were just strong enough to worry the opposition, to keep them in fighting trim.

The Jacksonians' failure at the polls, moreover, occurred at a time when there were plenty of conflicts to exploit. Industrialization and immigration were tearing the old social order to shreds, widening the gap between rich and poor, pitting workers against employers, Irish newcomers against old Yankees, Catholics against Protestants, zealous social reformers against hidebound traditionalists, burgeoning industrial towns against rural backwaters. Yet the Jacksonians continued to lose almost everywhere—in the large cities, in the old fishing villages, in the new factory towns, and in most farm communities. They made their best showings in towns that were literally "off the beaten path" and the least touched by change—in towns with no post office, no tavern, no church, no doctor, no lawyer.[41]

Their failure was partly their own making. As the national spokesmen for states' rights, limited government, economic retrenchment, and territorial expansion, Old Hickory and his followers never spoke to the issues that troubled most Massachusetts voters. Since the 1820s, "improvements" was the shibboleth of the age in the Bay State, among not only Boston Brahmins but also middle-class businessmen and lower middle-class artisans and shopkeepers. Interest groups fought over who got what and when, but not over fundamental economic policy. They all favored economic development; they all wanted the benefits of turnpikes and canals, more bridges and post offices, new and larger factories. And, almost instinctively, they shared with Adams the fundamental premise that all governments, state and federal, were duty-bound to improve the general welfare.[42]

Adams not only represented these widely held beliefs, but also benefited from the success of the "improvements" program in Massachusetts. His own followers in the 1820s, and the Webster men thereafter, ran the state adroitly. As the primary spokesmen for economic development and social progress, they made sure that "improvements" touched virtually every major town in the state, so that by the 1850s all but a dozen interior towns had railroad connections, and the Bay State as a whole had four times as much track per square mile as New York. They managed to do this, moreover, without running up a large public debt or placing a heavy burden on the state's taxpayers. The Boston elite, who as always dominated the state, eased the jealousies of small-town folk by providing them with liberal bank charters, letting them remain overrepresented in the state legislature, and supporting small-town talent for state office. Their shrewdness, along with the pervasiveness of industrial growth and the success of state-supported "improvements," effectively undercut most of Old Hickory's thunder. Elsewhere Jacksonian battle cries against "monopolies," economic favoritism, high taxes, and economic mismanagement rallied hundreds of thousands of voters to the polls; but in Massachusetts they fell largely on deaf ears.

Thus Adams, who was out of step with much of the nation when he was President, marched shoulder to shoulder with the dominant men in his home state. His dream of a national system of internal improvements, which so outraged the Old Republicans of Virginia, raised only a few eyebrows in Massachusetts. His program of economic development reflected the common New England view—a point of view that was wedded to the tariff, internal improvements, the "orderly" sale of public lands, and a strong national bank. Yet there was another reason why Adams won so easily in the heyday of Jacksonian Democracy. As we shall see in the next chapter, he was also the leading voice for the most powerful "democratic" movement in his district and the state as a whole.

CHAPTER II

Adams and Democracy

John Quincy Adams was a maverick. He ran for Congress as the best known National Republican in Massachusetts. The National Republicans were the "insiders" in Massachusetts politics, the voice of the establishment. By the time Adams took his seat in Congress, he had switched parties and was a "zealous Antimason." The Antimasons were anything but "insiders." They were, in their odd way, the voice of "democracy" in Massachusetts politics.

No word has been used more frequently than "democracy" in describing American politics after the War of 1812, but the word is seldom associated with the name of John Quincy Adams. On the contrary, it is almost invariably linked with his arch-enemy Andrew Jackson. Not only are there scores of books on this subject, but virtually every American history textbook has a chapter entitled "Jacksonian Democracy."

The expression "Jacksonian Democracy," however, has long been the source of much confusion. Although historians habitually use the phrase there is little agreement on what it means. In one book, the typical democrats are the urban masses; in another, simple farming folk and restless pioneers; in another, expectant capitalists; and in still another, a motley assortment of all three.[1]

Much of the confusion obviously stems from the fact that two distinct phenomena—the advent of democracy and triumph of Andrew Jackson—have been linked. Jackson was undoubtedly the most forceful and dramatic political figure between the

Battle of New Orleans and Civil War, the period when democracy became dogma. Jackson also differed from his predecessors. He was the first President from west of the Appalachians and the first since Washington who was not a college graduate. He was savage in his hatreds, and had been involved in numerous duels, stabbings, and other frays. His followers, moreover, shrewdly called themselves Democrats.

But such facts hardly provide solid ground for the common notion that the rise of Jackson and the advent of democracy went hand in hand. Jackson, as historians have pointed out frequently, was hardly on the side of the "common man" in his home state of Tennessee. He supported the well-to-do and had fought the "canebrake democracy" of General William Carroll, who became invincible in Tennessee politics despite Jackson's opposition.[2]

Actually, both Adams and Jackson operated in a political atmosphere where politicians of all stripes tried to gain power by proclaiming the virtues of white man's democracy. Advocates of white man's democracy suffered a crushing defeat in the Virginia Constitutional Convention of 1829, ran into trouble where Federalist conservatism still lingered on, and railed constantly against the evil machinations of insidious aristocrats. But generally most politicians, rich and poor alike, sang the praises of the ordinary white man. In this atmosphere the supporters of Jackson sometimes damned the aristocrats and celebrated the virtues of the ordinary white man with a bit more zeal than the supporters of Adams displayed, but at times they lagged behind and suffered the consequences. For democratic dogma came out of many streams and took some striking twists and turns.

Jackson propagandists, quite naturally, took advantage of this general atmosphere. They portrayed their favorite as a man of the people, even though he lived in one of the finest mansions in the country and owned well over one hundred slaves, and claimed that Adams was an eastern aristocrat who despised the poor. When Jackson won a smashing victory over Adams in 1828, piling up 178 electoral votes to Adams's 83, they claimed that the "people" had revolted against the privileged few, that the poor and unwashed had turned on the rich in democratic triumph, even though the election returns clearly indicated that Jackson was far more popular in "aristocratic" Virginia than he was in "democratic" Vermont and that he ran much better in the slave states of the South than the free states of the North. When on Inauguration Day hundreds of rollicking partisans romped through the Executive Mansion, muddying rugs, smashing china, and jumping enthusiastically to get a glimpse of Old Hickory, Jackson's supporters represented this thundering herd as a new democratic force in Washington politics. "It was a proud day for the *people*," exclaimed the Jacksonian propagandist Amos Kendall. "General Jackson is *their own* president."[3] Such remarks were repeated endlessly, often as gospel, in one historical account after another, and thus the notion gradually developed that democracy triumphed with Jackson's victory in 1828.

In retelling this old story, popular historians generally depicted Jackson and Adams as contrasting figures. Jackson came to symbolize those frontier qualities that many believed characterized the West (and perhaps the South) as a whole: physical courage, a willingness to fight for cherished values, intuitive wisdom as opposed to formal learning, and will power as hard as iron. In contrast, Adams was portrayed as an effete, Harvard-educated, eastern aristocrat who technically might have been a Jeffersonian Republican like Jackson, but was at heart really a Federalist who distrusted the people and favored a strong central government.[4]

It was sometimes noted that Adams was not a prim and proper Boston Brahmin, but the least ostentatious of our early Presidents, the first to wear long trousers rather than the knee-length pantaloons and white-topped boots of an earlier day, the epitome of republican simplicity in his dress and his treatment of servants, a man who skinny-dipped in the Potomac with his valet and raced around the Capitol for exercise in winter. Some historians, moreover, ridiculed the charges of Jackson's propagandists, who had often claimed that Adams's well-known nonchalance and Republican casualness were simply masks to hide his patrician tastes, that secretly he had spent public money on a billiard table and other unsavory luxuries, and that his style of living inside the President's "palace" was really that of an aristocrat.[5]

Actually, both Jackson and Adams were aristocrats by American standards. The election of 1828 did not pit a western democrat against an eastern Brahmin. Rather, it matched a slave-holding aristocrat against a Yankee aristocrat. And, as in the case of Jefferson versus John Adams in 1800, the Yankee aristocrat was overmatched. Jackson, needless to say, lauded the wisdom of the ordinary white men who supported him in 1828. But it is doubtful that he would have been so lavish in praising the "voice of democracy" had he lost the election.

Adams, for his part, might not have heaped praise on the electorate even if he had won. For in his eyes the triumph of democracy had its bad points as well as good. The incurable "vice" of democracy was that it was "swallowed up in the present" and paid no heed to either the future or the past. Among its chief virtues, he believed, was one that no politician with national ambitions would dare to mention: it was incompatible with slavery and bound "to shake the fetters of servitude." Indeed, Adams found it "extraordinary" that the supporters of slavery sang the praises of democracy. If they really thought they could set limits on democracy, so white men would always be free to lord it over blacks, they were dreaming. Limiting democracy, especially democracy founded upon the rights of man, was impossible. In the long run its predominance was "inevitable," and everything in its path would be crushed. Fighting it "in the present age" was like trying to hold back the tide. Democracy was obviously "ascendant, and gaining victory after victory," and there was nothing that he, Jackson, or anyone else could do to contain it.[6]

Based on his reading of classical history and philosophy, however, he thought it was an unworkable form of government. One major fault was that governments would ultimately fail if they responded continuously and directly to the immediate passions and enthusiasms of the people. Rather, a good government had to lead and educate the people to a recognition of their best interests and the best interests of their children and their children's children. A good government had to look to the future.[7]

Another major failing of democracy was that it focused too much on persons and too little on property. The government established by the Founding Fathers struck a balance between the two, as it was "instituted for protection both of persons and of property—to secure alike the rights of persons and the rights of things." By failing to maintain this balance, the tendency of democracy was to "degenerate into ochlocracy and Lynch law. . . ."[8] Indeed, when Adams wrote these words, mobs were springing up all over the country, tormenting unpopular minorities everywhere, sacking the homes of blacks in New York and Philadelphia, burning a convent in Massachusetts, attacking a bank in Baltimore, lynching gamblers in Mississippi. Were these to be the hallmarks of democracy?

Adams, like his father before him, thought the best government was one that struck a balance between the three basic forms of government: democracy, aristocracy, and monarchy. Each form had its virtues, but each had inherent limitations as well, and a government based solely on any one was bound to fall prey to that form's shortcomings. The ideal, therefore, was a government that combined the best features of the three. Virtually raised on this philosophy, Adams claimed time and again that it was not simply a reiteration of what he had learned from his father, or Thomas Jefferson, or the Federalist Papers. It was reinforced, he argued, by his long study of Aristotle and the Roman Republic.[9]

Adams, however, was hardly consistent in his thinking. Even though he stressed balance, and said that the triumph of democracy was inevitable, he often gave the most weight to the aristocratic element. He generally held the leadership responsible for what happened, good or bad. The Jacksonians were thus wrong in attributing everything good in society to the "people," just as the Federalists were wrong in blaming the "people" for all society's failings. The "people" were not even responsible for throwing him out of office; that he blamed largely on the slaveholding aristocracy and their northern allies. For him, as for Jefferson, what was needed was an aristocracy based on "moral properties"—and *not* a government of wealth, which was "very bad." The general populace needed not just leadership and guidance, but leaders with superior moral values.[10]

Much of his argument can be dismissed as mere cant. He claimed, for example, that the basic political struggle was not between the haves and have-nots but rather between leaders with "moral" vision like himself and demagogues motivated solely by naked self-interest. He had no doubt that his enemies, who were generally wealthy and powerful aristocrats, used the shibboleths of democracy for political gain, while he was generally blind to the fact that his own followers did the same thing.

Despite such glaring pretense, Adams had no illusions about who counted in American society. He told Alexis de Tocqueville, whose *Democracy in America* would later inspire many scholars to exaggerate the "equality of conditions" prevailing in the United States, that slavery had modified "the whole state of society" in the South so that all white men "were almost equally privileged." In the North, on the other hand, where there was "a great equality before the law . . . it ceases absolutely in the habits of life. There are upper classes and working classes."[11] He also knew that the influence of the southern planter, thanks in part to the three-fifths clause of the Constitution, counted more than that of a northern aristocrat, and for this reason the selfish interests of the slaveholding elite dominated Washington politics.[12]

Adams thus was galled by the fact that he would always be a second-class citizen in the national pecking order. But what about the northern pecking order? The Adams family identified with the northern aristocracy and wanted to be at the top of every social pyramid. Unfortunately, they were not, and this fact infuriated them. They had few equals in Quincy and Braintree—or in Washington—but in Boston they clearly ranked below the Otises, the Perkinses, the Lowells, and a dozen or so other families. Indeed, even the Quincys (at best their equals in Quincy) had social superiority in Boston. The situation was such that when the ex-President's son Charles Francis married the daughter of Peter Chardon Brooks in 1829, he was actually marrying "up" in the eyes of the Boston elite.[13]

The problem the Adams family had in Boston probably had more to do with politics than with either pedigree or money. They simply were not trusted politically. John Adams had been regarded as too independent for Federalist Boston, and John Quincy Adams had committed the unforgivable sin of apostasy. Sent to the United States Senate as a Federalist in 1803, he first infuriated Boston Federalists by supporting the Louisiana Purchase and criticizing Britain's actions on the high seas. "Like a Kite without a tail," declared banker Stephen Higginson, he was totally undependable.[14] Then in 1807 Adams advocated stern measures against England for attacking the U.S.S. *Chesapeake*, and he not only voted for Jefferson's Embargo Act but, worse, in 1808 attended the Republican caucus to nominate presidential and vice-presidential candidates. Federalist journalists denounced him as an "apostate," one of "Bonaparte's Senators," a "popularity seeker," a "traitor," a "party scavenger," a "Lucifer." The Massachusetts legislature publicly rebuked him by electing a replacement six months earlier than usual, and ordering both Massachusetts Senators to vote for the repeal of the embargo, thus forcing Adams to resign before his term was up.[15]

Thereafter Adams was a despicable "apostate" as far as Federalist Boston was concerned. Their hatred, in fact, grew as he rose in the ranks of the Republican party, and their voices continued to dominate Bay State politics, despite charges of treason hurled at them for their part in the Hartford Convention in 1814, and despite the death of Federalism in national politics. Then in 1824 Adams's bid for the Presidency split their beloved state party into two wings: those who saw him as the best hope for Massachusetts in national affairs and those who could never forgive his transgressions or his more recent denunciations of the Hartford Convention. The split was fatal, and by the third year of Adams's presidency Massachusetts Federalism was all but dead. Some old Federalists joined the National Republicans under Adams; others, like the unforgiving Theodore Lyman, joined the Jacksonian opposition.[16]

Fuel was added to the fire in 1829, when Adams entered a verbal war with thirteen Boston Federalists. The controversy grew out of two letters that were written by Thomas Jefferson in December 1825 to William Branch Giles, a Jacksonian who was trying to discredit Adams. In the first letter Jefferson had praised Adams for his conduct in 1808, relating in rather jumbled fashion that Adams had warned him that the Massachusetts Federalists were "in negotiation with agents of the British government" and that repeal of the embargo was necessary to remove "temptations" to New England separatism. The letter, written by an old man whose memory was failing him, obviously confused events that occurred during the War of 1812 with events before the war. The second letter, which Jefferson asked Giles not to publish, was a severe criticism of Adams's first annual message, expressing "deep affliction" at the rapid usurpation of power that Adams was embarking upon in his call for a national program of roads and canals, a national university, and the like. After Jefferson's death in 1826, Giles published the damaging letter, the one he was forbidden to publish, and tried to stifle the first letter which praised Adams for his patriotism in 1808. The Adams forces, working through Jefferson's grandson, got a copy of the first letter and saw that it too got into print.[17]

It is hard to say what the old Federalists of Boston would have done if Adams had not entered the fray. Jefferson's first letter, even though its facts were jumbled, essentially accused them of treason. But there is some evidence that they would have let the matter pass had Adams not authorized the *National Intelligencer*, in October 1828, to publish a statement in his name that corrected some obvious errors in Jefferson's recollections, while reaffirming the charge that Massachusetts Federalists in 1808 sought the cooperation of Britain toward the "dissolution of the Union, and the establishment of a separate confederation."[18]

This charge set off a furious debate in Boston. John Lowell, one of the more vehement Adams haters among the old Federalists, demanded a public investigation and warned Adams that unless he could substantiate his charge his character would "deeply suffer."[19] Theodore Lyman gave the charge a different political twist and tried to turn it to the advantage of the Jacksonians. He announced in the *Jackson Republican* that it was now clear that Daniel Webster and other Federalists had been "engaged in a plot to dissolve the Union and re-annex New England to Great Britain." Webster brought a criminal libel suit against Lyman, which ended in a hung jury. In the trial, the Solicitor General Daniel Davis denounced Adams for defaming "the good and the patriotic and the pious." Adams's statement, thundered Davis, "exhibits every abandonment of principle—of unutterable depravity."[20]

Simultaneously, Harrison Gray Otis and twelve other prominent Federalists demanded publicly that Adams name the Federalist leaders who had plotted secession and present "unequivocal evidence" to prove such a conspiracy. It was unjust, they argued, for a man in high office to make such charges without full documentation. Adams, who had just lost the presidential election, responded with a long public letter in which he refused to name names. But he went out of his way to sting Otis and his colleagues for their part in the Hartford Convention, which had indeed toyed with the idea of secession, and made it clear that they would be sorry if they pushed matters further. In January 1829, Otis and his confederates rejoined with the *Appeal to the Citizens of the United States*, in which they claimed to be speaking not just for themselves, nor for their distinguished ancestors, nor for the old Federalist party, but for the entire Commonwealth of Massachusetts. At some length they justified the Hartford Convention and reiterated their main point that it was an abomination for the President to make unsubstantiated charges of treason against them, their ancestors, and their state.[21]

By this time Adams was already at work on a long and detailed indictment of his old Massachusetts enemies. Devoting his early morning hours to the task, the out-going President searched his diary, examined his correspondence files, and wrote old friends to get further documentation. One of his best sources turned out to be William Plumer of New Hampshire, a fellow deserter from the Federalist party, who regretted the fact that he had once advocated New England separatism in response to Jeffersonian Democracy and the Louisiana Purchase, and wanted to make amends for his part in the conspiracy.[22] In time, Adams had much more than the names that Otis and his colleagues demanded. He compiled what amounted to a history of New England Federalism and various Federalist conspiracies from the time of the Louisiana Purchase in 1803 to the Hartford Convention in 1814, a document of some 84,000 words, which among other things fully justified his leaving the Federalist party when he did. Indeed, he had not deserted the Boston Federalists so much as they had deserted him and the Union.[23]

The long indictment was never published in Adams's lifetime. Once finished he showed it to several friends, who counseled him to think about it for a while and to let sleeping dogs lie. In time, Adams had other battles to fight, which necessitated his working even with arch-enemy Harrison Gray Otis. So the document did not become public knowledge until one-half century later, when his grandson, the talented historian Henry Adams, published an expurgated version that omitted some particularly nasty paragraphs pertaining to Otis.[24] Still, even though the long document did not appear until after all the principals were dead, it was well known in New England political circles that the old man had collected plenty of ammunition against his adversaries. So the Boston elite continued to regard Adams as a loose cannon, and Adams continued to hate them with a passion. Indeed, when he compiled a hate list in 1835, he placed Otis at the very top.[25]

Oddly enough, during all the years that he was fighting with Otis and other New England Federalists, he was never fully trusted by the Jeffersonian Republicans' Virginia leadership. Typically, when James Madison in 1809 offered Adams the post of Minister to Russia, John Taylor of Caroline remarked: "That both the Adams' are monarchists I never doubted. Whether monarchists, like pagans, can be converted by benefices, is a problem the solution of which I always feared Mr. Madison would attempt."[26] Virtually every year some Republican made a similar remark, accusing Adams of being either a monarchist or a Federalist, which were interchangeable terms in the minds of most Republicans. Even Jefferson himself, in response to Adams's first annual address in 1825, charged Adams with reviving Federalism and inching toward monarchy. And the Jacksonians never tired of repeating the old refrain that Adams, despite his casual dress and nonchalant manner, was really at heart a Federalist and a monarchist. So even though Adams was ostracized on State Street in Boston he was not acceptable to the other side.

In fact, Adams differed with both the Boston Federalists and the Virginia Republicans. He did not share the Federalists' detestation of the French Revolution, their corresponding attachment to Great Britain, their aversion to republics and contempt for ordinary people, or their belief that Jefferson and Madison were servilely devoted to France. He did share—and more so as he got older—their jealousy of southern power and their hatred for the three-fifths clause of the Constitution that provided for slave representation in both Congress and the Electoral College. He was at odds with the Virginia Republicans, too, when it came to their attachment to states' rights and strict construction of the Constitution, and their corresponding dread of a strong national government, which they feared would be the death of slavery. He did not love the "people" as much as some Republicans claimed they did, but he once noted in his diary that he had much more confidence in the calm judgment of the people than had his predecessor, James Monroe of Virginia.[27] He took the people into his confidence, moreover, in his first annual message when he laid out his dream of a strong national government building the nation's economy in rationally planned steps. He wore both his Republicanism and his Federalism, then, with a difference.

Thus Adams's reputation as a maverick was well established long before he cast his lot with the Antimasons in 1831. Indeed, in the eyes of his old Boston enemies, the news that Adams had joined the Antimasons merely confirmed the fact that the ex-President was a totally unprincipled renegade.

Historians, however, have generally had trouble coping with the idea that Adams became, in his own words, "a zealous Antimason." For, to most twentieth-century scholars, Adams was the epitome of learning, the elite scholar in politics, while the Antimasons were the forerunners of Senator Joseph McCarthy and all the right-wing witch-hunters of recent American politics. Until the 1970s, in fact, most historians dismissed the Antimasons as irrational, paranoid, conspiracy-minded bigots.[28]

How could a rational man like Adams, a Harvard-educated gentleman, join forces with such small minds? How could a man of reason become linked with "the politics of unreason"? Did he really believe that Freemasonry was the greatest political evil of his day, even more dangerous than the triumph of Andrew Jackson?

Many historians, in searching for the origins of red-baiting and "the paranoid style in American politics," were undoubtedly too hasty in labeling Antimasonry as an early version of "the politics of unreason." They were also led astray by Charles McCarthy's *The Antimasonic Party*, which was published in 1903 and remained the only comprehensive study that was readily available for the next eighty years. McCarthy made one enormous mistake. He dismissed the episode that was central to Adams and other Antimasons—namely, the kidnapping and probable murder of William Morgan—as "merely incidental" to the development of Antimasonry. He left later historians with the decided impression that only a handful of Masons had been involved in Morgan's abduction, and that the uproar over Morgan's disappearance had little to do with the development of political Antimasonry. Indeed, after reading McCarthy, one would hardly guess that Adams and other Antimasons had ample grounds for thinking that around three hundred Masons had been involved in the crimes against Morgan, and that the crimes were followed by a massive cover-up.[29]

Then, as now, the Masons were a secret, exclusive fraternal organization. Some men were asked to join; others were blackballed; most were never even considered. Tracing its origins to medieval England and Scotland, American Masonry was formally established in Boston in 1733, spread from port cities to commercial towns in the backcountry, and flourished after the turn of the nineteenth century. Over the years, the Masons had developed the reputation of accepting only the "better sort": George Washington and Benjamin Franklin had been members, and so were Andrew Jackson and Henry Clay. Masons had boasted for several decades that they held "almost every place of power where POWER IS OF ANY IMPORTANCE," and that their membership consisted of "men of RANK, wealth, office and talent, in power and out of power." They had bragged, too, of their ability to work in concert. There was undoubtedly some truth to their boasts, but how much is still a matter of conjecture. A study of Woodstock, Connecticut, indicates that Masons held many more public offices than their numbers would warrant, and another study of Genesee County, New York, the site of Morgan's kidnapping, shows that over half the key members in both political parties were Masons.[30]

Antimasonry was almost as old as Masonry itself. From the beginning, Freemasonry's critics worried about the fraternity's secrecy, suspecting that Masons were conducting drunken orgies, making unsavory business deals, plotting subversion. As the secrets leaked out, critics denounced Masons for their blood-curdling oaths, which among other things called for vows of silence "under no less penalty" than having one's "throat cut from ear to ear," "tongue plucked out by the roots," "bowels taken out and burned to ashes," "body dissected into four equal parts." Angry churchmen sometimes accused Masonic lodges of being either enemies of Christianity or surrogate churches usurping the domain of true religious bodies by providing moral, charitable, and social leadership. Women also resented Masonic lodges, not only because they were exclusively male, but also because they challenged women's role as guardians of social morality. Democrats and egalitarians chastised Masons for their elitism, their exclusiveness, their alleged control of public offices, and their use of titles such as "King," "High Priest," and "Master."

The first concerted attack on Freemasonry in the United States occurred in the 1790s in New England, where the Federalist hierarchy and the Congregational clergy had begun to associate Masonry with the French Revolution, atheism, and Jeffersonian Republicanism. Led by the renowned geographer and clergyman Jedidiah Morse, they tried to establish a connection between Masonic lodges in the United States and a notorious secret organization in Europe known as the "Bavarian Illuminati," which was accused of subverting authority and promoting anarchy and revolution. Morse singled out a lodge in Virginia, which was composed of French exiles, as living proof that the Illuminati intended to assault American political and religious institutions. The charge proved to be spurious, however, and the hysteria quickly died down, even though some New Englanders continued to believe that the Masons were unprincipled schemers.

After the turn of the nineteenth century, Antimasonry was dormant and Masonry flourished throughout most of the United States. From the port of Boston to remote towns in the backwoods of Michigan, men enjoyed the heady pleasure of membership in an organization with such exalted heroes as Washington, Franklin, and the Marquis de Lafayette. Meanwhile, the historic complaints against Freemasonry were treated with contempt. Did anyone actually believe that the noble Washington would join a wicked conspiracy against the laws of God or man? Was anyone foolish enough to believe that Ben Franklin would have a man's tongue ripped out for divulging the secrets of Masonry? Clearly, the bloody oaths were allegorical, and the secret rituals and high-sounding titles such as "High Priest" and "King" were innocuous.

Such arguments carried the day until 1826, when a large group of Masons in western New York tried to stop William Morgan of Batavia, New York, from publishing an exposé of the three Blue Lodge degrees. Morgan, of course, was not the first to publish a book which revealed all the secret signs, grips, passwords, and obligations. There were numerous exposés of Masonry already in print, including *Jachin and Boaz*, which was first printed in London in 1762 and still readily available on both sides of the Atlantic. News of Morgan's apostasy nevertheless infuriated Masons throughout western New York, and they retaliated with several crimes that bore all the marks of a highly organized lynching.

In the late summer of 1826 bands of Masons botched several attempts to steal the manuscript and to burn down the publisher's print shop. Then on a trumped-up charge brought by a prominent head Mason in Canandaigua, a town forty-eight miles east of Batavia, Morgan was arrested and taken to Canandaigua, where the magistrate released him for lack of evidence. He was re-arrested immediately for owing an innkeeper $2.69 and thrown into the Canandaigua jail. The next evening the local head Mason and two assistants talked the jailer's wife into releasing Morgan upon payment of the debt. No sooner had he been freed than he was seized by four men and thrown into a waiting carriage, whisked off into the night, and taken to Fort Niagara which was roughly one hundred fifty miles by road to the west. On the long journey to Fort Niagara the kidnappers had plenty of help and were provided with food, fresh horses, different carriages, and new personnel. After they reached Fort Niagara no one knows for certain what they did to Morgan, but evidence indicates that they drowned him, weighted and tied, in the Niagara River. His body was never found.[32]

The crime attracted an unusual amount of attention for several reasons. There were, first of all, a large number of men involved. The authorities eventually indicted fifty-four men, but at least twice that number had a hand in the various crimes against Morgan. Another reason was that the kidnapping and other crimes covered most of western New York. Seven counties were involved, and the culprits came from scores of towns from Canandaigua to Fort Niagara. They left such a wide trail of evidence, moreover, that indignant citizens in four counties immediately launched investigations to find out what happened to Morgan. Most importantly, all the participants were Masons, men who had sworn bloody oaths to punish any apostate who revealed their secrets. So Morgan's abduction and probable murder never seemed to be an isolated act of violence by a few crackpots, as so many twentieth-century historians once assumed. On the contrary, it had all the earmarks of a massive and highly organized conspiracy.

The idea that it was the work of a conspiracy, however, probably would have lost credence if justice had been meted out quickly. For the initial reaction to the crime was intense but not hysterical. Most people simply assumed that the culprits would be rapidly arrested, tried, and punished—and that would be the end of it. There were, after all, scores of eyewitnesses who were willing to testify against the kidnappers, and amateur sleuths everywhere were uncovering incriminating evidence. Yet the wheels of justice barely moved at all. It seemed that indignant citizens were blocked at every turn by Masonic judges, Masonic sheriffs, and Masonic officeholders who sought to squelch the affair. When indictments were finally secured, Masonic jurors frequently would not convict. When juries did convict, judges handed down sentences that were incredibly light. Indeed, the jail terms for the ten men who were finally convicted ranged from just thirty days to twenty-eight months. Stung by the apparent breakdown of law and order, many law-abiding citizens in western New York became convinced that the whole legal system was in the hands of an insidious Masonic empire.

Meanwhile, the Masonic lodges in western New York did nothing to calm people's nerves. On the contrary, once they got over the initial shock of Morgan's "murder," they began to battle the protesters with renewed zeal. They refused to expel members who were clearly guilty of kidnapping, while they threw out other members who criticized them for foot-dragging and obstruction of justice. In time many prominent Masons became so outraged by the conduct of the lodges that they renounced their membership and joined ad hoc groups that were calling for the removal of all Masons from positions of authority.[33] Of these seceding Masons the most important figure was the Reverend Elder David Bernard, pastor of a Baptist church in Warsaw, a dozen miles from Batavia, who subsequently published *Light on Masonry*, which became the "bible of Antimasonry."

Hence Antimasonry was reborn. To the dismay of seasoned politicans it spread like wildfire, first through New York and then through Vermont, Connecticut, Massachusetts, Pennsylvania, Ohio, and the Michigan Territory. Suddenly, men met in conventions and pledged that they would never again knowingly vote for a Mason for any public office. Ordinary citizens began counting the Masons in town and state offices. There were hundreds. Indeed, in some states lists of lodge members resembled a roll call of the legislature and the bar. Were they conspiring against the people, too? All Antimasons had to do was take some well-known Masonic boasts, quote from the confessions of seceding Masons such as David Bernard, and rail against "this vile conspiracy which benefited the *few* at the expense of the *many*," which preferred "corrupt 'brothers' to honest citizens in appointments to office," which "hated democracy and cherished aristocratic and regal forms of power."

To this basic argument, evangelical Antimasons added that Masonry was "an infidel society at war with true Christianity."[34]

The results were startling. In the fall election of 1827, just a year after Morgan's abduction, Antimasons carried fifteen assembly seats in central and western New York. "The result of the election," wrote one commentator, "astonished all—even the Anti-Masons themselves—and opened the eyes of politicians to the growing power of the new political group."[35] By 1830 Antimasons could boast of 124 newspapers across the country; 45 percent of the gubernatorial vote in Pennsylvania, 48 percent in New York, and 35 percent in Vermont. Skillful leaders like Thurlow Weed and William Seward of New York and Thaddeus Stevens of Pennsylvania emerged to head the charge. Half of the Masonic lodges in Pennsylvania "voluntarily" surrendered their charters; the number of active lodges in New York dropped from 480 to 82; the Grand Lodge in Vermont went underground for ten years, and local lodges virtually ceased to exist. Nationally Masonic membership declined from more than one hundred thousand in the mid-1820s to some forty thousand a decade later.[36]

Antimasonry swept into Massachusetts just as Adams was finishing his term as President. Dividing churches and town meetings, it gained momentum from the summer of 1828 through the winter of 1829. It became particularly strong in the Connecticut River Valley of western Massachusetts and in the growing industrial centers just south of Boston. About half the towns that Adams would represent in Congress became hotbeds of Antimasonry, and in all but one or two of the other towns Antimasons were a significant minority.

The Antimasons in Adams's home district joined forces with like-minded citizens elsewhere in the state, establishing newspapers, meeting in county conventions, and sending delegates to state conventions at Faneuil Hall in Boston. The Faneuil Hall meetings, in turn, passed the usual Antimasonic resolutions. The first convention asked the Grand Lodge of Massachusetts to sever all ties with "grand" Masonic lodges in New York and to renounce the bloody oaths and system of Freemasonry. After the Grand Lodge ignored such appeals, a subsequent conven-

tion demanded that Masonic affiliation be grounds for disqual-
ifying jurors in cases where only one party was a Mason, that
extrajudicial oaths be declared illegal, and that "all zealous ad-
hering Masons" be barred from holding state or federal offices.
The state convention also established a steering committee, called
the Suffolk committee, which became famous nationally for its
bitter attacks on Masonry.[37]

Adams was a latecomer, not a leader, in this crusade. While
Antimasonry was capturing the hearts and minds of his neighbors in Braintree and Quincy, as well as in the surrounding
towns of Milton, Randolph, Stoughton, Abington, and Weymouth, he was concerned with other matters. He was preoc-
cupied in 1828 and 1829 with his loss to Jackson, the death of
his son George, his financial affairs, and his battle with Otis
and the Boston Federalists. In June 1829 he was asked to subscribe to an Antimasonic newspaper that was being established
in Pawtucket, Rhode Island. He turned down the request, explaining to the editor that "until recently" he never thought
favorably or unfavorably about Masonry, and although he now
"thought it mischievous and hoped it would be voluntarily
given up," he was not "disposed to countenance any persecution against it or against any of its members."[38] A year later
he was asked to subscribe to another Antimasonic newspaper
published in Boston. This time, in refusing the offer, he took
a tougher stance against Freemasonry, denouncing its secrecy
and calling for suppression of Masonic oaths. Still, he made it
clear that he was too old to join the battle.[39]

Why, then, did he decide within the year to cast his lot with
the Antimasons? It is hard to say for certain. It could be argued,
in part, that politically he had no choice. By the time he was
elected to Congress in November 1830, the Antimasons were
clearly a force in the politics of his district, and they could no
longer be treated as merely an adjunct of the National Republican party. By the following spring it was impossible to ignore
the "brawl" that had broken out between the Antimasons and
the Masons in Massachusetts politics.[40] The Antimasons were
screaming persecution. They had carried 150 out of 490 assembly districts and were certain that the state legislature had cheated
them out of seats in the state senate. Under Massachusetts law,

whenever the winner of a popular election failed to get an absolute majority, the decision went to the legislature—and in each of many cases the legislature decided in favor of the Masonic candidate with fewer popular votes than the frontrunning Antimason. Could Adams afford to remain neutral under these circumstances? He had no need to worry about his district turning him out in favor of a Jacksonian Democrat. But might he be turned out in favor of an outspoken Antimason? The Antimasons enjoyed an absolute majority in eleven of the twenty-four towns in his district.[41] Could he ignore that fact? If he did, he might suffer the ignominy of being not only a one-term President, but also a one-term Congressman.

His political self-interest, moreover, coincided with his own inclinations. He had no love for the Masons. He had been defeated in his bid for a second term in the White House by an active Mason, the former Grand Master of the Grand Lodge of Tennessee, who went out of his way to scorn Antimasons. In addition, many of his old Boston enemies were dedicated Masons. He also had no doubt that Masons in western New York had killed Morgan and had literally gotten away with murder. He was angry, too, about the high-handed way Masons in his own National Republican party had treated Antimasons in the state elections. He still thought it wrong to persecute individual Masons, and he was careful not to alienate long-time supporters in the National Republican party. But he was now willing to accept the idea that the Masonic influence in politics had to be eliminated. So he abandoned his public position of neutrality, attended an Antimasonic convention at Faneuil Hall in May 1831, and admitted to being a "zealous Antimason" in September.[42]

His new party, like the weaker Jacksonian Democrats, consisted mostly of outsiders challenging the Massachusetts establishment. Even the delegates to state conventions, he noted in his diary, were unknown men with little wealth and plebeian origins.[43] They, like the hated Jacksonians, counted on the common man to crush the "aristocracy" at the ballot box and developed political apparatuses to bring thousands of ordinary citizens out of factory hamlets, up from millstreams, and to the polls. They were like Jacksonians, too, in denouncing "privilege" and "exclusivism" while insisting that some Americans be excluded from "democracy." They differed only in their choice of victims, saving their venom for Masons, while the Jacksonians generally tormented free blacks. Elsewhere the Jacksonians often took the lead in championing popular government, but in Massachusetts the followers of Old Hickory were barely heard, and the strongest voices in behalf of the common man were those of "zealous Antimasons."

Adams, though a long-time member of the national establishment, never seemed disturbed by his new compatriots' denunciations of elitism. As far as he was concerned, they wanted only to rid politics of "corrupt" aristocrats who made backroom deals at the expense of ordinary citizens. They had no quarrel with leaders with superior "moral" values. They were not indirectly attacking him. Indeed, they were obviously happy to have him on their side.

Adams immediately took up his pen in behalf of his new party. An old friend in Philadelphia, Edward Ingersoll, had written asking if his sympathies extended to "political Antimasonry," noting that the movement was dividing the opposition against Jackson and persecuting many good and patriotic Masons for the excesses of a few. Adams fired back with three long letters that found their way into the newspapers. Was not Freemasonry, he asked, clearly responsible for a wide assortment of crimes including arson, conspiracy, fraud, slander, libel, fraudulent abuse, false imprisonment, perjury, kidnapping and murder? Had not these crimes gone unpunished? And had not Freemasonry stood in the way of justice?[44]

Ingersoll, who hardly wanted the job of defending Masonry against Adams's slashing attack, suggested that others were better qualified to answer those charges. The task finally went to William Leete Stone, editor of the New York *Commercial Advertiser*, who was looking for a way to recount the entire controversy. He published a series of letters which were so unsatisfactory in the eyes of his fellow Masons that he eventually had to quit the fraternity. Adams responded to Stone's defense of Masonry, and this led to another exchange of letters, which Stone published in the *Commercial Advertiser* and which were widely reprinted throughout the country.[45]

After cutting his teeth on Ingersoll and Stone, Adams went after Edward Livingston, a distinguished jurist and humanitarian. Besides serving as Jackson's Secretary of State, Livingston held the highest Masonic office in the country, General Grand High Priest of the General Royal Arch Chapter of the United States. In his inaugural address, Livingston had branded the charges against Freemasonry as lies and had denounced the current "persecution" of the fraternity.[46] Adams, using the address as a whipping post, hammered away at Livingston in a series of public letters, hoping to get the General Grand High Priest into a public controversy. To Adams's chagrin, Livingston let the charges go unanswered. The ex-President's charges were reprinted time and again, however, and gained wide currency.[47]

In all these public confrontations Adams was careful to treat individual Masons with respect while blasting away at the "Institution" of Freemasonry. He had no doubt, he said, that many good and honorable men were Masons. But why did so many lodges remain silent in the face of the kidnapping and murder of William Morgan? The Morgan crimes made it "the solemn and sacred, civic and social duty of every Masonic Lodge in the United States, either to dissolve itself, or to discard forever . . . all oaths, all penalties, all secrets, and all fantastic titles, exhibitions and ceremonies hitherto used in the Institution." Adams also acknowledged that many honest and intelligent Masons did not take seriously the blood-curdling oaths, penalties, and obligations. But how, he asked, could any humanitarian justify the retention of oaths that were so barbaric they put a "common cannibal" to shame? And what was the "fruit" of these oaths, their obligations, and their penalties? Was it not Masons who did the kidnapping, who committed the "foul and midnight murder"?[48]

Adams also made much of the elitism and favoritism of Masonry. Always addressing Masonic leaders by their elaborate titles, he never let his readers forget that Masonry was a hierarchical and aristocratic organization that was at odds with true democracy and majority rule. He did not see how any believer in republican simplicity or true democracy could allow himself to be called "sovereign Master," or "Most Excellent Prelate," or "Knight Templar," or "Royal Arch Companion," or "Grand High Priest." This royal brotherhood, moreover, met behind closed doors and secretly took sacred vows to promote a brother's political advancement at the expense of the rest of the community. As a result, "wherever a lodge or chapter has existed, at least three fourths of all the elective offices in the place were held by worthy brethren and companions of the craft, chosen by men, multitudes of whom knew not themselves the influence under which their votes were cast."

Adams also pounced upon the charge that Antimasons had "persecuted" Masons, claiming that Edward Livingston had no right to make such an accusation. Surely, as "General Grand High Priest," he knew that Masonic lodges influenced elections in favor of their brethren, and that Masonic judges, jurors, and legislators discriminated in favor of Masons and against Antimasons. If Masons had the right to secretly influence elections in behalf of one another, certainly Antimasons had the right to openly counter this "conspiracy of exclusive privilege." How, he wondered, could Antimasons be accused of "persecution" for voting against legislators and judges who corrupted the civil order in favor of Morgan's murderers?

Besides defending Antimasonry, Adams also allowed the Antimasons to nominate him for several offices. There was much talk, in 1831, of nominating him for President. But this effort was blocked by the party's New York leadership, William Seward and Thurlow Weed, who thought that choosing such a well-known "loser" would be "disastrous" to the party's chances in the Empire State.[49] Shortly thereafter, many prominent Massachusetts Antimasons started touting the old warrior as a potential gubernatorial candidate, and in September 1833 the state Antimasonic convention nominated him with 219 out of 288 votes. Adams accepted the nomination, knowing full well that the Antimasons lacked the votes to carry the state, but hoping privately that his old party, the National Republicans, would endorse him at their October convention. The Boston *Advocate*, the leading journal of the Antimasons, declared that the National Republicans now had the chance "to prove what they often assert, that their party is not identified with Masonry. . . ."[50]

But National Republicans wanted no part of this proposed coalition. Boston Masons were "in complete combustion" at Adams's nomination, and thirty-five Masons won seats in the city's sixty-three-man delegation to the state nominating convention. The state committee chairman, moreover, was William Sullivan, one of Adams's old Federalist enemies, whom Adams claimed had "the double venom of Hartford Convention federalism and of spurious Masonry in his blood." The Boston *Atlas*, the leading newspaper of the National Republicans, heaped abuse on Adams, denouncing him as a "renowned renegade" and "the tool and dupe of a desperate faction." The state convention, to no one's surprise, rejected Adams and chose John Davis, a Congressman from Worcester, as the party's standard bearer.[51]

In the November election Davis won 40 percent of the vote, Adams 29 percent, and the Democratic candidate Marcus Morton 25 percent.[52] With no candidate winning a popular majority, the election went to the state legislature, where National Republicans and Davis men dominated both chambers. Adams sent a note to the Speaker of the House requesting that his name be withdrawn, claiming that he would rather not be elected by the legislature if he could not be elected by the people.[53]

Despite his problems statewide, Adams had little trouble forging a coalition between his old party and his new one in his home district of Plymouth. Elected as a National Republican, he took his seat in Congress in December 1831 as a full-fledged Antimason and for the next several years identified with fifteen to twenty fellow Antimasons in the House of Representatives, attending their strategy sessions and voting with them roll call after roll call. And, like his fellow Antimasons, he refused to support "Grand Master" Henry Clay in the presidential election of 1832. Still, he never acknowledged that he had broken with the National Republicans, only with the Clay or Masonic faction of the party. At first he portrayed the Antimasons as just an adjunct of the National Republican party—and then later as the forward-looking, egalitarian, and responsible wing of the party. This perception, which made some sense in other states where

Antimasons and National Republicans had banded together against the Jacksonians, made little sense in Massachusetts, where National Republicans were the main opposition to Antimasonry. Yet at a time when party politics was at best frail and elusive, and mavericks and party bolters were commonplace, Adams had little trouble getting away with this argument in his home district. In fact, he ran as well as Henry Clay and Daniel Webster in the district's Republican towns, while in the Antimasonic strongholds he outpolled both of these Republican stalwarts by some 50 percent. As a result he had little serious opposition in the 1830s and won by several thousand votes in a district that Clay lost in 1832 by fifty-eight votes and Webster carried in 1836 by a mere five votes.[54]

Adams's success at home was also due to growing lethargy among Masons. In Massachusetts, as elsewhere in the North, Masons lost the will to fight many months before Antimasons gave up their crusade. Local Masons found it impossible to simply meet the criticisms of their neighbors with "dignified silence," as Edward Livingston and other national leaders suggested, and they were often on the defensive, either apologizing profusely for the excessive zeal of the New Yorkers, or admitting that the hallowed traditions of their fraternity were silly and meaningless. Wherever Antimasonry flourished, they abandoned their lodges in droves. Indeed, so many Massachusetts Masons took to the pulpit to announce their secession that by 1834 the Grand Lodge felt compelled to forbid this practice, announcing that there were "more becoming ways of withdrawing." Although statistics are scarce and estimates vary, most Massachusetts lodges lost at least two-thirds of their members, and with reduced membership the great majority were forced to shut down. Thus, in many communities, Antimasons soon found themselves thundering against an undemocratic, un-Christian "monster" that in fact had ceased to exist.[55]

Once it became clear that swarms of Masons were deserting the battlefield, statehouse politicians took steps to placate the Antimasons. They hardly went so far as to make amends for excluding Antimasons from the state senate or for failing to endorse the nomination of Adams for Governor. Indeed, they continued to stand in the way of Antimasonic politicians and to thwart the demands of the more radical Antimasons. But in 1834 they finally launched an investigation of Freemasonry, forced the Grand Lodge in Boston to surrender its civil charter of incorporation, and passed legislation outlawing extrajudicial oaths. Even zealous Masons supported several of these measures, hoping that a few token victories would satisfy the more moderate Antimasons, which in turn would bring about the demise of Antimasonic agitation.[56]

Antimasonic agitation, in fact, was on the wane by 1834. Historians usually mark its death soon after the presidential election of 1832, when its national candidate, William Wirt, captured only Vermont and a few dozen congressional districts such as the Plymouth district of Massachusetts. Yet in many parts of the Northeast candidates continued to run until the 1850s as "Antimason and Whig" or "Antimason and Democrat," and for many voters that was the badge of an honest man. Moreover, Wirt's dismal campaign only obscures what was really happening in northern society. Socially, the power of Antimasonry was awesome, destroying lodges in one town after another and literally bringing Freemasonry to its knees. The rout was so overwhelming that many Antimasons, like the famous evangelist Charles Grandison Finney, thought that Freemasonry "was dead, and had no idea that it could ever revive."[57]

Success, probably more than anything else, killed Antimasonry. That was the view of most of Adams's fellow Antimasons in Congress. In March 1834, at their monthly strategy meeting, they heard a report on how victory had decimated the "spirit" of Antimasonry in western New York, and how it was "utterly impossible" to maintain a distinct organized Antimasonic party with "no adversary left to contend with." The Pennsylvania Congressmen were more optimistic than the New Yorkers, but apparently most of the fourteen men in attendance agreed that victory socially meant trouble politically. Their party would have to build coalitions with others—or die.[58]

Although Adams shared this point of view, he was so distressed by the course of events in his home state that he soon lost his Antimasonic ardor. He wanted to build a statewide coalition,

but not with the Jacksonian Democrats. He would have had
few worries on this score if he lived elsewhere, for in most
northern states the Jacksonians followed the lead of Old Hickory
and heaped abuse on Antimasonry.

But Massachusetts was different. The Jackson party in Massachusetts was so weak and the leadership so incompetent that
it hardly counted in state politics, and the National Republican
party was so dominant it had little need for allies. Adams worked
hard to reconcile the two antagonists, but National Republicans
in the state legislature were willing to make only token concessions, while blocking the election of Antimasons to the state
senate and the Governor's council. By late February 1834 Adams
lost hope for healing this breach, believing that statehouse Republicans had done everything possible to "fret and exasperate"
the Antimasons and drive them into Jackson's party. The editorials of Benjamin Hallett of the Boston *Advocate* now called
for an alliance with the Jacksonians.[59]

The last chance for reconciliation with the old National Republicans came in 1835. Nathaniel Silsbee resigned from the
United States Senate, and the two houses of the Massachusetts
legislature had to choose a replacement to sit alongside the
"god-like" Daniel Webster, who was hoping to win the Presidency in 1836. No one, said the Antimasons, was better qualified than John Quincy Adams, and they pushed his candidacy
with all the enthusiasm they could muster.

Adams, who was as eager for victory as they were, initially
took a substantial lead in the state senate, but in the lower
house trailed John Davis, the incumbent Governor, by a few
votes. Then, briefly, a deal seemed to be in the making. At the
urging of Adams and his son Charles, the Antimasons in the
legislature touted the nomination for Governor of Edward Everett, the obvious choice of many National Republicans. The
Antimasons and the old National Republicans appeared to be
merging into a new anti-Jackson party, called the Whigs, as
was happening in other northeastern states.

But such was not the case. Secretly, from Washington, Daniel
Webster urged his Massachusetts supporters to join the Antimasons in backing Everett to the hilt but to block Adams's
election to the Senate.[60] And in time, Adams supplied many

hesitant Webster men with an excuse for voting against him. The issue was an old one, concerning claims against the French for depredations on American shipping during the Napoleonic wars. After years of negotiation the French had finally agreed to pay in six installments, but then delayed payment when the first installment was due. In anger, Jackson recommended reprisals on French property in his annual message of December 1834. Webster and Henry Clay fulminated against Jackson's proposal in the United States Senate, making Old Hickory out to be a bungler and a warmonger. When the issue came before the House of Representatives, however, Adams threw his considerable prestige as the nation's foremost diplomat behind Jackson's get-tough policy. That, along with the coincidental news that Adams had sold his New England Insurance stock, shocked many Bostonians, particularly merchants who had dire visions of a naval war against France and the loss of ships laden with goods. It also provided many a statehouse politician with a convenient excuse to switch his vote from Adams to Davis, and thus Adams was defeated.[61]

Shortly thereafter the Antimasons formally nominated Everett for Governor, just two days before the National Republicans did, and Everett tried to line up Antimasonic support for Webster's presidential candidacy. The double-dealing, however, eventually backfired. Adams knew that Webster was behind his defeat, and other Antimasons came to share his bitterness. When the state Antimasonic convention met in October 1835, the delegates declared that the previous endorsement of Everett did not bind them to support other nominees of the new Whig party, and they went on to nominate a Democrat, William Foster, for Lieutenant Governor. And instead of endorsing the pride of Massachusetts, Daniel Webster, for President, they threw their support behind the scheming Jacksonian, Martin Van Buren of New York.

Antimasons in other states were livid, denouncing Benjamin Hallett as the "Boston Benedict Arnold," and likening the endorsement of Van Buren to high treason. How, they asked, could any Antimason cast his vote for Van Buren, the "sly fox" who had orchestrated Adams's defeat in the 1828 presidential election? Such advice went unheeded. Even Charles Francis

Adams was so eager for revenge that he advocated an alliance with the Jacksonians.[62]

Would John Quincy Adams follow his son's lead? He pretended that he was better off serving in the House than in the Senate. But he fooled no one: he was clearly bitter at losing the potential Senate seat and wanted retribution. Yet even though he despised Webster and yearned for revenge, he could not bring himself to advocate the unthinkable, a full-scale alliance with the crafty New Yorker who was aggressively courting the plantation South. Parting company with his son and many local Antimasons, he remained publicly neutral during the election campaign of 1836.[63]

On election day he undoubtedly gloated over the news that the "god-like" Daniel barely won 50 percent of the vote in the Plymouth district, while he won handily with 83 percent.[64] His emotions were mixed, however, when he learned that the state was carried by Webster and remained under Whig control, while Van Buren won the national election. For, like most of his fellow Antimasons in Congress, he had cast his lot with the new Whig party, but was hardly a Whig of the Webster-Clay school.

Adams's sojourn with the voice of democracy in Massachusetts politics thus came to an end. Although he would never admit it, he had been swept up in the democratic tide and had benefited from it at the polls. He lost some of this support after the 1836 election, when Antimasons in the Plymouth district flocked into the Democratic party. While he had no trouble beating the Democratic challenger, William Jackson, he never again enjoyed the victory margins of his Antimasonic days. His share of the total vote dropped from 83 percent in 1836 to 59 percent in 1838 to 54 percent in 1840; then his district was altered and his total dropped another two percentage points.[65]

Yet, while he lost touch with many of his Antimasonic followers back home, he kept in step with his fellow Antimasons in Congress, who never doubted for a moment that Old Hickory and his followers were scoundrels. Like Adams they perceived a new evil on the horizon, a monstrous "Slave Power," which threatened to fasten fetters upon the entire nation. Unlike their fellow Whigs they joined Adams in fighting the Slave Power on every issue, not sporadically, but consistently for years to come.

CHAPTER III

Guardian of the Future

When Adams went to Congress in 1831, party organizations were feeble and electoral coalitions in disarray. The two-party system of Jefferson's day was dead. A new one had yet to evolve.

Both the friends and foes of Jackson's administration called themselves "Republican." The use of modifiers, such as "Democratic Republican" for the supporters of Jackson and "National Republican" for the followers of Clay, was neither popular nor commonplace. The terms commonly used to distinguish various Republican factions were "Administration men" and "Anti-Administration men"—or "Jackson men," "Clay men," and "Antimasons." Not until 1834–35, at the earliest, did the lines of party cleavage begin to solidify. Even then many Congressmen were reluctant to give up the good old name of "Republican" and accept such new designations as "Democrat" or "Whig." Many were still uncommitted, voting with the administration half the time, and against it the other half.

That was not the case with Adams. From the day he entered Congress he was an Anti-Administration man, and everyone in Congress knew it and acted accordingly. True, he never saw himself as a "Clay man" and made the familiar claim, heard from many politicians, that he was "above" politics and "always" an independent. His history-conscious family would later seize upon such remarks, underscore them, and painstakingly portray him as an independent who was never tied down by party politics. Their viewpoint came to dominate most historical

writing and still persists in historical literature. But it turned
reality virtually on its head: Adams was much more of a party
warrior than he or his family acknowledged, and he was anything but independent when it came to the Jackson administration.

His choices were thus limited. He preferred to fight with
Antimasons at his side, against the followers of Webster and
Clay in his home state of Massachusetts and against the supporters of Jackson in the nation's capital. He enjoyed excoriating
Boston Brahmins as well as Tennessee slavemasters, Harrison
Gray Otis as well as Andrew Jackson. He hated Otis even more
than Jackson, and loathed Jackson, Clay, and Webster with
almost equal ferocity. But when political Antimasonry crum-
bled, he had to join forces with men he despised—with Clay,
Webster, and even Otis—against the Administration party. He
voted with the Jackson administration on a few celebrated occasions, but nine times out of ten he voted with the opposition.
And, as he was quick to point out, "the call for yeas and nays
is the bugle-horn of party, and never fails to rally the pack."[1]

The "bugle-horn of party," in fact, was clearly more important
to Adams than to most members of Congress. He was not
surrounded, as his family and many historians have maintained, by a motley assortment of party hacks who blindly
followed the dictates of their party. Quite the contrary, most
Congressmen in the early 1830s were non-party voters. Typical
of the majority was James Findlay, a Jackson man from Ohio,
who served with Adams from 1831 to 1833. Findlay voted against
the Jackson administration almost as often as he voted with it.[2]

The idea that Jackson had a well-disciplined party in Congress
that heeded his every whim was another figment of the Adams
family's imagination. The Jacksonians were even less disci-
plined than the opposition. This was partly because Congressmen from the West and South, where Old Hickory was particularly popular, often ignored the party "bugle-horn." Far more
attentive were Antimasons and Northeasterners, who had the
best records in Congress as good, reliable party men. Adams,
a member of both categories, was a stalwart member of the
pack.

In voting against the Jackson administration, Adams was in

step with both his fellow Antimasons and the dominant voices in New England. Castigated as a rebel for supporting the Antimasons in state politics, he was invariably on the side of the Webster men when the "yeas and nays" were called in Congress. He differed with them in debate, placing more emphasis on internal improvements and building for the future and less on the virtues of the past, the sanctity of established institutions, the wisdom of the Founding Fathers, and the need for high tariffs. He was also less diplomatic in his dealings with the South, savagely blaming Jackson's entire program on "slaveholding exterminators of Indians," and constantly stressing the fact that Old Hickory's support of states' rights, small government, an old-fashioned agrarian economy, and agricultural expansion best suited the South and slavery. Nevertheless, like most Webster men, he was wedded to the dominant New England view of economic development and was a staunch believer in protective tariffs, internal improvements, the "orderly" sale of public lands, and a strong national bank. Thus, when it came time to vote, he was generally in accord with Webster's followers, roll call after roll call, year after year.

Not only did Adams enjoy considerable support when he began his career in Congress, he also started from a position of power. Seven days after the swearing-in ceremony he was appointed chairman of the Committee of Manufactures and thrust into Washington politics with a chance to again shape the future of the nation.

His quick rise to prominence was partly due to the workings of Congress. It was structured in such a way that newcomers could rapidly reach positions of authority—and frequently did. Seniority, a troublesome problem in Congress today, had little significance. Most Congressmen served only a term or two. The turnover rate was such that Adams was one of 89 newcomers in a House of 213 members. Only 46 of Adams's fellow freshmen would return for a second term, and only 26 for a third. In his second term, thanks partly to a new apportionment decreed by the census, there were 152 new faces in a larger House of 240 members. Two years after that, there were another 115 new names to learn.[3]

The high turnover rate, in itself, was probably enough to

force the Speaker of the House to appoint some freshmen to key committees. But it worked in conjunction with an unwritten House rule that each major committee must have geographical and factional balance. In practice, the system enhanced the power of newcomers from small states with a high turnover rate at the expense of Congressmen from states with a large number of Representatives, namely New York and Pennsylvania. At times, to satisfy requirements of geographical suitability, a Speaker would have to appoint unknown freshmen to committees in preference to sitting members. Thus usually one-third to one-half of a committee's members were serving their first term, and the average amount of experience on even a major committee, such as Adams's Committee of Manufactures, was only two or three years.

Under these circumstances, if the Speaker valued experience at all, he often had to turn to seasoned veterans in the opposition party to head a few committees. Putting a man with Adams's experience in charge of a major committee, therefore, was unusual only in that Adams was such a prominent member of the opposition. But Speaker Andrew Stevenson, a good Jackson man, was hardly blind to the dictates of partisan politics. He could have appointed Adams to the Foreign Affairs committee, where he obviously belonged. Instead Stevenson appointed Adams to Manufactures, where he might embarrass himself, and refused to let him switch places with another Massachusetts Representative, Edward Everett, who had been assigned to Foreign Affairs.

Adams complained bitterly about Stevenson's behavior in his diary,[4] but he knew that he was starting from a position of power. Furthermore, he could hardly argue that foreign affairs were more important to his constituents than manufactures. Foreign affairs were clearly secondary in the life of the nation. The hottest issues were economic, and everything that Adams's administration had stood for—internal improvements, the tariff, the Second Bank of the United States—was being attacked.

Adams brought to the battle a firm commitment to national planning but no economic philosophy, per se. Regarding most economic theorists as little more than charlatans and sophists, he had no interest in economic theory, and without much thought or deliberation rejected the philosophy of *laissez-faire*. His knowledge of Adam Smith, the great economic philosopher of his youth, was vague and incomplete at best. He knew nothing about the contemporary theorists David Ricardo and Thomas Malthus, and freely admitted his ignorance. Nor did he have any interest in any of the popularizers of his day. He read bits and pieces from the writings of Mathew and Henry Carey, Tench Coxe, Daniel Raymond, William Gouge, Hezekiah Niles, and other Americans who wrote on economic matters, but he had no respect for their work and no desire to read more. He preferred to rely on ancient homilies and his own instincts.[5]

Particularly in the dark when it came to money and banking, two of the biggest issues of the day, he did nothing to rectify his lack of knowledge. The more complex functions of banks and the credit system thus remained a mystery to him. He knew more, perhaps, than the average man who waited in long lines during periodic bank panics, cursing the bankers and the "whole rotten paper system," hoping to redeem a pocketful of bank notes for hard coin. But like the average man he operated largely on the gut level, and his thinking was primitive. Mindful of the Biblical injunction that money was "the root of all evil," he distrusted all bankers, regarded most as swindlers and thieves, and thought the whole banking system was a "necessary evil" that had to be controlled. There was no room in his thinking for unexpected vagaries of the economy, the ups and downs of the business cycle, or even honest mistakes. Everything that went wrong was the fault of the rascals in charge. If a local bank was forced to temporarily suspend specie payment, that was a sin, the result of misconduct on the part of the banker. If banks across the country suddenly had to shut their doors, that too was the result of moral turpitude.[6]

Overall, he championed Alexander Hamilton's banking policies without accepting Hamilton's central premise. Hamilton, in his 1790 *Report on a National Bank,* had emphasized the monetary function of a national bank, pointing out that a bank "in good credit" could issue more notes than it could cover, and thus could expand the nation's money supply far beyond the available base in gold and silver. A national bank, therefore, could promote and control economic growth.

Hamilton's report stimulated a wide-ranging debate among

Adams's fellow New Englanders over what was the optimum safe ratio. That is, should a bank issue three, four, or five times what it had in the vault? But Hamilton's basic premise troubled the Adams family. Snarled John Adams in 1809: "Every dollar of a bank bill that is issued beyond the quantity of gold and silver in the vault represents nothing and is therefore a cheat upon somebody."[7] Echoed his son John Quincy in 1832: "All paper circulated beyond the amount representing the precious metals is fictitious capital."[8] What ratio, then, would he recommend? He never addressed the question directly, but often left the decided impression that the only proper ratio was one-to-one.

If that was the case, his instincts matched those of the Jeffersonian agrarians who clamored for the destruction of all banks and the whole paper system. But he was on Hamilton's side, and his main reason was that a strong national bank could be an agency of restraint, holding in check the smaller state banks, stopping them from issuing hordes of bank notes. It was far better, moreover, that the federal government rather than the states control the money market.

But who would control the national bankers? If bankers as a breed were cheaters and highwaymen, surely it made no sense to trust national bankers any more than state bankers. Indeed, the checkered career of the Second Bank of the United States proved that national bankers were apt to cheat, to issue twice as many notes as the law allowed, to foster wild speculation and financial chaos. Could the federal government, any more than state governments, overcome the power and influence of bankers and bring them under control? Surely federal politicians were just as subject to bribery and corruption as state politicians. But such logic fell on deaf ears, for the whole question of a national bank was one of passion more than reason, and Adams was just as illogical in his vehement support of a national bank as others were in their desire to destroy it.

While Adams approached the great economic issues of his day with only a smattering of economic knowledge and even less theory, he had a national vision that few others could match. From his extensive travels throughout the Atlantic world, as well as his life-long study of the ancient classics, he recognized the value of economic diversity. To develop national strength and remain an independent republic, he argued, the United States through the agency of the federal government must achieve more self-sufficiency and greater economic balance.

He thus became the champion of manufacturing long before mills sprang up in his native New England, indeed at a time when Daniel Webster and most of State Street were strongly biased against manufacturing and in favor of commerce. Although he never advocated the full gamut of programs recommended in Hamilton's *Report on Manufactures*, he insisted that the federal government must provide a favorable climate for industrial growth through tariff protection. If the government protected domestic manufacturing against foreign competition, he felt that other problems, such as capital accumulation and labor supply, would take care of themselves. Labor and capital would move to wherever money was to be made.

Like many other Americans who traveled widely in Europe, Adams knew that industrialization had its ugly side. To his brother in 1800 he described in detail what life was like in Silesia, Germany. In most cases, he noted with dismay, industrialization had degraded the worker and enriched the entrepreneur beyond belief. Factory owners, by their control over the manufacturing process, had diverted the lion's share of the profits into their own pockets and paid their workers only bare subsistence wages. The average family had hardly enough to "keep soul and body together." He wondered whether such baleful consequences could be avoided; whether the United States could industrialize and break free of its dependence on European factory goods without creating such gross misery and opulence. An example Americans might follow, Adams told his brother, was the mill town of Grunberg, where some six or seven hundred looms were owned by a corporation of the workers, and the profits were distributed widely rather than to the favored few.[9]

Yet apart from expressing hope that the United States avoid the wretched living conditions he found in Silesia and elsewhere in Europe, Adams was generally oblivious to the social impact of industrialization. New England industrialized in the first half of the nineteenth century, roughly the last fifty years of his life, and the great profits hardly found their way into the pockets of workers as in Grunberg. On the contrary, the richest 10 percent of the Massachusetts population watched gleefully as its share of the economic pie grew from less than half to more than three-fourths.[10] The pie as a whole, to be sure, grew enormously, and thus many workingmen enjoyed a higher standard of living than their forebears. The great industrial towns of New England, moreover, managed to ward off the dire poverty that was so common in Manchester, England, or in Silesia during the early nineteenth century. Still, industrial growth brought a host of problems to the Bay State, and there was much worry about working conditions, wages, strikes, urban growth, and Irish immigration.[11] Adams, however, devoted little time to such problems.

What he worried about, above all else, was national support for internal improvement. It was not enough to just establish manufacturing. The federal government had to knit together various parts of the economy, not only to create a bigger national market, but also to foster a sense of cohesion among the sections of the country. It was not simply a matter of farmers needing roads and canals to get their wheat and corn to market, and industrialists needing the same roads and canals to get pots, pans, and cotton goods to inland farmers. The nation itself was too big, too diverse, and if steps were not taken to tie it together, it would soon break into pieces.

Adams saw himself as the instigator of the entire national system of internal improvement. He told one correspondent in 1824: "I offered to the Senate . . . the first resolution . . . that ever was presented to Congress contemplating a *general system* of internal improvement." He told another in 1837: "I laid the foundation of it all." What he had in mind was a resolution he presented in 1807 calling on the Secretary of the Treasury to present a "plan" of internal improvements on a grand scale. Even though this resolution was voted down, it triggered another, which eventually led to the pathbreaking Report of 1808 by Albert Gallatin. To Adams's chagrin, however, much of the credit for a national system of internal improvement went to Henry Clay, who was hailed and cursed throughout the nation as the father of the "American System." As Adams saw it, his brainchild had fallen into the "hands of other and younger men" because he spent so much time abroad after 1808—and during this period his system "thrived and prospered and made their political fortunes, and kindled their vaulting ambition."[12]

His plan for improvement, he noted with pride, was far broader than that of the latecomers who stole his thunder. He was interested in more than roads and canals. His conception of "internal improvement," a phrase which he always used in the singular, included not only transportation and communication projects, but also a vast array of scientific and educational endeavors. The government's job was to use federal revenues to improve the condition of the people—physically, economically, intellectually, morally, and politically.

Funding this brainchild presented no problem for Adams. The necessary capital would come from the sale of public lands and from the tariff. Agreeing with Jackson that the government's first obligation was to pay off the public debt, he noted gleefully that the day was rapidly approaching when the entire national debt would be discharged. Then "the swelling tide of wealth" pouring into the federal treasury from government land offices and custom houses could "be made to reflow in unfailing streams of improvement from the Atlantic to the Pacific Ocean." The results would be marvelous: railroads and canals would checker the entire Union in ten years, hundreds of thousands of workers would have constant employment and higher wages, and every dollar spent would repay itself "four fold in the enhanced value of the Public Lands."[13]

This dream, in turn, meant that the federal government had to have a public land policy—as well as a tariff policy—designed to raise revenue. That, in Adams's mind, was only fair, because the land had been purchased with the money and blood of the entire nation and thus the whole nation should reap the benefits. But the idea that the land should raise revenue put Adams at odds with Thomas Hart Benton, the forceful Senator from Missouri, who since 1820 claimed to speak for the "New West" in demanding that the lands be sold quickly and cheaply for the benefit of actual settlers. Benton and others also clamored for "pre-emption," which would give squatters on government lands the right to buy 160 acres at the minimum price of $1.25 an acre without having to participate in a government auction, where they might be outbid by outsiders. With less success, Benton campaigned vigorously for the concept of "graduation," which would not only reduce the price on those lands that remained unsold year after year, but also would give away "refuse lands" that could not be sold at a reduced price. Adams was horrified: "The whole drift" of Benton's proposal, he noted in 1826, "was to excite and encourage hopes among the western people that they can extort the lands from the Government for nothing."[14]

Adams, although he denounced western extortion and demanded that public lands be sold for their "true value," agreed with Benton that public lands must be distributed to private citizens. He had no patience with Boston Federalists who claimed that the rise of the West would lead to the demise of New England in national politics. They were shortsighted. As long as Yankees went west in droves, and the West benefited from Yankee benevolence, it was bound to enhance New England's influence in the Union—not undermine it.[15]

Nor did he ever seriously consider the suggestion of his Secretary of the Treasury, Richard Rush, that migration westward had pernicious economic consequences, in that it drew off eastern capital and labor and thus retarded the industrial development of the nation.[16] Even though some modern analysts agree with Rush,[17] the federal government, with virtually no army and no bureaucracy, simply could not have stopped people from going west and "squatting" on public lands. Legally, squatting was trespassing, and Congress in 1807 had given the army the duty of driving trespassers off the public lands. But this obligation proved impossible to carry out.

Adams's dream, in any event, depended on the sale of public lands. He hoped to create a beneficent circle whereby land sales would pay for improvements, and improvements in turn would quadruple the value of public lands, and so on—so in time his children's children would reap the benefits of a more bountiful Republic. He thus saw the vast expanse of vacant lands in the West, under the benevolent hand of the federal government, coming into cultivation and bringing prosperity not only to Benton's settlers but to the entire nation.[18]

Adams, in short, was an economic nationalist. The benevolent hand of government was the linch-pin of all his dreams. *Laissez-faire* was anathema: only fools or traitors would let the nation's economy be governed by the invisible hand of the international marketplace. The federal government, to be sure, should never discourage individual enterprise, nor meddle with the sacred right of private property. But if the United States were to follow Adam Smith's doctrine and concentrate on what it could produce best and most efficiently, meeting the rest of its needs through trade, then it would remain a nation of cotton planters and farmers at the mercy of industrial England. To insure political independence, as well as the economic well-being of future generations, the federal government had to take positive steps to develop a balanced, self-sufficient economy. That, indeed, was its sacred duty.[19]

Adams doubted that Andrew Jackson would follow such an enlightened course. Indeed, he went to Congress certain that Old Hickory wanted to destroy the whole concept of a positive state. Adams saw a host of demons on the horizon, including John C. Calhoun of South Carolina, who wanted to kill the tariff; Thomas Hart Benton of Missouri, who hoped to plunder the public domain; and the Old Republicans of Virginia, who detested the very concept of an energetic national government. In May 1830, Adams sat down with Richard Rush to predict the future: "We agreed," Adams noted in his diary, "that the Indians are already sacrificed; that the public lands will be given away; that domestic industry and internal improvement will be strangled; and when the public debt will be paid off and the bank charter expired, there will be no great interest left upon which the action of the General Government will operate. The future must be consigned to 'the sweet little cherub that sits up aloft.' "[20]

As chairman of the Committee of Manufactures, Adams was in a position to draw blood in the fight against Jackson, Benton, and Calhoun. But whose blood? That was uncertain when the biennial problem of tariff revision was turned over to Adams's committee in December 1831. For there were three lines of battle, often shifting, always entangled.

One was over the extinction of the federal debt. The national debt was being paid off at a rate that would extinguish it entirely within a year or so, and it was Jackson's passion to have it paid in full by the end of his first term. Adams had no desire to fight the President on this issue. Never sharing the Hamiltonian view that a well-funded debt had advantages, he basically agreed with Jackson that it was bad morally and practically for the country to be in debt. Hence he told Henry Clay, who thought Jackson's goal should be disregarded, that whether or not the President's desire was "the wisest idea that ever entered the heart of man," it "ought to be indulged, rather than opposed."[21]

The second issue, which was intertwined with the first, was the cotton states' demand for tariff concessions. Since Jackson's victory over Adams in 1828, the followers of Vice-President Calhoun had counted on the Jackson administration to drastically cut the Tariff of 1828, the so-called Tariff of Abominations. But that would have cost Jackson support in such crucial pro-tariff states as Pennsylvania and Ohio and delay payment of the national debt. So Jackson had urged his first Congress to use the "utmost caution" in handling tariff reform; and Congress had responded in 1830 with revisions that barely touched the worst features of the Tariff of Abominations.

The Vice-President's South Carolina followers were outraged. They blamed the tariff for all their woes. Their fathers and forefathers had become rich planting rice, indigo, and sea island cotton, and they had done well themselves with the addition of upland cotton. The depression of the early 1820s, however, not only disrupted their economy but also coincided with the rise of New Orleans and the more bountiful cotton states in the Southwest. Now Charleston, once the pride of the South, was a mere dwarf alongside New Orleans; and now South Carolina, which had once produced more cotton than the rest of the South combined, was being overshadowed by Georgia, Alabama, and Mississippi. Even worse, after the furious congressional debate over the gradual abolition of slavery in Missouri, their most trusted slaves had become rebellious.

Who was to blame for their troubles? In the early 1820s a rival states' rights faction had pointed to Calhoun, claiming that his enthusiastic nationalism and support for protective tariffs after the War of 1812 had brought the state's decline. Soon they raised such a howl that the Calhounites, to save themselves from political extinction, abandoned all traces of economic nationalism. Indeed, they suddenly became the most radical states' righters in the entire South, screaming even louder than their rivals against the evils of protective tariffs and an energetic federal government. In 1828 they denounced the Tariff of Abominations in the *South Carolina Exposition and Protest*. Secretly written by Calhoun, it set forth the famous doctrine of nullification. The states, so the nullifiers argued, were sovereign; they had created the federal government, and thus were the only proper judges of whether it had overstepped its powers. Should a state judge an act of Congress to be in violation of the Constitution, it could declare the act unconstitutional and prevent enforcement within its borders. Only an amendment to the Constitution, which would necessitate the approval of at least two-thirds of the states, could override a state's objection.

Nullification was just a threat until it became clear that the Jackson administration had no intention of gutting the tariff. After the Jacksonians failed to do so by 1830, the nullifiers called for action, but everything went wrong. Totally mystified by the fine legal points of Calhoun's argument, even South Carolinians dismissed "nullification" as just a fancy word for "treason" or "revolution." And Andrew Jackson, who boasted of being a South Carolinian "by birth," made it clear where he stood. While toasting the Union at the Jefferson Day dinner he glared at Calhoun with overt hostility, signaling to all that he regarded his Vice-President as a traitor or madman, not a compatriot.

By the time Adams reached Congress the nullifiers had regrouped and were better prepared for action. Their opportunity came when Jackson, in his presidential message in December 1831, called on Congress to relieve the people of unnecessary taxation once the federal debt was extinguished. This proposal was turned over to the Committee of Ways and Means, which was chaired by George McDuffie of South Carolina. McDuffie was not just a nullifier but a spell-binding orator who had managed to convince thousands of South Carolinians that Yankee manufacturers, through import duties, were in effect stealing forty bales of cotton out of every hundred the South produced. Indeed, although completely fallacious, his forty-bale theory had proved to be political dynamite, far more explosive than the legal intricacies of Calhoun's argument.

In January 1832, quickly and to no one's surprise, McDuffie's committee came forth with a sure-fire way to cut taxes. Not only did federal custom houses, bellowed McDuffie, collect more revenue than all other federal agencies combined, but every principle of justice, patriotism, and sound policy dictated the elimination of protective tariffs, for they were ruining the South, injuring the West, and benefiting only the manufacturing states. Accordingly, his committee proposed that duties on all protected articles be reduced in three steps to a flat rate of 12½ percent by June 30, 1833.[22]

That, however, was far more than Jackson wanted. The Old General wanted to reduce the tariff, but just enough to completely cut the ground from under the nullifiers, so that if they raised a howl they would have few followers and thus could be crushed. Adams too was willing to cut the tariff, less drastically than Jackson but enough to make some concessions to the South and eliminate what he considered obvious injustices in the Tariff of Abominations, a document which he signed as President but never regarded as above reproach. He therefore accepted his committee's recommendation, made at its first meeting, that he work with Jackson's Secretary of the Treasury, Louis McLane, to determine what sort of bill the administration would support.

Although Adams got along well with McLane, he worried constantly about the administration's plans, especially after several months passed and McLane had yet to come forth with a set of proposals. Would Jackson harken to the shrill voices of his native South? Would he expect northern industrialists to bear the major burden for national harmony and accept sharp cuts in the tariff? That depended in part on how he responded to the third major issue, the one that was dearest to Adams's heart.

This was the issue of internal improvement. In Adams's mind

it was not only tied to the extinction of the national debt, but it was the solution to the big problem facing all protariff men. The problem was the pending surplus: once the debt was paid, the federal government would be in the awkward position of collecting far more revenue than it was obliged to spend. How, under these circumstances, could protariff men justify high taxes on imports? The problem, hard for us to even imagine, caused thousands of sleepless nights.

There were two obvious solutions. One, championed by Henry Clay, was to cut tariff revenues to $7 or $8 million annually by increasing duties on some protected articles to such a high rate that it became prohibitively expensive to buy foreign imports. Adams, although intrigued by Clay's solution, concluded that it was too harsh and inflammatory, that it would enrage the nullifiers and drive more southern hotspurs into their camp. A much better remedy, he thought, was to keep tariff revenues relatively high, and once the debt was extinguished to start channeling millions of tariff dollars into internal improvements.[23]

That solution, along with protecting manufacturers in his home district, was central to Adams's battle plan. When Thomas R. Mitchell, a free-trader from South Carolina, proposed that tariff revenues be cut to $13 million a year, Adams insisted that revenues could not fall below $20 million, and not because he was a "worshipper of the tariff, but of internal improvement." Similarly, he told McLane that his intention was to keep tariff revenues high enough, once the debt was paid, to "reserve as much as five millions a year" for internal improvement.[24]

Neither Adams nor McLane thought there was much chance that Jackson would go along. The President had not only vetoed Clay's pet project, the Maysville Road Bill, in May 1830, but also questioned repeatedly the constitutionality of federally sponsored internal improvements. The constitutional argument, in Adams's mind, was obviously fraudulent. He had no patience with Jackson or any other "strict constructionist" who claimed that the Constitution did not give the federal government the right to build roads and canals. Indeed, after Jefferson had spent $15 million to purchase Louisiana, southern platitudes about the limited powers of the federal government were merely impudent. So too was Jackson's pious suggestion that internal improvements would be feasible if the proper constitutional amendment were passed. He knew very well that such an amendment would be voted down in his native South.[25]

Did Adams misjudge Jackson? Some twentieth-century historians have dismissed Jackson's constitutional reservations, in the words of George Rogers Taylor, as "forced and unreal, little more than forensic shadowboxing." Despite all his constitutional quibbling, notes Taylor, Jackson increased appropriations for internal improvements by some $600,000 a year.[26] Such an argument, however, never would have convinced Adams, for in his mind the Jackson administration had the golden opportunity to spend far more on internal improvements than any previous administration, thanks to the extinction of the national debt. And what did Jackson do? He spent his time establishing a major roadblock, talking up the need for a constitutional amendment! The constitutional argument, snarled Adams, had no merit to it whatever; it was entirely self-serving, designed to mask selfish interests, particularly those of Jackson and other slavemasters who feared that internal improvements would bring unending progress to the free states and the downfall of the plantation South.[27]

Finally, in April 1832, after an agonizing delay of nearly five months, McLane came forth with a set of proposals. As predicted, there was no call for major expenditures on roads and canals. McLane recommended that present tariff schedules be slashed by $10 million, from roughly $22 million per year to $12 million. This would be accomplished mainly by reducing average rates from 45 percent to 27 percent.[28] While this proposal was hardly as radical as McDuffie's, it put the major burden for national harmony on northern manufacturers. It was a compromise, but with a distinct southern bias.

With a set of proposals finally before them, Adams's committee went to work drafting legislation. The committee members already knew that they were at odds on virtually every issue. Indeed, according to James Findlay of Ohio, the Speaker of the House could "not have selected seven members from the whole house so effectively suited to disagree with one another as the seven members of the committee of manufacturers."[29] The squabbling had already caused Adams, on several occasions, to try to be excused as chairman. But Adams and the other six were told repeatedly that their work was essential, that the nation desperately needed a "compromise" tariff, that the very future of the nation depended on their handiwork. So they met daily for nearly a month, hearing testimony, placating scores of interest groups, juggling numbers. The labor was herculean, so exhausting that it played into Adams's hands. For despite his constant grumbling he had the stamina to maintain the upper hand; while others went home early, or dreamed of rest and relaxation, he worked and pushed for "compromise." Finally the majority agreed on a general bill, without agreeing on any of its specific parts, and "indulged" their chairman to present his report.[30]

So on May 23, 1832, Adams in behalf of his committee reported House Bill 584 to revise the tariff laws of the United States. Examining the entire history of the tariff, from virtually every possible angle, the old warrior claimed repeatedly that the bill was a "compromise" based largely on the administration's recommendations and that it granted the South major concessions. In fact, Adams's bill deviated substantially from the administration's recommendations, cutting total revenues by only $5 million, and establishing a reserve for "defense" and internal improvements. Duties on the "average" protected article would be cut, but only about half as much as the administration wanted. The cuts, moreover, were hardly across the board: indeed, even though overall tariff rates would decline, the crucial levies on iron, cotton goods, and fine woolens would remain high, and the "average" reduction was achieved in large part by placing items not made in the United States on the duty-free list. But the South, argued Adams, should be particularly pleased, and especially by the elimination of all "minimum" levies and the remission of duties on coarse wool and coarse woolens, so-called "Negro clothes," which slavemasters bought for their slaves.[31]

The nullifiers were not pleased, and neither were New England sheep farmers and woolens manufacturers. The producers of cheap woolens claimed that they would be "utterly ruined." The nullifiers insisted that Adams's bill was a sham, that

sharp reductions on iron, cottons, and all woolens were absolutely necessary, that overall duties would actually be increased
by $1 million. So Adams had to work long hours, hearing
complaints from both sides, listening to speeches that often
began at 10 o'clock in the morning and lasted well into the
evening, and sometimes continued the next day and the day
after. "I am chained to my seat," he wrote his wife, "as long
as the Tariff is before the House."[32]

The final bill, to Adams's surprise, fared much better among
southern Representatives than among his fellow New Englanders. Half of the New England delegation voted against the bill,
not because they disliked the bill as a whole, but because they
did not want to go on record as making concessions to the
South at the expense of some of their own constituents. A
majority of southern Representatives, on the other hand, voted
for the bill, still complaining about the continued protection for
northern industry, but realizing that generally lower import
duties would result in lower prices.[33] The bill passed by a two-
to-one margin, and in many quarters Adams was hailed as a
hero who had resolved a national crisis. Even Harrison Gray
Otis sang his praises![34]

While Adams was basking in glory, however, George McDuffie
and the other nullifiers in Congress returned home proclaiming
that a great injustice had been done. And John C. Calhoun,
who by this time had broken completely with Jackson, urged
his fellow Carolinians to action. In the fall elections, the nullifiers won the two-thirds majority in the South Carolina legislature necessary to call a special state convention. Meeting in
November 1832, the convention swiftly nullified the tariff acts
of 1828 and 1832, forbade the collection of duties within the
state beginning February 1833, called on the state legislature to
undertake all necessary military preparations, and threatened
secession and war should Washington resort to arms. In antic-
ipation, hotheads prepared for battle.

Adams predicted disaster. South Carolina was clearly acting
like a bully, trying to dictate legislation at the point of a bayonet.
But the big danger, in his judgment, was in Washington. He
was certain that Jackson, even though he obviously detested

Calhoun, was collaborating with the nullifiers. Although Jackson talked tough, denounced the nullifiers as traitors, threatened to hang Calhoun, put the forts in Charleston harbor on alert, and ordered General Winfield Scott to take command of the forces in South Carolina, he was just posturing, thought Adams; in the end Jackson would give the nullifiers everything they wanted—the protection of industry, internal improvements, the Adams tariff. All would be sacrificed, just as the Indians had been.[35]

When Congress reopened in December 1832, events only confirmed Adams's worst fears. Jackson's annual message called on Congress to examine the tariff question once again, to cut duties even further, to do away with the "inequalities" that caused so much trouble in "one quarter of the United States." In addition, the President suggested selling public lands at cost rather than for revenue. He indicated, moreover, that he would approve federal internal improvements only if the states requested a constitutional amendment sanctioning them. The message, noted Adams, "surrenders the whole Union to the nullifiers of the South and the land-robbers of the West."[36]

Six days later, to Adams's surprise, Jackson issued a ringing proclamation against the nullifiers, in words that Adams himself might have written, sternly warning South Carolinians against resisting the laws of the Union. Yet despite the strength of the President's proclamation Adams was still certain that the words were merely words and no action would be taken against South Carolina. He had learned "in secret," he told New Jersey Governor Samuel Southard, "that no measure of compulsion is intended. . . . The policy of the Administration is to surrender the whole Union to Nullification at discretion, and to crush John C. Calhoun and five or six Scoundrels."[37]

The turn of events in Congress, argued Adams, bore out his gloomy forecast. The Speaker, in choosing members for Adams's committee, replaced "a real friend to the Protective system," Charles Dayan of New York, with another New Yorker, Michael Hoffman, "the most anti-manufacturing man in the house." To Adams's dismay, Hoffman succeeded in checkmating Adams and the manufacturing interests, and the task of proposing new tariff legislation fell entirely into the hands of

the Committee of Ways and Means, now chaired by a loyal
Jacksonian, Gulian C. Verplanck of New York.[38] In short order
Verplanck's committee brought forth a bill written by the
administration that would cut tariff revenues in half by 1834,
reduce total revenues by nearly $7 million, and totally eliminate
Adams's beloved long-range plan for internal improvements.

Shortly thereafter, while Adams was desperately trying to
derail the Verplanck bill, Jackson asked Congress to enact a bill
to make it easier to use force against South Carolina if that
should become necessary. Dismissed by Adams as just another
smokescreen, the Force Bill went to the Senate where Calhoun,
now a Senator, rose to his feet and lashed away at Jackson,
generating a full-scale constitutional debate. Soon the Jacksonians were fighting on several fronts, trying to get the Force Bill
through the Senate and the Verplanck Tariff through the House.
Stumbling badly, they eventually lost the initiative in tariff reform to their old nemesis, Senator Henry Clay, who combined
forces with Calhoun and pushed through the Compromise Tariff of 1833. Tariff rates would go down, in gradual steps over
a nine-year period, to a uniform rate of 20 percent. Simultaneously Congress passed a Force Bill, and Old Hickory signed
both measures on the same day. Ten days later, the South
Carolina convention reassembled, rescinded its ordinance of
nullification, and in a final gesture of defiance voted to nullify
the Force Bill.

The outcome, then, was inconclusive. Most modern historians hold that the nullification crisis ended in a great victory for
Jackson, democratic nationalism, and majority rule. The Old
General's firmness and toughness, so it has been argued repeatedly, forced the nullifiers to back down. That, of course,
was not the way Adams saw it. Using a simile that was very
close to home, he likened the nullifiers to an old dowager who
ruled her family by throwing hysterical fainting fits, and claimed
that Jackson, in calling for the repeal of the Adams Tariff, ignored the whole concept of majority rule and in fact stifled "the
firm and manly voice of nineteen-twentieths of our constituents,
to satisfy the brainsick doubts, or appease the menacing clamors
of less than one-twentieth."[39] Adams, it should be noted, was
not the only one who had such a negative view. Among others,

Alexis de Tocqueville was absolutely certain that the federal government had been defeated. Washington, in his judgment, was just too feeble to enforce the law. Once Congress was faced with angry citizens "with arms in their hands," it "completely abandoned the principle of the tariff," and "to conceal its defeat" passed the Force Bill.[40]

While Adams's harsh assessment of Jackson's behavior has been rejected by most historians, his perception of the underlying issue has gained favor. Like many twentieth-century commentators, he always maintained that the furor over the tariff reflected more virulent tensions over slavery. The "anti-tariff policy of the South," he said, was at heart a "slaveholding policy." The great slaveowners were afraid that the free states would prosper, gain the upper hand, and bring the slavemasters' domination of the nation to an end.[41]

The only reason there was any confusion on this point, he argued, was that the slavemasters' chief spokesmen, Jackson and Calhoun, were personally at sword's point. The Jackson men in Congress were thus confused. They had trouble reconciling "two incoherent elements, subserviency to the slaveholding policy and the personal animosities of President Jackson against Vice-President Calhoun." But despite the hatred between the Jacksonians and the Calhounites, "the real question now convulsing the Union was, whether a population spread over an immense territory, consisting of one great division all freemen, and another of masters and slaves, could exist permanently together as members of one community or not; that, to go a step further back, the question at issue was slavery."[42]

If the nullification crisis ended in a smashing victory for slavemasters determined to maintain the upper hand, Jackson's concurrent decision to destroy the Second Bank of the United States marked yet another triumph for the forces of stagnation. The major difference, in Adams's mind, was that Jackson's war against the Bank not only catered to the "brainsick doubts" of strict constructionists in the South but also satisfied the venal interests of state bankers in the North and particularly the money barons of Wall Street. In both cases the losers were the voices of progress, nationalists like himself who believed that the federal government was duty-bound to improve the condition of the people, while the victors were states' righters who dreaded the future and desperately wanted to preserve the past.[43]

Adams played a curious role in the Bank War. He said on several occasions that the Bank was more important than the tariff, but his actions often indicated the contrary. At times he was very active in the controversy; at other times he was almost a passive observer. One explanation, of course, is that he lacked the requisite knowledge to handle the fine points of the Bank controversy. Another is that he was so involved in the concurrent dispute over the tariff that he had neither the time nor the energy to fight for the Bank.

The tariff, moreover, was clearly far more important to his constituents than was the Bank. Ordinary people in the Plymouth district had little reason to be concerned about the Second Bank. The notes of the Second Bank were not the principal means of exchange, as they were in the Southwest and the West; indeed, state bank notes completely dominated the means of exchange, more so in Massachusetts than anywhere else in the Union, so that a typical Plymouth storekeeper in 1832 handled thirty-three times as many state notes as federal notes. By the same token, no one in Adams's district looked to the Second Bank to keep the wildcat bankers in line, or to ride herd on bankers who issued far more notes than they could cover. That job was being done by the Suffolk Bank system of Boston.[44] So while Adams had to worry about his stand on the tariff, an issue so sensitive that manufacturers and workers in his district might even turn him out of office if tariff levies were slashed, that was not the case with the Bank.

On the other hand, Adams liked the way the Second Bank was being run. Chartered in 1816, it had gotten off to a rocky start, first overexpanding its notes and contributing to wild speculation under the loose direction of William Jones, and then when hard times came in 1819 driving debtors and state bankers to the wall under the tight-fisted policies of Langdon Cheeves. The Bank, in fact, made a host of enemies in those trying times. But after Nicholas Biddle took over the Bank's presidency in 1823, the Bank ran smoothly, and the national money market at last seemed to have a semblance of order.

Adams, moreover, thought highly of Biddle. He owned fifteen shares of stock in the Bank, and whenever he stopped at the Bank's main office on Chestnut Street in Philadelphia to pick up his dividends, Biddle himself waited on him. A cultured aristocrat, Biddle shared Adams's taste for poetry and the classics, exchanged dinner engagements with the Adamses, and wrote flattering letters. Needless to say, he never mentioned that he had voted against Adams in both 1824 and 1828.[45] Had Adams known that fact, he undoubtedly would have thought less of Biddle and his bank. As it was, Adams was one of the banker's staunchest admirers when he set off for Congress in the fall of 1831.

By that time it was clear to all that Biddle's bank was in trouble. Jackson had made it known on numerous occasions that he was against renewing the Bank's charter, and the odds were that he would be re-elected and still President when the charter expired in 1836. Renewal, some speculated, might even become an issue in the 1832 election. So on his way to Washington Adams stopped at Philadelphia and had Biddle sell his stock, partly to divest himself of a potential conflict of interest and partly to pay off some Boston debts.[46] Upon arriving in Washington, Adams was uncertain as to what the Bank ought to do, first arguing that it would be stupid to push for recharter four years in advance of the expiration date and then changing his mind and arguing the opposite.[47]

He was not the only one who had trouble deciding what to do. Jackson, in his annual message, told Congress that he wanted the Bank abolished. Then several days later, to the astonishment of Old Hickory's supporters in Congress, Secretary of the Treasury Louis McLane recommended that the Bank's charter be renewed. While dumbfounded Jacksonians wondered whether the administration had changed its position, Nicholas Biddle received all sorts of contrary advice on what course of action the Bank ought to take. Henry Clay, who planned to run against Jackson in 1832, urged Biddle to push for recharter before the election on the grounds that Jackson might not dare a veto in an election year. Secretary McLane and other friends of the Bank argued that such a move would be folly: it would not only prove Jackson's contention that the Bank was a powerful political agency that tried to shove the government around, but also goad him into a veto. Biddle also suspected a veto, but finally decided to gamble and make the Bank an election issue if the need arose. So on January 9, 1832, he petitioned for recharter.

In the House, the Bank's petition was turned over to George McDuffie's Committee of Ways and Means, which reported out a bill in favor of the Bank a month later. Adams, busy with the tariff controversy, took little note of the proceedings. He expected the Bank Bill to pass, but had "inside information" that Jackson would veto it.[48]

Then in mid-February it became clear that the Jacksonians intended to do everything possible to discredit the Bank—and perhaps to stop the Bank Bill from even getting through Congress and to the President's desk. Congressman Augustine S. Clayton of Georgia, working in concert with Senator Thomas Hart Benton of Missouri, called on the House to appoint a select committee to investigate the misconduct of the Bank, listing seven instances of charter violation "involving forfeiture," and fifteen instances of abuse "requiring correction." Clayton wanted a wide-ranging investigation that would look at everything, the wrong-doings of branch banks as well as the mother bank in Philadelphia, old offenses that occurred before Biddle's tenure as well as recent violations. If McDuffie and other pro-Bank Congressmen opposed such an investigation, the Jacksonians would then accuse them of trying to cover up the Bank's misdeeds.[49]

Prompted by Biddle and concerned about the fate of the Bank Bill, Adams finally stepped in to set limits on Clayton's witchhunt. He pushed through an amendment that limited inquiry to operations of the mother bank, thereby omitting the twenty-seven branches, including the nearby Baltimore branch, which had a notorious reputation for favoritism, chicanery, and corruption. Also, through his amendment, he limited investigation to breaches of the Bank's charter, thus eliminating the fifteen abuses "requiring correction," and forced the committee to complete its investigation in just five weeks. Having partly defanged Clayton's investigation, he grumbled loudly when Speaker Stevenson appointed him to serve as one of the seven investigators, along with Clayton and three other anti-Bank men, and McDuffie and one other Bank supporter.[50]

The seven-man committee then went off to Philadelphia. Apart from the fact that the committee members got along splendidly, their three-week investigation produced no surprises. Biddle cooperated with the minority but not the majority. The majority tried to dig up as much dirt as possible, probing deeply into alleged abuses as well as charter violations, while the minority defended the Bank and tried to set limits on the majority's inquisition. Adams complained that the majority ignored the restrictions placed on the investigation; the majority, in turn, claimed that they were hamstrung by the five-week deadline and their inability to take their investigation to Baltimore and other cities.

The committee produced three reports. The majority report, in calling for the Bank's termination, accused the Bank of a host of sins, including usury, selling coin, building houses to sell or rent, and buying the support of Congressmen and newsmen through favorable loans. Written by Clayton, a freshman Congressman, the majority report was so flimsy that a neutral newspaper, *Niles' Weekly Register*, called it "the strangest mixture of *water-gruel and vinegar*, the most awkward and clumsy and exaggerated *ex-parte* production that we ever read."[51] Thus McDuffie, who wrote the minority report, had little trouble refuting the majority's charges. Adams signed McDuffie's report, which was brief and plain spoken, but he felt compelled to submit a much longer report of his own, in which he not only defended the Bank at great length but also made several charges against the Bank's enemies.[52]

These charges, in turn, were to have enormous impact on historical literature. Adams claimed, for example, that Jackson's attack on Biddle's bank was not just the handiwork of strict constructionists in the South. It was also the work of capitalists in "every state of the Union" who had invested heavily "in stocks of multiplied state banks. Most of these are rivals in business with the Bank of the United States, and they have all boards of directors and most of them are colleagued with newspapers, all eager for the destruction of the Bank. . . ." This was particularly true of New York bankers, thought Adams, who

found the Bank "doubly obnoxious" because it effectively cut
into their profits. Indeed, he believed the animosity of New
York bankers was "so great as even to spread its influence into
the legislature of the State."[53] Years later, Bray Hammond and
other historians would seize upon such remarks and portray
the Bank War as a struggle between rival business interests,
between irresponsible state bankers and the fiscally responsible
Nicholas Biddle, between Wall Street speculators and the staid
national bank on Chestnut Street.[54]

However, Adams probably did not know what he was talking
about. He was clearly guilty of oversimplification, picturing
virtually all state bankers as financial wild men, and lumping
virtually all state banks together as opponents of Biddle's bank.
Recent research has shown that many state bankers—especially
in such commercial centers as New Orleans, Cincinnati, Baltimore, and Philadelphia—were strong supporters of the national
bank. Also, rather than being wild speculators, most state bankers were fiscal conservatives, particularly those in New York
and other eastern cities. And while most of New York's leading
politicians were against Biddle's bank, they hardly took their
cues from Wall Street; if anything, they followed the dictates
of Martin Van Buren, the state's foremost politician.[55]

In any event, Adams's scathing indictment of the Bank's
enemies had more effect on future historians than on his fellow
Congressmen. Nicholas Biddle had six thousand copies printed
and widely distributed. While the Bank's supporters sang Adams's praises, the Richmond *Enquirer* and the Boston *Courier*
subjected him to blistering editorials. But in Congress, where
pro-Bank men already had votes to spare, the situation remained the same. Having helped to get the Bank Bill around
Clayton's attempted roadblock, Adams turned his attention once
again to the tariff controversy. That, along with the overbearing
Washington heat, sapped most of his energy as the Bank Bill
made its way through Congress. The bill finally passed on July
3, 1832, enjoying solid support among all congressional dele-
gations except those from New York and the South. Seven days
later, Jackson responded with a ringing veto. That too was
expected, and it concerned Adams far less than the fate of the
tariff bill, which Jackson had yet to sign into law.[56]

Unable to override the veto, Congress adjourned on July 16,

and Adams returned to Quincy. Elsewhere in the nation, the Bank veto quickly became a hot issue in the upcoming presidential election, with Jackson's friends embracing it as a second Declaration of Independence, claiming that the "humbler members of society" at last had a President who stood for even-handed justice and against special favors for the rich, and the followers of Clay lambasting it as the worst form of demagoguery. In Adams's home district, however, Jackson had no chance at all on election day, and the only issue of importance to Adams was whether the Antimasons would capture more votes than the "Clay Masons." Once the 1832 election was over and Jackson won handily in the nation as a whole, Adams presumed that the Bank War was over—that Biddle had gambled and lost and that the Bank was now a dead issue.

Adams presumed wrong. Even though Jackson won easily, receiving nearly 55 percent of the popular vote, the Old General was angry. He had expected to win by more, to crush Clay by a much bigger margin than he had beaten Adams by in 1828. But he had failed to match his 1828 victory margin, and thus his re-election was tainted by a decline in popular approval. The Bank veto had cost him votes, especially in Pennsylvania, and he was furious at Biddle not only for forcing his hand but for spending thousands to defeat him. Denied the triumph he felt he deserved, Jackson was determined to get even, to kill the Bank before it killed him.

At the same time, however, he had the nullifiers to deal with. So when Congress resumed in December, Adams found two issues on the President's agenda. The most pressing was the nullification crisis, and that was what occupied most of Adams's time. But the President, in his message to Congress, made it clear that he was still out to get the Bank, calling for another investigation and suggesting that the government's deposits were not safe in the Bank's hands. In due course, the House declared on March 2, 1833, by an overwhelming vote, that the government's deposits were perfectly safe in the Bank's vaults and ought to be left there. Adams, bemoaning the triumph of the South's antitariff policy, took little comfort in the President's defeat.[57]

Jackson himself was disgusted. And by this time Clay and

Calhoun had combined forces, snatched away his lead in tariff legislation, and pushed through the Compromise Tariff of 1833. Furious at the turn of events, Jackson blamed the Bank for his congressional troubles. That "hydra of corruption," he claimed, had bought congressional goodwill and put together the "corrupt" coalition between Clay and Calhoun to damage him. With the elimination of the national debt, moreover, federal money would pile up in the Bank's vaults and enhance Biddle's power, giving him more money to buy congressional votes to topple the verdict of 1832. Hence, once the nullification crisis was over and Congress went home, Jackson decided to strangle the Bank and present Congress with a *fait accompli*. He would remove the government's mounting deposits before the legislature convened again in December 1833.

That decision disrupted the Jacksonian coalition. Many members of the administration, including Louis McLane, vehemently opposed it and predicted disaster if Old Hickory went through with such a radical proposal. Since removal required the signature of the Treasury secretary, McLane had to be kicked upstairs into the State Department. William Duane of Pennsylvania was brought in to do the job, but after several state banks had been chosen to receive government deposits he defied Jackson and refused to authorize the transfer. So he too had to be removed. Finally, with the supportive Roger B. Taney of Maryland as his Secretary of the Treasury, Jackson in September 1833 ordered that all future government deposits be placed in selected state banks.

Biddle responded by turning the full economic power of the Bank against the government. He ordered a general curtailment of loans by all branches of the Bank, hoping thereby to create such a severe contraction of credit that public pressure would force Congress to restore the deposits—and perhaps even renew the charter. Mounting bankruptcies, unemployment, and widespread panic did put enormous pressure on the Jacksonians in Congress, and many deserted the fold during the winter of 1833–34. Along with Clay's supporters and many Antimasons they formed a new party, which they called Whig to signify their opposition to executive tyranny. Like the Whigs of England they claimed to be fighting an Old World despot who placed his will above that of the Constitution, the courts, the legislature, and the good of the country. Crowning Jackson "King Andrew I," the Whigs soon had enough votes in the Senate to censure Jackson in March 1834 for misuse of presidential power.

In the House, however, Jackson's supporters maintained the upper hand and eventually pushed through four resolutions sustaining the administration's Bank policy. Adams, slow in accepting the label "Whig," planned to deliver a scorching last-minute speech that would sway a few key votes. But he was outmaneuvered when Jackson's supporters called the previous question and brought debate to an end. Storming mad and claiming that his right to speak had been suppressed, Adams went the next day to the office of the *National Register*, which agreed not only to publish the exhortation but to print it in such a form that it could be turned into a pamphlet and hawked throughout the country as a "suppressed" speech. The harangue thus found its way into thousands of Whig households and gained enormous attention.[56]

The speech, for the most part, hammered away on the typical Whig argument that the removal of deposits was illegal. Adams also added his own special bite when he delved into Old Hickory's motives. The official explanation, he said, was humbug. The removal of deposits had nothing to do with the approaching expiration of the Bank's charter, or the safety of the government's money, or the alleged corruption of the Bank's leadership. Each charge was ridiculous on its face, based on insubstantial and deliberately misinterpreted evidence, and obviously contrived. The real reason for Jackson's actions was that he wanted to destroy every vestige of a strong national government, reduce government to a "simple machine," in accordance with a plan worked out long before he took office. The goal was to strengthen the hand of wealthy landholders, particularly the great slavemasters, by deliberately destroying the government's ability to help other elements of the population such as industrialists, merchants, and northern workingmen. "The destruction of the Bank," concluded Adams, "was necessary both to the simplification of the machine and to the accomplishment of the end."[59]

In addition to Jackson's long-term policy of enhancing the slavemasters' hegemony at the expense of the rest of the nation, Adams saw simple greed at work. The state banks now receiving federal deposits clearly had been chosen for political and personal reasons—and rightly deserved the popular nickname "pet banks."[60] Indeed, said Adams, the only interest many of Old Hickory's closest advisors had in the Bank War was fattening their own pocketbooks and getting federal deposits into their own hands. Secretary of the Treasury Roger B. Taney, for example, hardly acted out of "pure and disinterested patriotism in transferring the use of the public funds from the Bank of the United States, where they were profitable to the people, to the Union Bank of Baltimore, where they were profitable to himself." Even worse was Martin Van Buren, the new Vice-President, who now had the "whole treasury of the United States" at his mercy "to use in electioneering for himself when and where he pleases."[61]

Such stinging criticism bothered Democratic leaders in Congress, who lived in fear of a full-scale party revolt and worried about the tarnished image of the "pet bank" system. But it was of no use to Biddle's bank. Jackson refused to budge, his anti-Bank majority in the House held firm, and the Bank was doomed.

Inflows of British capital, moreover, offset the dire effects of Biddle's contraction. Indeed, thanks to the Chinese desire for opium, British investors suddenly had plenty of silver for overseas investment and began pumping capital into the American economy. With the British buying state canal bonds and other American securities, eagerly financing one new venture after another, the American economy began to boom: commodity prices rose at a rate of 13 percent a year in 1835 and 1836; government land sales skyrocketed from 3.8 million acres in 1833 to 20 million acres in 1836; and the money supply shot up 64 percent in the same years.

During the boom years Adams alternately felt broken-hearted, angry, and helpless. The Bank was dead, and out of the bulging federal surplus in the "pet bank" system "political swindlers" like Reuben M. Whitney and Amos Kendall were "replenishing their own coffers and making princely fortunes." The expanding economy, meanwhile, was like an overinflated balloon that was bound to burst. But what could he do? There were not enough votes in Congress to stop "the reign of subaltern knaves" who were "fattening upon land jobs and money jobs."[62] Predicting disaster, he ranted and raved one day, and was completely despondent the next.

The predicted disaster finally came at the end of Jackson's reign. In June 1836, when the speculative fury was at its peak, Congress voted to distribute the mounting federal surplus of nearly $40 million among the states. Two months later, to satisfy hard-money men in his party and to put a brake on land speculation and runaway inflation, Jackson issued the Specie Circular ordering the Public Land Offices to accept only hard money and Virginia land scrip as payment in land transactions. Then within months the economy turned sour: cotton prices fell, British officials took steps to curb overseas investments of silver, and English investors cut down their capital exports to the United States. In May 1837, shortly after Jackson left office, a financial crisis in England triggered a run on the banks in the United States, and quickly forced banks to suspend redemption of their notes for gold. The Panic of 1837 was dramatic but brief, and within the year banks were again redeeming their notes in gold and prices began to rise. But then came a second financial crisis and another wave of bank failures followed by a long depression that lasted well into the 1840s.

Who was to blame? Actually, neither Jackson nor Biddle was in any position to control the external forces that generated the boom and then the bust. But that fact had no effect on contemporary Americans who refused to believe that the nation's economy, small and open to outside forces, was largely at the mercy of the giants in the international marketplace. Even Adams, who spent much of his life in international diplomacy, assumed that the United States was fully capable of controlling its economic destiny.

So Americans looked for home-grown villains. Thomas Hart Benton and other hard-money Jacksonians fulminated against the evils of paper currency. Once again, they argued, it had generated a disastrous boom-bust cycle, and the only solution was the destruction of all commercial, note-issuing banks. Adams and his fellow Whigs, on the other hand, railed against

Jackson. By destroying Biddle's power, they argued, Old Hickory had eliminated the only effective check on wildcat bankers
and other scoundrels. Without the Bank to police them, state
bankers had madly expanded their note issues, lending money
even to the most reckless speculators, increasing both the quantity of money in circulation and the danger of massive bank
failures. Then Jackson, with his drastic Specie Circular, popped
the land boom and precipitated a financial crisis. What was
needed, said Adams and his fellow Whigs, was another national
bank to keep the economy running on an even keel.

The Whig interpretation captured the fancy of many historians and endured for decades as historical truth. Now, however, historians know that it was factually wrong.[33] State bankers were not the wild men Adams and others made them out
to be, and very few changed their practices with the destruction
of Biddle's power. A few, to be sure, undertook dangerous new
loans and decreased their reserves. But others, apparently responding to the uncertainty created by Jackson's policies, became more conservative in their business practices and less
prone to take risks. In any event, new specie from abroad rather
than the bankers' practices caused the massive growth in money
supply in the mid-1830s. By the same token, the hard times
that followed were triggered largely by the rapid decline of
outside capital.

In reality Jackson and Biddle were only bit players in an international economic drama, and Adams and other Americans
grossly exaggerated their importance. Nonetheless, with Whigs
clamoring for a third national bank and hard-money Democrats
denouncing all note-issuing banks, Jackson's policies became a
staple of American politics on both the national and the state
levels. As a result, some states continued as before; others
turned banking over to a state-owned monopoly or a mixed
public-private bank; a few outlawed banks entirely. Meanwhile,
on the national level, Adams and his fellow Whigs tried and
failed year after year to establish a third national bank, while
Jackson's successor Van Buren, who was left to cope with the
Panic of 1837, championed the cause of hard money.[64]

In September 1837, in a special message to Congress, Van

Buren criticized state-chartered banks, advocated a hard currency, and called on Congress to sever the bond between the federal government and private banks. Instead of placing its money in private banks and supporting the "paper" system, the government in effect ought to wash its hands of all responsibility for a banking system, put its money in "independent treasury" offices, and do business only in gold and silver.

Van Buren's Divorce Bill aroused the bitter opposition of not only Adams and his fellow Whigs, but also soft-money Democrats. So Adams was often on the side of the majority in the fight over the "independent treasury." After years of squabbling, hard-money Democrats finally got the independent treasury bill passed in 1840 only to see it promptly repealed the next year. Then, after five more years of wrangling, the independent treasury was reinstated in 1846 and remained the law of the land until the Civil War.

Adams spent little time arguing about the practical aspects of the bill. What horrified him, he said, was the very idea of a divorce of bank and state. Only a raving lunatic, he believed, could have come up with such a plan. Next there would be a "divorce of Trade and Shipping" or a "divorce of Army and Fire Arms in the face of an invading enemy" or a "divorce of Laws and a bench of judges." No one in the community needed "so much and so constantly the aid of banking operations as the Government." What was needed, above all, was a national bank like the one Jackson "strangled."[65]

Yet in the privacy of his study and in his correspondence, Adams was no longer as certain as he once had been. In 1837 he confessed to a New York businessman that he really had no idea what was going on. The "subject of banking, exchange, currency, circulation and credits is so complicated that the doctrine of fluxions and the infinite series which I never could understand appears to me plain sailing in comparison with it." Yet as a Congressman "I must have something to do with it, and I am groping like a blind man to find my way, feeling for a table or chair, or bed post as I go, to save myself from stumbling over them—and what I want most of all, is counsel, from those who do know something about it—practically."[66]

What shook his faith, among other things, was the failure of

Biddle's bank.[67] After losing its federal charter, Biddle's bank
got a charter from the state of Pennsylvania, and like many
other banks suspended specie payment in 1837, struggled along
for several years, and finally closed its doors in 1841. Resigning
as the bank's president in 1839, Biddle was hounded by law-
suits, irate stockholders, and the sheriff until he died in 1844.
Was Biddle the high roller, the reckless banker that his critics
pictured? Did he deserve to die in a penitentiary as the Jacksonians claimed? Adams never agreed with Biddle's enemies,
but he did have trouble understanding how any honest, well-
run bank could fail. What troubled him most was what would
have happened to the government's money if all $50 million of
it had still been entrusted to Biddle's bank.

This uncertainty, however, had no effect on his voting. He
remained a good Whig until the day he died, voting the party
line on one bank bill after another. But he seldom entered into
the incessant debates over banking. For by this time he was
involved in other matters, saving his tongue and his invective
for the debate over the gag rule, the expansion of slavery, and
the Slave Power conspiracy.

CHAPTER IV

The Rise of
Organized Antislavery

On the same day that Adams became chairman of the Committee of Manufactures, the job that consumed most of his energy during his early years in Congress and increased his bitterness against the South, he presented fifteen petitions to the House. The petitions, signed by citizens of Pennsylvania, called for the abolition of slavery and the slave trade in the District of Columbia.

When Adams rose to speak he had no idea that such petitions would play a major role in his congressional career, add to his stature, and cause his name to be hailed and cursed in the years ahead. Presenting petitions framed by ordinary citizens was just one of the perfunctory duties of every Congressman. The practice in the House was to routinely call for petitions, beginning with Maine and moving southward. Congressmen were expected to be brief, to state only the titles or the subjects of their petitions, note the number of signatures and the places from which they came, and move that the petitions be referred to committee.

Antislavery petitions were also commonplace. They had been received by Congress since Washington's administration. They invariably irritated some Southerners, but the antislavery movement was small and weak, hardly worth getting excited about, and the rule was to avoid discussion of the slavery question whenever possible. Accordingly, antislavery petitions were usually received without comment and buried in committee.

But Adams had not spoken before a legislative body in years,

and his once rich and resonant voice was now enfeebled by
age, sometimes even fitful and quivering. So he decided to test
his voice, to read one of the petitions and make a few remarks,
rather than follow the usual practice of dispensing with the
reading and simply moving that the petitions be turned over
to the proper committee. He spoke for five minutes, explaining
that he opposed those parts of the petitions calling for the
abolition of slavery in the nation's capital, and implying that
he favored the elimination of the slave trade. To his relief, his
fellow Congressmen listened with "great attention." He sat
down pleased with himself, grateful that he had overcome his
"small and trivial" worry.[1]

Meanwhile, Congress followed the long-standing tradition of
ignoring the petitioners. The fifteen petitions were received
without comment, referred to committee, and quietly forgotten.

That was 1831. Four years later there was no easy way for
Congress to ignore antislavery petitions. By the summer of 1835,
the antislavery movement seemed to have the power, money,
and organization to bring drastic change to the social order,
and the country was in a state of panic. From Maine to Missouri
scores of prominent citizens took to the podium to denounce
the American Anti-Slavery Society, and millions of ordinary
citizens heard and repeated commonplaces about the danger of
disunion and civil war, slave insurrections and race war, and
the downfall of white America. Fiery speeches and anti-abolition mobs were everyday news. Southern vigilance committees
patrolled the quarters of blacks, questioned strangers, and
searched post offices, stages, and ships for antislavery literature.
Several southern communities even put a price on the head of
Arthur Tappan, the president of the American Anti-Slavery
Society. "The abolitionists," reported James Gordon Bennett of
the New York *Herald*, "a few thousand crazy blockheads have
actually frightened fifteen million people out of their senses."[2]

Why the hysteria? For one thing, antislavery clearly had momentum throughout the Western world, and the old institution
of slavery, which had once been "normal" from New England
to the tip of South America, had begun to give way rapidly.
By 1804 all northern states had either freed their slaves or adopted

a program of gradual emancipation. In Haiti black revolutionaries abolished slavery in 1804. Argentina and Columbia adopted
gradual emancipation in 1813 and 1814; Chile abolished slavery
in 1823; Central America in 1824; Mexico in 1829; Bolivia in
1831. England, which always served as an example for many
Americans, began using its naval power to suppress the Atlantic
slave trade in 1820, and after years of intensive lobbying British
abolitionists in 1833 finally got Parliament to abolish slavery in
the British West Indies.

Shortly thereafter, two of the British movement's leading agitators, Charles Stuart and George Thompson, turned their attention to the United States. That raised the suspicions of many
Americans, who feared the British were trying to foster slave
rebellions, to pit North against South, and to bring about disunion and civil war.[3]

Men of power also worried incessantly about the vast number
of native-born "crackpots" and "troublemakers" who tromped
across the northern countryside. Indeed, parts of New England,
New York, and the Ohio Valley seemed to be overrun with
revivalists, reformers, and enthusiasts espousing one cause or
another. "Reform" was in the air after the War of 1812, especially in the North, and by the mid-1830s the more "radical"
reformers seemed to have the upper hand. These outspoken
men and women paid little attention to the values of polite
society, stepped on the toes of the rich as well as the poor, and
often challenged the authority of traditional church and community leaders. They claimed that church and civil leaders were
too permissive, too tolerant of "SIN," too lax in enforcing Christian standards. They wanted tougher standards, tighter social
controls. They wanted their churches to excommunicate gentlemen who had an occasional after-dinner drink as well as the
town drunk. They wanted to close the brothels of the rich and
well born as well as those that catered to sailors and rough-
necks.

Often pictured by historians as rampant individualists, these
militant reformers were anything but that. Primarily men and
women with rising social prospects and a deep commitment to
evangelical Protestantism, most zealous reformers belonged to
organizations that put a premium upon concerted action, the

power of numbers rather than individual initiative. These organizations wanted to build up massive followings, which
through pressure group tactics would force others into line and
eventually rid American society of such "sins" as ungodliness,
immorality, prostitution, and liquor.

The largest movement by far was the crusade against liquor,
which by 1834 had over five thousand local auxiliaries. Temperance advocates kept interest at a fever pitch through the use
of sensational propaganda, women lecturers, children's pa-
rades, and reformed drunks. Like most other reformers they
became more demanding as time passed, first calling for moderation, then total abstinence, then prohibition. The list of forbidden drinks also expanded, from "ardent spirits" like rum
and whiskey to "all intoxicating liquors" including beer, wine,
and cider. The crusade left scores of politicians and church
leaders reeling in its wake.

Yet while the campaign against Demon Rum shook up many
northern leaders it failed to shake the nation as a whole. That
honor fell to northern abolitionists who, using the same methods as temperance advocates, proclaimed that slavery was "SIN,"
the South a "brothel," and the only remedy was "immediate
abolition." The "immediate abolitionists" rose to prominence
in the early 1830s as a result of a series of battles with the
American Colonization Society.[4] This organization had claimed
since 1817 that the solution to the slavery question lay in shipping free blacks "back to Africa." African colonization, so it
was argued, was God's plan to rid the country of the poor and
despised free blacks, provide a nucleus of black missionaries to
carry the Gospel to the Dark Continent, and simultaneously
encourage planters to emancipate their slaves. The society had
the support of such illustrious men as Henry Clay, Chief Justice
John Marshall, and former President James Madison. It was, in
the eyes of most northern gentlemen, the epitome of a "respectable" reform.

But free blacks hated the society. After an uphill struggle of
many years, some finally convinced a twenty-three-year-old
white newsman, William Lloyd Garrison, that African colonization was just a plot by northern racists and southern slavemasters to drive free blacks out of the country. Shortly thereafter

Garrison launched the Boston *Liberator*, which came out for the "immediate abolition" of slavery "without expatriation." The Colonization Society, exclaimed Garrison, was a "monster" that had to be destroyed. It was "a libel upon humanity and justice— a libel upon republicanism—a libel upon the Declaration of Independence—a libel upon Christianity." It dulled the nation's conscience concerning the "sin of slavery" and "shamefully duped" many men of good intention, while it bolstered slavery by the removal of free blacks, by annually sending "hundreds of worn-out slaves . . . off to die, like old horses."[5]

Yet while Garrison's attacks alarmed many colonizationists and some Southerners, he was at first just a small voice shouting in the wilderness. In an age of primitive and costly communications it took money and know-how just to be heard. Until canals, railways, the telegraph, and a steam-powered press made travel and communications cheap and almost instantaneous, it was incredibly difficult to build a network of well-coordinated pressure groups. Not only was the country vast, but there were still scores of isolated communities in the East, like the Berkshires in Massachusetts, that had nothing to do with the rest of their states.[6] Poor and costly communications worked against all attempts—and especially those of poor men like Garrison— to draw people with similar opinions or parallel interests into cooperative activities.

It took a few fat pocketbooks and a national organization to make Garrison's *Liberator* a household name across the country. That was achieved when a few influential whites like the Tappan brothers of New York City were won over to the cause. The Tappans, Garrison, and other converts to "immediate abolition" waited until news of British emancipation reached the eastern seaboard in late 1833 before launching the American Anti-Slavery Society. Such timing, they reasoned, would give the movement momentum and the appearance of being part of a worldwide crusade. They were particularly anxious to be identified with the British movement and thus left themselves open to the charge of being part of a gigantic British conspiracy to sow discord in the United States and foster slave rebellions, disunion, and civil war.

Trained mainly in evangelistic work and seasoned in temperance and other reform movements, the abolitionists proved to be experts in the art of communications. With men of power determined to stop them, and only a shoestring budget, they managed to convince hundreds of thousands that the average planter was a brute who took advantage of black women, mutilated his slaves, and sold his own mulatto children "down river." They reworked the southern image so well that "Christian women of the North" immediately thought of the whip and the slave trade whenever they heard the word "South."

To get their message across, abolitionists took full advantage of every advance in communications. Like Methodist circuit riders, antislavery preachers went from village to village organizing men, women, and children into antislavery societies— thus increasing the antislavery network from forty-seven societies in 1833 to over one thousand by late 1836. Intensive organizing invariably led to mob violence, which usually scared off faint-hearted merchants who feared the loss of trade, but radicalized others and provided the antislavery movement with enormous newspaper coverage. Playing up anti-abolitionist violence, abolitionists repeatedly turned it to their advantage and touched the guilt-laden consciences of many Northerners. And scores of men and women joined the movement only after seeing a traveling preacher, Bible in hand and denouncing the "sin" of slavery, stand up to an angry mob.

Antislavery organizers also followed the example of the leading evangelists of the day in relying heavily on churchwomen. While women lacked the right to vote, and technically had no political voice, they were generally regarded as inherently more moral than men, and hence their opinions on moral questions were highly respected. Capitalizing on this sentiment, the American Anti-Slavery Society encouraged women to gather signatures for massive petitions to Congress. Carrying petitions from door to door proved most effective in mobilizing support, in getting people to think and talk about antislavery principles, and in keeping the slavery issue in the public mind. After the names were gathered they were usually pasted onto a standardized form addressed to the "Fathers and Rulers of the Country" and forwarded to Washington.

The petitions, however, were not what caused the furor in

1835. More important was the decision of the American Anti-Slavery Society to take full advantage of a dramatic revolution in printing. Almost overnight the introduction of steam-powered presses and other technological developments cut the cost of printing in New York City virtually in half. Moving quickly, Arthur Tappan and his New York associates increased their publications by nine times and tried to flood the country with tracts, newspapers, kerchiefs, medals, emblems, and even blue chocolate wrappers bearing the antislavery message. Capitalizing on the cheap postal rates that newspapers had long enjoyed, the Tappan group mailed several hundred thousand free papers to communities North and South. By late July 1835 the tracts and newspapers reached southern ports. The South exploded, and overnight organized antislavery became the hottest issue of the day.

Up until this time, Adams was just a role player in the American Anti-Slavery Society's strategy. The society's leaders chose him to present their petitions mainly to capture the limelight. Anything the ex-President did was certain to be newsworthy. Even if he presented the petitions and denounced the contents that was far better than having the petitions presented by an unknown enthusiast. Also they knew that the sharp-tongued old man loved a good fight and was beyond caring what the South thought of him. And, in contrast to most northern politicians, he had never gone out of his way to attack them. Southerners thought he was secretly on the society's side. Most abolitionists, however, had their doubts. His record on the slavery question left much to be desired.

Where, indeed, did he stand on such issues as slavery and race? Two facts immediately catch the eye. First, though he had a reputation for being tolerant, he was actually a bundle of prejudices. Like many upper-class Yankees of his day, he thought Anglo-Saxon males were superior to everyone else, tended to be paternalistic to all "inferiors," and made disparaging remarks about Jews, Spaniards, Mexicans, blacks, Indians, and women.

During his youth these remarks sometimes got him into trouble, particularly with his mother, who excoriated him for denigrating women. Indeed, her scathing lectures may have caused him to moderate his thoughts—or at least keep his mouth shut and accept the fact that his mother and some other women were very outspoken and determined to be more than man's helpmate. In later life, despite outbursts of male chauvinism, he showed his mother's influence in encouraging women to become better educated and urging them to speak out on political matters. In this he differed strikingly from other politicians of his day.[7]

From his mother, too, he learned as a child to treat the black help on the family's farm in a condescending but kind way. She also taught him by example to be considerate to the some sixty blacks who lived in the Quincy area. He had no contact with Indians as a child, but from books and hearsay came to regard them as hopeless misfits. As an adult he usually thought of them as occupying the bottom of the racial ladder, several rungs below Africans and far below Anglo-Saxons. In offhand remarks he often linked Indians with savagery, Africans with a society somewhere between pastoralism and primitive agriculture, and Anglo-Saxons with advanced civilization. At no time, moreover, did he seriously question the prevailing white man's assumption that Indian culture had to give way to Christianity, that "savagery" had to succumb to "civilization."[8]

How, then, did Adams ever earn his reputation for unusual tolerance? In part this was due to his forebears, particularly his mother, who was known locally not only as a forceful advocate of women's rights but also for her role in integrating the Quincy school. In 1797, after spending some time educating a black child in her parlor, she put him in school. Several days later some townfolk sent "Neighbor Faxon" to her house to complain, and immediately she put him on the defensive. Was Faxon not a patriot? Was he not committed to the sacred values of the Revolution—to liberty and equality and Christian brotherhood? Surely a black face should not bar a fellow citizen from instruction. How else was the boy to be prepared to make a living? To her delight, Faxon was dumbfounded and quickly backed down.[9]

While such incidents redounded to Adams's credit, even more important to his reputation was the changing temper of the times. Racism became so virulent after the War of 1812 that kindly white men, even when they were condescending, seemed like virtual saints in comparison with the vast hordes of newsmen and politicians who spewed forth a constant stream of venom against the dark-skinned, raised mobs to terrorize blacks, and led crusades to strip black men of their voting rights. Several times a decade in Providence, New York, Philadelphia, and Cincinnati, white mobs razed black homes and churches. Irish immigrants seized the jobs of urban blacks and drove them to the outer fringes of the job market. Blacks were barred from voting in all the new western states and lost their right to vote in four of the original northern states: Connecticut, New York, New Jersey, and Pennsylvania. By 1840, in the five states where they still could vote, white voters scorned and spat upon them and drove them away from the polls. Meanwhile, Indians were forced off their ancestral lands, and celebrated Indian killers such as Andrew Jackson and Richard M. Johnson enjoyed widespread popularity.

In this atmosphere, black and red men turned to Adams for help. He was condescending, and he was "disgusted" by the thought of a white woman like Shakespeare's Desdemona pursuing a "nigger" like Othello.[10] But he was not vicious, not violent, and he would never encourage a mob to demolish black churches or burn black orphanages. Harder to explain away, perhaps, were his harsh comments about Indians. Following Jackon's invasion of Spanish Florida in 1819 he had even justified Jackson's execution of Indian prisoners without trial. Such statements, thundred Benjamin Watkins Leigh of Virginia, were just as monstrous as Jackson's acts of violence.[11] But others dismissed Adams's remarks as merely tough talk made during the heat of battle to gain an edge on Britain and Spain at the negotiating table, pointing out that Adams had aggressively defended all of Jackson's actions, including Old Hickory's summary execution of two Englishmen as well as his execution of Indian prisoners.[12] Whatever the reasoning, Leigh's argument had little impact, and Indian leaders as well as other underdogs looked to Adams for help.

Adams, who dismissed Leigh's observations as just "lawyer's arguments," knew very well that he was on the side of the angels. During the 1820s most of the race-baiting politicians and newsmen in the North gravitated to the Jackson camp, and by the mid-1830s the Jacksonians and the Whigs could be differentiated on the issue of race. Not every Whig, to be sure, was a paternalist like Adams. Indeed, one of the worst race-baiting editors in the North, James Watson Webb of the New York *Courier and Enquirer*, was a Whig. But some Whig leaders clearly sympathized with the plight of the dark-skinned, and about half agreed with Adams that as long as white "rabble" had the right to vote so should free blacks. Others were too busy denouncing the Irish and the Catholic Church to have any time for "nigger-knocking." The Jacksonians, by contrast, were generally of one mind, defending the Catholic Irish on the one hand while cursing black suffrage and catering to the worst strains in northern racism on the other.[13]

Adams was certain where the trouble lay. His opponents had somehow convinced themselves that the basic rights of man applied only to whites. How they managed to do so was beyond his imagination. As he saw it there was no way an intelligent man, or a man of high Christian principles or humanitarian sentiments, could reach such a conclusion. The scriptures made it clear that all races descended from common ancestors, first Adam and Eve and then Noah and his wife, and nature itself testified that the non-white races were "people." Nevertheless, from personal experience, he knew that some very discerning and moral men, like John C. Calhoun of South Carolina, managed to identify universal principles such as "liberty" and "equality" with the color of a man's skin. Once in 1820, after walking home from a Cabinet meeting with Calhoun, he tried to account for the South Carolinian's thinking—and finally concluded that one of the evils of slavery was "that it taints the very sources of moral principle."[14]

The northern Jacksonians, as Adams viewed them, were cut from the same cloth as Calhoun. They, too, assumed that the Declaration of Independence applied only to white men. He made the point to George Bancroft, a 35-year-old Harvard graduate who claimed that Jacksonian Democracy was the embodiment of liberty, justice, and humanity. Did Bancroft, wrote Adams, include slaves and free blacks in his concept of "government *by the people*"? Or did the Jacksonian version of democracy include only whites? The obvious exclusion of blacks, added Adams, reminded him of an impulse he once had when listening to Calhoun toast *"universal education."* He had been tempted to correct Calhoun, to interrupt and suggest that the South Carolinian add the qualifying words *"skin deep."* But instead he kept still and contemplated the revolutionary effect a true policy of universal education would have on South Carolina.[15]

Adams was not always so cautious. He spoke out when the Washington police singled out black prisoners for abuse. During his Presidency he set an example by always receiving blacks and Indians, stating that he much preferred hearing their grievances than dealing with the endless line of white office seekers.[16] Moreover, he was flattered whenever those who championed human rights, such as the petitioners from Pennsylvania, appealed to him for help. He liked to think of himself as a guardian of the rights of the oppressed; this was central to his self-image.

The second fact that jumps from the ex-President's record is that until the 1830s his position on slavery was hard to fathom. To be sure, he made all the usual comments about slavery, denouncing it as an evil, a "foul stain" on the Republic's good name. But like most politicians of his day his strong pronunciations against slavery in the abstract led to very little action. Up until the 1830s, in fact, he behaved like a typical presidential aspirant, constantly courting southern support.

The planters, of course, never trusted him. But they were generally suspicious of all Yankees, and their distrust of him was based largely on suspicion rather than overt acts. In fact, there was very little in his record that could be construed as hostile to slavery—and much that could be seen as favorable. Indeed, if he had died in 1831, rather than started a new career in Congress, he might have come down in history books as a fence straddler, or even a proslavery Northerner, rather than an antislavery man.

Adams's diplomatic record, from an antislavery perspective, was dismal. In his various diplomatic roles he affirmed on numerous occasions that slaves were property. He frequently assisted slaveholders who were trying to extradite runaway slaves from Canada. More importantly, he fought hard for masters whose slaves fled to British warships and forts during the War of 1812. The federal government had failed to get compensation for thousands of slaves carried off by the British at the end of the American Revolution. But this time, with Adams playing a key role, a decade of negotiations ended in the British paying more than one million dollars in indemnities.[17]

More worrisome still was his record on the Atlantic slave trade. Nearly every humanitarian in the country, North and South, had agreed that the trade in slaves between Africa and the New World was a despicable business, a monstrous evil that had to be destroyed. Yet Adams, instead of taking a lead in eradicating this abomination, was a noticeable foot-dragger. In 1804, as a young Senator from Massachusetts, he opposed legislation outlawing the importation of African slaves into Louisiana. He also insisted that Congress abide by the letter of the Constitution and not pass any legislation prohibiting the importation of slaves until 1808. In both instances his reasons were legalistic.[18]

His record of foot-dragging continued once the United States joined Britain and Denmark in outlawing the Atlantic slave trade. At first the slave traders were liable to fines; then jail sentence; and finally in 1820 they were declared "pirates" and thus punishable by death. But the main problem, always, was catching them. The United States, with virtually no navy, was incapable of policing the high seas. The only country that could run down the slave traders was Great Britain, which was eager to suppress the trade, but needed legal authorization to search slave ships flying the colors of other nations. To a limited degree Portugal, Spain, and the Netherlands gave the British navy that right in 1817 and 1818. American politicians, however, worried incessantly about the long history of British warships stopping American vessels and impressing American seamen.

Adams became their chief spokesman. Unless Great Britain, he argued, was bound by an article "as strong and explicit as language can make it" never again to take a man from an American vessel in time of war, the United States could not even consider granting the right of visit and search. Adams was so stubborn on this issue that at one point the British minister to the United States, Stratford Canning, suspected that he had ties with the various slave traders operating out of Newport, Salem, and other Yankee ports. After visiting New England and finding no connections, Canning concluded that Adams was using the issue to further his presidential ambitions. Nothing else made any sense.

Finally in 1823, after Congress passed a resolution by a vote of 131 to 9 calling for an effective agreement to rid the world of slave-trading "pirates," Adams came to terms with the British minister. The resultant treaty, however, was gutted by the Senate, and it was not until the Lincoln administration some forty years later that the United States finally granted Britain the power to effectively suppress the Atlantic slave trade.[19]

Adams's record was also suspicious when it came to the expansion of slavery. As a Senator in 1804 he was conspicuous in voting against a series of antislavery amendments to a bill establishing territorial status for the southern portion of the Louisiana Purchase. The driving force behind the amendments was Senator James Hillhouse of Connecticut, an ardent Federalist who had vehemently opposed the acquisition of Louisiana. Some said that Hillhouse just wanted to cause trouble for the Jeffersonian Republicans, who fancied themselves as the torchbearers of liberty and equality in the Atlantic world but were in fact heavily dependent upon slaveholding interests. But he was also probably sincere in saying that he hated slavery and wanted to curb its growth whenever possible. In any event, his amendments were designed to strike a blow against the Atlantic slave trade and to severely limit the growth of slavery west of the Mississippi River.[20]

At the time, Adams claimed the measures were "insufficient." Years later, when he was running for President and had to account for his past, Adams explained away his negative votes by arguing that under Hillhouse's scheme slaves could be brought from Africa to South Carolina—and then shipped legally into Louisiana.[21] In fact, one of Hillhouse's provisions was specifically designed to close the South Carolina loophole.

Also curious was Adams's reasoning with regard to Florida. More than anyone else, with the possible exception of Andrew

Jackson, Adams was responsible for the acquisition of Florida from Spain in 1819. Yet even while drawing up the treaty he was troubled by the fact that Florida was going to be another addition to the slaveholders' domain. He told Senator Ninian Edwards of Illinois that if he were in the House or the Senate he would oppose the treaty with Spain unless an article was added "prohibiting and excluding slavery from the territory to be acquired." He was not, however, a member of Congress. He was Secretary of State, and as such "a servant of the whole Union."[22] So he refrained from adding an article, or suggesting that anyone do so. It was not his job to make trouble for his own treaty.

Adams tried to avoid trouble as well in the furious battle that broke out in 1819 over admitting Missouri as a slave state. He was caught by surprise when James Tallmadge, an obscure freshman Congressman from New York, offered an amendment to the statehood bill prohibiting "the further introduction of slavery" into Missouri and providing that all slaves born in Missouri after it became a state "shall be free, but may be held to service until the age of twenty-five years." But Adams quickly realized that Tallmadge had hit the chink in the South's armor, particularly that of Jeffersonian liberals, who for years had denounced slavery in the abstract and now were being asked to live up to their words. How, he wondered, could they object to Tallmadge's proposal? It merely extended to Missouri the same program of gradual emancipation that the revolutionary generation had enacted in New York, New Jersey, and other northern states—and the proportion of slaves in Missouri was no greater than it had once been in New York. So why let slavery engulf Missouri? Why disgrace the Republican heritage? "The discussion of the Missouri question," noted Adams, "has betrayed the secret of their souls. In the abstract they admit that slavery is an evil. . . . but when probed to the quick upon it, they show at the bottom of their souls pride and vainglory in their condition of masterdom."[23]

Adams also quickly realized that the Jeffersonian leadership would not be able to sidestep the issue. In the past they had always succeeded in blaming disgruntled Federalists for raising the slavery question. But Tallmadge was not a high Federalist like James Hillhouse. He was a Jeffersonian Republican, and he obviously had the backing of many Jeffersonian Republicans in the North, who were tired of the South's long domination of the Union and clearly feared that the rapid expansion of King Cotton would further enhance the slaveholders' power in national affairs. Here, noted Adams, was "the basis for a new organization of parties terrible to the whole Union, but portentously terrible to the South—threatening in its progress the emancipation of all their slaves, threatening in its immediate effect that southern domination which has swayed the Union for the last twenty years." "I take it for granted," he added in his diary, "that the present question is a mere preamble—a title page to a great tragic volume."[24]

At the time Adams thought about meeting the issue head on. He knew very well that anything that entailed the "total abolition" of slavery would necessitate the "dissolution" of the Union. But even that might be worthwhile, he mused, for the nation then might be "reorganized upon the fundamental principle of emancipation," and a life devoted to that object "would be nobly spent or sacrificed." Furthermore, if the Union had to be dissolved, slavery was "precisely the question upon which it ought to break." So in the long run resisting the expansion of slavery into Missouri was probably "the wiser as well as the bolder course."[25]

This, however, was not the course Adams followed. Under the pressure of his presidential ambitions and practical politics, he kept these bold thoughts to himself and privately urged members of the New England congressional delegation to compromise the Missouri question. "If a provision could be obtained excluding the introduction of slaves into future territories," he told two New Hampshire Representatives, "it will be a great and important object secured."[26] He was relieved when a settlement was finally manipulated through Congress, admitting Missouri as a slave state, Maine as a free state, and "forever" prohibiting slavery in the remainder of the Louisiana Purchase north of latitude 36°30' (the southern border of Missouri). The settlement, he reasoned, was morally bad—but necessary because of defects in the Constitution regarding slavery. It was not, therefore, a step backward.[27]

This reasoning broke down completely, however, when Missouri subsequently presented a constitution for congressional approval. The Missouri constitution included a clause *requiring* the state legislature to pass laws barring free blacks and mulattoes from entering the state "under any pretext whatsoever." And that, without question, was a giant step backward. The clause clearly violated the federal constitution, which declared that "the citizens of each State shall be entitled to the privileges and immunities of the citizens of the several States." While there was no universally accepted definition of "citizen," there was also no doubt that blacks and mulattoes were citizens in some states when the Constitution was framed in 1787, as well as in 1821 when Missouri presented its constitution. And one of these states was Massachusetts.

To give way on this issue, concluded Adams, was to give too much. So he encouraged William Eustis, the Congressman from his home district, to present a resolution declaring that Missouri would be admitted to the Union only after it expunged the repugnant clause from its constitution. Also he told Henry Baldwin, a Pennsylvania Congressman, that if he were a member of the Massachusetts legislature he would move a declaratory act that as long as "the colored citizens" of Massachusetts were deprived of "their rights as citizens of the United States within the State of Missouri . . . the white citizens of Missouri shall be held as aliens within the Commonwealth of Massachusetts." On second thought, he added, he would go even further and "prohibit by law the delivery of any fugitive slave upon the claim of his master." As Secretary of State, however, he was not in a position to be so outspoken.[28]

His chance to speak out came in 1822. In the wake of the Denmark Vesey slave conspiracy, frightened South Carolinians passed a series of laws to stop the spread of "incendiary" ideas. One problem, as they saw it, was that black sailors from the North and foreign countries had the free run of Charleston whenever they were on shore leave. Fearing they might spread notions of freedom and rebellion among the slaves, the South Carolina legislature required that black and mulatto sailors be held in jail as long as their ships were in port. The new law violated not only the rights of "colored citizens" from Massa-

chusetts and other seafaring states but also a treaty between
the United States and Great Britain guaranteeing equal treatment of their seamen.

With the British badgering him constantly, Adams protested
vigorously to the Governor of South Carolina and at one point
got the law suspended. But angry Charleston aristocrats soon
had the law reinstated, and after that Adams's trenchant protests were to no avail. To increase the pressure he obtained a
ruling from Attorney General William Wirt that the statute was
unconstitutional, that it violated both the treaty and Congress's
exclusive control over commerce. Yet despite Wirt's ruling and
Adams's continued pressure the Charleston sheriff kept jailing
black sailors. Other southern states soon copied the South Carolina statute, and by the time of Jackson's Presidency a half-
dozen states were flagrantly nullifying both the treaty and Wirt's
ruling. To Adams's dismay, Jackson's Attorneys General in 1831
and 1832 overruled Wirt, sided with South Carolina, and in
effect declared that free blacks had no rights as "citizens" under
the Constitution. Subsequently the British were told that the
entire matter was "beyond the reach of any power vested in
the President."[29]

What, then, were antislavery men and women to make of
Adams's record? His fruitless efforts in behalf of black seamen
certainly set him apart from the Jacksonians. Undoubtedly he
was willing to fight for basic human rights whenever the Constitution so dictated. Yet whenever there was a conflict between
liberty and the law, or liberty and his position in government,
or liberty and his political career, the cause of liberty was abandoned. Even after Adams became a Congressman, when he
was speaking just for a northern district rather than the whole
nation, he was reluctant to become embroiled in the dispute
over slavery and invariably criticized the aims of antislavery
petitioners.

Why did he act this way? That question troubled many antislavery men, and in 1833 Moses Brown, a rich Providence
Quaker, demanded an answer. Why, asked Brown, did Adams
berate petitioners who called for the abolition of slavery in the
nation's capital? Adams explained that while he shared Brown's
distaste for slavery he opposed the petitioners' request on three

grounds. First, the petitioners had no right to call for changes that affected citizens living in other states and territories. Second, the issue that the petitioners kept raising would only "stir up ill blood" and might even cause the South to pass harsher slave codes. Third, the majority of the people in his home district were against stirring up the slavery question.[30]

In 1833, when Adams wrote this explanation, organized antislavery had scarcely penetrated his home district. Only the manufacturing town of Kingston had even the makings of an antislavery society. But shortly thereafter, abolitionists quickly gained a foothold in the "Old Colony," particularly in manufacturing hamlets and Antimasonic strongholds, two of his key constituencies. By the mid-1830s there were eight auxiliaries, including two "ladies" groups and one "juvenile female" society, within ten miles of his home—and a total of twenty-five antislavery societies within his district.[31] And by 1837 there was no longer much sympathy in his district for anti-abolitionist violence. When a mob attacked the antislavery preacher Ichabod Codding at the Robinson Church in Plymouth, the Grand Jury refused to ignore the incident, which was the common practice throughout the North, and instead brought charges against the High Sheriff for failing to disperse the mob.[32]

Nevertheless, even though local abolitionists became more numerous and consequential as time passed, they never had the power to force Adams's hand. Not only were they always a controversial minority, but they could swing only a few votes. Even ardent abolitionists disregarded the *Liberator's* battle cry to "scatter the vote" and instead they cast their ballots for Adams, a nationally renowned fighter, rather than a local nobody. So, like it or not, antislavery leaders had to play Adams's game, let him present their petitions and then tolerate his criticisms.

Adams's antislavery critics, of course, had only his public record to go by. They had no idea what he was writing in his diary during the Missouri crisis, or what he was telling other politicians. If they knew, they might have realized that on some issues he was definitely a fellow traveler.

One key issue was African colonization. Unlike most patricians of his day, Adams never had a kind word for the Colonization Society. He thought the whole project was crazy, and the philanthropists who believed that it would help end slavery were "weak-minded." Moreover, in his eyes, not all colonizationists were well meaning. Many were speculators hoping to make a political or economic killing, and many more were slaveholders who simply wanted to get rid of free blacks at public expense and increase the market value of their slaves. Most revealing, thought Adams, was the Virginia legislature's rationale for recommending that public money be spent to colonize free blacks. Clearly, Virginia politicians had no interest in ending slavery; they just wanted to expel free blacks, the pariahs of southern society, who were accused of stealing and making slaves rebellious.[33]

Adams was anxious to keep these thoughts to himself. Many of his close associates were colonizationists, including President Monroe, and he had no desire to offend them. But in a Cabinet meeting in 1819 he opposed giving the Colonization Society government money to purchase land on the Guinea coast, and he feared that the "fanatics" within the society would force him to take a public stand. To his dismay, his silence caused both friends and foes of the Colonization Society to assume that he supported the movement. In 1831 Jackson even accused him of squandering government money on the society's colony of Liberia. Even more irritating was listening to the "visionaries of that fraudulent charitable institution" who came to him expecting a helping hand. He told one that African colonization would not "diminish the number of slaves in the United States by a single individual." He told another that the whole plan was "an abortion."[34]

Adams was hardly upset, then, when Garrison and other abolitionists launched a full scale campaign to destroy the Colonization Society. Other politicians responded to the society's cries for help, ranted and raved, and denounced Garrison for his "calumnies" and "misrepresentations." Some even took to the streets and led mobs against the abolitionists. But Adams secretly agreed with Garrison. He, too, thought the Colonization Society was a moral cancer that had to be destroyed. Indeed, having reached that conclusion a decade before Garrison, he delighted in recording the society's failures.

In rejecting colonization, Adams was also in accord with the abolitionists on the bedrock issue of "amalgamation." Deep down, in the marrow of their bones, many Americans were certain that the only alternative to slavery was the mixture of the races. Blacks and whites, they assumed, could never live together peacefully as free men; either one race would exterminate the other, or racial differences would have to be wiped out through intermarriage and interbreeding. Such thinking, in fact, inspired scores of half-baked schemes to ship emancipated blacks out of the country. The trouble was that there were millions of blacks, and it hardly made sense for a nation that was short of both capital and labor to be spending millions getting rid of workers.

The abolitionists, however, not only rejected colonization as a hare-brained solution but went out of their way to destroy the Colonization Society. Why did they save their sharpest barbs for the society? What was their solution to America's race problem?

The answer, thundered colonizationists and racists, was "amalgamation." The abolitionists obviously intended to end race hatred in America by destroying the differences between the races, by marrying black to white, by "mulattoizing our posterity." That was why they gathered free blacks in their societies. That was why they let Frederick Douglass, a runaway slave, become one of their leading agitators and star attractions. That was why they opened schools in such places as "Bucktown," "Little Africa," and "Nigger Hill."[35]

Such reasoning plagued abolitionists continually from the 1830s through the Civil War. They repeatedly denied the charges, arguing that abolishing slavery would end miscegenation in America. Look, they said, at Thomas Jefferson's mulatto children. Look at Vice President Richard M. Johnson's black consort and half-white offspring. The life of the slaveholder, wrote Garrison, "is but one of unbridled lust, of filthy amalgamation."[36] Yet, try as they might, they never overcame the charge of being "amalgamators." No charge was repeated more tenaciously, and none was more effective in stirring up the rancor and brutality of anti-abolitionist mobs.

How did Adams respond to all this? On the one hand, the mere thought of miscegenation disgusted him. He reacted initially to the interracial love scenes in Shakespeare's *Othello* in much the same way as his mother had fifty years before. In 1785, when she saw the play, she confessed: "My whole soul shuddered when I saw the sooty Moor touch the fair Desdemona." Yet while his mother had reproached herself for harboring such deep racial prejudice and not having a more "liberal mind," Adams took a different tack. He maintained in 1835 that the moral lesson of this tragedy was that "black and white blood cannot be intermingled in marriage without a gross outrage upon the law of nature, and that in such violations nature will vindicate her laws." His reaction, he thus argued, was in accord with nature.[37]

Yet like many Americans Adams also looked upon miscegenation as an obvious solution to the country's problem. Unlike most of his compatriots, however, he did not find it more repulsive than any other solution. In his judgment slavery was worse, race war was worse, and African colonization was such a pipe dream that it was unworthy of serious consideration. He definitely would have preferred racial homogeneity if that were possible; but given the conditions in the United States, the actual effect of racial mixing would be less disastrous than the continuation of slavery. Indeed, whites outnumbered blacks by such an enormous margin that the black race would be eliminated by the "bleaching process of intermixture," and the remaining white population would have just "a dash of African blood"—like several of his fellow Congressmen.[38]

Adams sensed, moreover, that he differed from many on this issue. The "dash of African blood," he noted in his diary, was more than enough to disqualify David Levy, the delegate from the Territory of Florida, in the eyes of many members of Congress.[39] But to Adams, the more noteworthy fact was that the man was a Jew. And whenever he referred to Levy, a political enemy, he invariably used terms such as the "Jew delegate from Florida," "the alien Jew," "the squealing . . . Jew delegate," and paid no heed to the alleged "African blood."[40]

On the visceral level, therefore, Adams's reaction to the antislavery crusade was far less intense than that of most politicians. The campaign for "immediate emancipation without expatriation" touched raw nerves in both North and South, and caused thousands of Northerners to take to the streets to destroy the "amalgamators." Yet even in the fall of 1835, when politicians from Massachusetts to Missouri hysterically denounced Arthur Tappan and "the infuriate demoniacs associated with him," Adams was hardly alarmed. He told one correspondent: "With the Slave and Abolition whirligig I hope to have no concern."[41]

By the same token, he was also insensitive to the charge that organized antislavery would lead to disunion and perhaps civil war. He had already concluded, at the time of the Missouri crisis, that disunion was probably inevitable, and that any kind of civil war would lead to the destruction of slavery. Indeed, in his judgment, there was no institution on earth less adapted to survive an internal war than slavery.[42] He certainly did not want the South to break from the Union, but if that were to be the nation's fate, so be it. Slavery was still "precisely the question upon which it ought to break."

So neither the charge of "amalgamation" nor the fear of "disunion" and "war" moved Adams to take drastic action. In 1835, at the height of the frenzy over organized antislavery, he was conspicuously absent when an overflow crowd gathered in Boston's Faneuil Hall, the "cradle of liberty," to hear New England's finest denounce the abolitionists.

The meeting had the backing of the Boston *Atlas*, the Webster Paper, and the *Morning Post*, the Jackson and Van Buren paper. The high point of the meeting was a speech by Adams's old enemy, Harrison Gray Otis, who warned his fellow citizens that "a *revolutionary society*" had arisen, formed combinations with auxiliaries in every community and state, organized women and children as well as men, even "interrogated" one Congressman, and now clearly endangered the Union. "I pray," said Otis, " . . . that my grave may close over me before the union descends into hers."[43]

At the same time, the Boston *Courier* ran a serial entitled

"Letters Against Immediate Abolition" by Thomas Russell Sullivan, a resident of New Hampshire. Sullivan had no love for the "man-owners at the South," but the methods of the abolitionists infuriated him. How, he asked, could "our own New England men" descend to such practices? They *"ought* to know how we do business in the new world." Yet, contrary to "our republican forms," they have tried to stir up the passions of every man, woman, and child "through organized societies, public meetings, authorized agents, foreign emissaries, regular publications, and incessant circulation of cheap tracts, pamphlets, handbills, &c." They have begun *"the agitation of legal, constitutional, or political reform . . . by measures adopted to inflame the passions of the multitude,* including the women and children, the boarding-school misses and the factory girls . . ." To stop them, he wrote, penal legislation would be necessary.[44]

Meanwhile Adams was home in nearby Quincy, noting the events in his diary. His youngest son's father-in-law, Peter Chardon Brooks, made a special trip from his Medford home to attend the Boston town meeting. But in Adams's judgment it was a waste of time. Not only had the "theory of the rights of man" taken "deep root in the soil of civil society," but it had "linked itself with religious doctrine and religious fervor" and "armed itself with the strength of organized association." As a result the country was now in a state of turmoil, with Mississippi mobs lynching blacks suspected of insurgency and whites suspected of helping them, with South Carolina mobs of "slave-holding gentlemen" intercepting the mail and destroying antislavery pamphlets, and with the abolitionists "making every possible exertion to kindle the flame of insurrection among the slaves." Brooks, Otis, and others thus might pass "resolutions against the abolitionists to soothe and conciliate the temper of southern slave-holders," but "the disease is deeper than can be healed by town-meeting resolutions."[45]

Was there any way to stop the "disease"? Adams preferred to let it run its course. He could not foresee its end; the country was then at peace and "over-pampered with prosperity," yet the "elements of exterminating war" were also in "vehement fermentation." His own guess was that eventually the planters would "separate from the Union, in terror of the emancipation of their slaves," and that then the slaves would "emancipate themselves by servile war." But all that, he mused, might be in the "remote" future. At that moment it was more likely that the Jackson coalition of southern slavemasters and western land robbers would continue to plunder the nation and to stifle economic progress.[46]

So Adams differed with other northern politicians in his response to the abolitionists' pamphlet campaign of 1835. The campaign troubled him, and he was certain that the abolitionists wanted to start slave insurrections, but he was not about to join the South or the colonizationists in an attempt to silence them. Nor was he willing to attend a Boston meeting to "soothe and conciliate" the slaveholders. Too conservative to become an abolitionist, he was also temperamentally incapable of joining the anti-abolitionists.

But he would continue to present antislavery petitions when Congress met in December 1835. And that guaranteed that he would be in the center of the fireworks.

CHAPTER V

The New Folk Hero

When Congress convened in December 1835, Adams still hoped to stay out of the "Slave and Abolition whirligig." But that was just wishful thinking. The South was still in a state of panic; some $200,000 had been placed on the head of Arthur Tappan, dead or alive; mobs had sprung up in New England as well as in the Deep South; and even the Massachusetts legislature had to consider measures designed to silence the abolitionists.[1]

Andrew Jackson, in his annual message, set the tone for Congress. Denouncing the abolitionists as "incendiaries," Old Hickory called for "severe penalties" to suppress their "unconstitutional and wicked" activities, and praised those Northerners who mobbed antislavery lecturers, broke up abolitionist meetings, and destroyed antislavery presses. He recommended that postmasters publish the names of everyone who subscribed to antislavery papers "for there are few so hardened in villainy, as to withstand the frowns of all good men." He called for a national censorship law to stop Arthur Tappan and his associates from sending "incendiary" literature through the mails into the South.[2]

Such legislation was merely a legal nicety. The Jackson administration had already taken extralegal steps to deny Tappan and his associates access to the mails. As soon as the pamphlet controversy developed, Postmaster General Amos Kendall, with Jackson's blessing, encouraged postmasters to ignore federal postal regulations and exclude antislavery pamphlets from the mail. They did so gladly. Indeed, anticipating Kendall's support, the postmaster of New York had already enacted measures to stop abolitionist tracts and newspapers at their point of origin. That alone killed the pamphlet campaign.[3]

At the same time, the federal law guaranteeing the free transmission of the mails had become largely a dead letter in the slave states. Statehouse politicians across the South had quickly found old ordinances or written new ones to stop the circulation of "incendiary" literature. South Carolina relied on an 1820 law that promised a year in jail and a $1,000 fine to any white man who brought "inflammatory" papers into the state; Kentucky turned to statutes passed in 1799 and 1831; North Carolina to an 1830 law; Louisiana and Mississippi to 1831 legislation; Alabama to an 1832 statute; while Virginia drafted new legislation requiring postmasters to call all "obnoxious" publications to the attention of the local justice of the peace, who in turn would determine if such writings were "incendiary," have them burned in his presence, and arrest the addressees. Though patently illegal, these measures had the blessing of Postmaster General Kendall, who in his annual report declared that such laws should be obeyed by all officials of the federal government.[4]

Ironically, while Kendall's extralegal arrangements had the full support of the South, Jackson's call for legal sanctions against the abolitionists did not. The idea of a national censorship law enraged Senator John C. Calhoun and his states' rights radicals almost as much as it infuriated northern abolitionists. The South Carolina Senator wanted the separate states, not the federal government, to be given discretionary authority to decide what papers were "incendiary" and "to prohibit their circulation through the mails." If Congress—and not the states—had that right, then a northern majority might refuse to censor abolitionist tracts and insist on their delivery through the mails. And by permitting antislavery pamphlets to flood the South, a northern majority could break "all barriers which the slaveholding states have erected for the protection of their lives and property." Jackson's proposal, therefore, would virtually "clothe Congress with the power to abolish slavery."[5]

The result was a quick stalemate. Calhoun easily derailed Jackson's proposal, but lacked the votes to get his own measure enacted. After months of futile debate, eighteen Senators sided

with Calhoun, and a bill authorizing state censorship of the
federal mails came within four votes of passing the Senate. But
the issue was never in doubt. Asking northern politicians to
turn their heads, ignore postal regulations, and let the South
illegally seize and destroy antislavery mail was permissible.
Only a handful had any sympathy for the abolitionists whose
civil rights were being trampled upon, and even they had no
hope of actually forcing the Jackson administration to deliver
abolitionist mail. Still, few northern politicians were willing to
go so far as to *legally* authorize state censorship of the federal
mails. That was asking too much![6]

Once the deadlock developed, the Jackson administration decided to abide by the extralegal arrangements that Kendall had
sanctioned. Though clearly unlawful, Kendall's methods had
stifled the pamphlet campaign, and as long as they worked
there was no need for congressional legislation. Why stir up a
hornet's nest? Jackson's successors adopted the same pragmatic
approach, and thus Kendall's policy remained in effect until the
Civil War.

The issue of antislavery petitions, however, had to be faced.
Northern Congressmen might think it hopeless to fight for freedom of the mails, but their right to present petitions was clearly
a different matter. What would Congress do when a Congressman from Maine or Massachusetts stood up with a handful of
petitions calling for the abolition of slavery and the slave trade
in the District of Columbia? Gone were the days when such
petitions could simply be ignored. Now there was bound to be
tumult and shouting, indeed a furor that would make the Bank
War seem like a teapot tempest. Would organized antislavery
finally gain a foothold in the political arena? Would Congress
let that happen?

The battle over petitions began immediately. On December 16,
Congressman John Fairfield of Maine presented a petition pray-
ing for the abolition of slavery in the nation's capital. John Y.
Mason of Virginia quickly moved that the petition be laid on
the table. The House agreed by a vote of 180 to 31, and for a
moment it appeared that Congress would follow its traditional
procedure of hearing and then quickly turning aside antislavery

petitions. Two days later, however, when William Jackson of Massachusetts presented a similar petition, South Carolina's John Henry Hammond demanded that the House "put a more decided seal of reprobation" on abolitionist petitions. Denying that Congress had any constitutional right whatsoever to abolish slavery in the District of Columbia, Hammond moved that such petitions be rejected "peremptorily" without a hearing.[7]

Suddenly, two constitutional issues were at stake. Did Congress have the constitutional right to abolish slavery in the nation's capital? And could antislavery petitions be rejected "peremptorily" without a hearing? Hammond, in raising these issues, later said that he had acted "more from impulse than reflection," but because Calhoun led a similar fight in the Senate, most Congressmen assumed that Hammond was doing the Great Nullifier's bidding.[8] In any case, Hammond expressed the views of hotspurs throughout the South. Memorials from one slaveholding state after another not only backed Hammond's demands to the hilt but also called on northern states to pass penal laws that would silence forever Arthur Tappan and any other "incendiary" who dared to hurl "firebrands" at the South.[9]

Again, however, southern hotspurs were demanding too much. In the eyes of most northerners, the power of Congress to govern the District of Columbia included the power to abolish slavery, and the constitutional right of petition included the right to be heard. Even Congressman Samuel Beardsley of New York, who in October had led a mob against the abolitionists,[10] found Hammond's motion totally objectionable. The right of petition, argued Beardsley, was "a sacred right, guaranteed to the citizens of the United States by the constitution, and was one, therefore, that the House was bound to respect." The House might send back a petition if it were "in insulting terms"; but if it "was respectful in its language" and the House disapproved only of its prayer, then the House had to "lay it on the table, or reject the prayer." Rejecting it outright, without even a hearing, was tantamount to denying the sacred right of petition.[11]

Such objections led to one legal argument after another. Did the right of petition imply the right to be heard? No, argued

Henry Wise of Virginia. The First Amendment prohibited Congress only from passing any "law" denying the right of petition. So long as legislation was not enacted, Congress had the right to reject abolitionist memorials out of hand. But what good, then, was the right of petition if citizens had no right to be heard? And what about the constitutional provision giving Congress jurisdiction over the District of Columbia in "all cases whatsoever"? Surely those words gave the people the right to ask Congress to abolish slavery in the district. No, bellowed Wise and others. The power that Congress had as the district's local legislature could not exceed its powers as a national legislature. But, then, why did the Founding Fathers "in their wisdom" choose the words in "all cases whatsoever"? Surely they would have chosen other words if the power of Congress were truly limited. And so it went, back and forth, for nearly six weeks.[12]

Southern firebrands, however, were in no mood for constitutional objections. One after another made it clear that regardless of the law the abolitionists had to be stopped. The Union, indeed, was in "imminent peril" as long as the abolitionists were allowed to stir up "the passions of the slaves," stimulate them to "midnight murders" and "servile rebellion," and "deluge our country with blood." Nor would Southerners stand still while slavery was attacked in the District of Columbia, for the abolition of slavery there would trigger bloody slave insurrections in the neighboring states of Virginia and Maryland, and soon the entire South would be engulfed in "all the horrors of servile war." There was only one way to deal with "fanaticism," declared Francis Pickens of South Carolina, and that was to "strangle it in its infancy."[13]

The tenor of the early debate angered Adams. It "has been all on one side," he reported to his son in mid-December. "The voice of Freedom has not yet been heard; and I am earnestly urged to speak in her name. She will be trampled under foot if I do not, and I shall be trampled under foot if I do. . . . What can I do?"[14] On December 21, he spoke against Hammond's motion and suggested that the petitions be referred to the standing committee on the District of Columbia, where they were certain "to sleep the sleep of death." But for the most part he

kept still and listened, voted "no" at the appropriate opportunities, and let a fellow Antimason, William Slade, speak in
freedom's name.

Slade was both willing and able. A former clerk in the State
Department under Adams, the forty-nine-year-old Vermonter
minced few words. Two days before Christmas he vividly described the horrors of slavery and slave trade in the nation's
capital; he asserted that blacks had the same natural rights as
whites; and he claimed that the South's hysteria regarding antislavery was due more to a guilty conscience than the fear of
slave revolts. His was by far the boldest voice in behalf of
freedom.[15]

Shortly after New Year's Day, Adams finally became embroiled in the controversy. On January 4 he tried to present an
antislavery petition from 153 inhabitants of Millbury, Massachusetts. Because the petition was "couched in the same language" as one the House had tabled the previous day, he
intended to just state its contents and move that it also be
tabled. But his neighbor in the next seat, John M. Patton of
Virginia, interrupted him and demanded to know whether the
petition had been received. Speaker James K. Polk of Tennessee
ruled that it had not, and then allowed a new member from
Georgia, Thomas Glascock, to make a speech against receiving
antislavery petitions.

Jumping to his feet, Adams called Glascock to order for vi-
olating the House rule against debating petitions on the day
they were presented. But the Speaker sided with Glascock,
ruling that the interdiction was not in effect because the petition
had not been received. Adams challenged Polk's ruling, made
a formal appeal to the House and asked for the yeas and nays.
That led to a clamorous debate which consumed the rest of the
day and dragged on sporadically for weeks.[16]

Then on January 18, while Polk's ruling was still at issue,
Adams presented a petition from 363 inhabitants of Weymouth,
a town in his own district, calling for the abolition of slavery
and the slave trade in the District of Columbia. This time Hammond interrupted and moved that the petition not be received.
Polk ruled Hammond out of order. Moments later Henry L.
Pinckney, another South Carolina nullifier, approached Adams

and asked if he would agree to a motion to postpone the entire question of receiving petitions so the day's business might proceed. Adams consented. He then presented another antislavery memorial from 158 Massachusetts women, and listened quietly as other members presented similar petitions.[17]

Pinckney, it turned out, was about to break with Hammond and Calhoun. Their dubious constitutional arguments, in his judgment, had become a major obstacle to any action the House might take to stop the flood of abolitionist memorials. Their arguments were doing the South more harm than good, he thought; they had to be discarded. As an alternative he proposed in early February that all petitions be referred to a select committee, which would be instructed to report that Congress had no authority over slavery in the states and that Congress "ought not" to interfere with slavery in the District of Columbia, not necessarily because it was unconstitutional, but because it was "unwise," "impolitic," and "dangerous to the Union."[18]

Pinckney's action infuriated his fellow nullifiers. Denouncing him as a "traitor" whose proposal had sacrificed the very citadel of southern rights, the Calhounites claimed that he was seeking the limelight or selling out to the Jacksonian presidential hopeful, Martin Van Buren, who clearly wanted to bury the constitutional question.[19] Whatever Pinckney's motives, his scheme was hardly the "compromise" that some historians have maintained. It only seemed that way because of the storm of protest in his home state.

Actually, from the standpoint of the abolitionists, Pinckney's scheme was far more dangerous than Hammond's. Total rejection, as proposed by Hammond, never had a chance of passing the House in 1836, and as long as the South clung to Hammond's proposal there was no way of silencing the abolitionists. A small coterie of northern Congressmen would continue to present abolitionist petitions and keep the explosive slavery issue before the House.

But once Pinckney offered an alternative, the situation changed dramatically. Within the week he had the votes to get a select committee established. Half the southern members voted for it; and with the other half screaming that Pinckney had completely abandoned "the principles of the South," every Northerner but one supported the beleaguered South Carolinian. Even Adams was willing to give him a chance.[20]

Polk, a Tennessee slaveholder and a staunch Jackson man, quickly made certain that the committee would come forth with a proposal that both Southerners and northern Jackson men could support. He stacked the committee with eight administration men and one border-state Whig. Pinckney himself was made chairman. Once the committee was established, debate on the question should have been suspended until the committee reported back. But Polk, for some unknown reason, allowed Virginia's Henry Wise to deliver a final blistering attack against the "traitor" Pinckney.[21]

The issue was in committee for more than three months. Meanwhile, in the Senate, Calhoun carried on the fight for total rejection and proved beyond doubt that it was a lost cause. Finally, on May 18, Pinckney's select committee reported three resolutions to the House. While short of Calhoun's dreams, all were pro-South. The first repeated a maxim that politicians, North and South, had long supported: that Congress had no constitutional authority to interfere with slavery in the slave-holding states. Even antislavery "radicals" were expected to agree with this resolution. Indeed, would anyone dare to vote "no"? The second proposal merely affirmed the points that Pinckney had made at length earlier: that to tamper "in any way" with slavery in the nation's capital would be unwise, impolitic, and dangerous—and therefore Congress "ought not" to do it. The final resolution was much tougher than Adams and many others had expected. Known from the beginning as the "gag rule," it prohibited the House of Representatives from printing, discussing, or even mentioning the contents of any petitions related "in any way" to the subject of slavery. Such petitions were to be "laid on the table" with "no further action whatever." The main purpose of this rule, said Pinckney, was "to arrest discussion of the subject of slavery within these walls."[22]

All three resolutions had the full support of the Jackson administration. Speaker Polk, a most determined man, never let debate get out of hand. He allowed several Southerners to vent their anger against Pinckney and claim that the entire package was too weak, that the second resolution in particular was a virtual capitulation to the abolitionists, that it wrongly implied that the House had constitutional authority over slavery in the District of Columbia. But when Adams rose to speak, the wily Polk quickly recognized George W. Owens of Georgia, a member of Pinckney's committee, who moved the previous question. The House, in turn, promptly adopted the motion, terminating debate. And so, after a one-sided debate, the Pinckney resolutions went to a vote.

Furious, Adams tried to gain the floor. He screamed at Polk for not recognizing him and for shutting off debate before he had a chance to speak. "Am I gagged or am I not?" demanded the ex-President. "Order! Order!" cried several voices. Polk, noting that debate had been terminated, ruled Adams out of order. Adams appealed to the House and lost by a 109 to 89 vote. When the clerk called his name on the first resolution, he asked for just "five minutes . . . to prove that resolution false and utterly untrue." Again came the cries: "Order! Order! Order!" And again he was denied the floor. Thus, over the vehement protests of Adams and others, the vote continued.[23]

In the end, all three of Pinckney's resolutions passed by large majorities. Yet despite the lopsided margins the three votes are worthy of careful analysis. For they reveal party cleavages that would persist for years, and as much as anything else they reveal precisely where Adams stood with respect to other politicians of the day.

There are, in fact, two persistent myths about Adams that the votes help to dispel. One is that the old curmudgeon was simply a courageous moderate of the old school, a lover of the Constitution and the Union, who insisted on protecting the Constitution and the rights of his constituents against the outrageous assaults of southern hotspurs. Without question, Adams often pictured himself this way; he liked to think of himself as a judicious man who was forced to fight in behalf of northern rights and the Constitution. But he also referred to the Constitution as a "menstrous rag"[24]—and indicated on numerous occasions that the Union under the domination of slavemasters was hardly worth preserving. Clearly, his vast diary has left us with a picture that is a bit blurry, confused, and perhaps distorted.

Are his enemies any help? Obviously, southern Congressmen had a far different view of him than the many biographers who have portrayed him as a noble defender of basic constitutional liberties. Indeed, often bearing the brunt of his invective, Southerners never thought of him as a "moderate." Nor did they envision him as an ardent defender of the Constitution. There was more to his passion than that. Among other things, they knew that he blamed them for ruining his Presidency, for shattering his program of internal improvements, for standing in the way of everything he held dear. And they were certain that he wanted his pound of flesh in return.

They were at least partly right. Adams's response to Pinckney's first resolution indicates that he was far more hostile toward the South than were most Northerners, yearning to make trouble for the great planter-politicians whom he deeply resented, secretly hoping for their destruction. At first glance, the resolution had nothing to do with anything in dispute. It merely repeated the old precept that politicians had supported since Washington's day: that Congress had no constitutional right to interfere with slavery in the slaveholding states. Lincoln would support this principle even on the eve of the Civil War. Most antislavery radicals accepted it as true. Yet in 1836 Adams and eight other northern Whigs voted against it.[25]

Indeed, Adams not only voted against it, but went out of his way to proclaim that Congress, in certain circumstances, had the power to destroy slavery in the South. After failing to get "five minutes" during the vote to speak against the resolution, he found an opportunity shortly afterwards when Congress took up an entirely different matter, a resolution enabling the President to provide relief rations to white victims of Indian hostilities in Georgia and Alabama.

He was hardly diplomatic. Sharp and caustic, he lectured southern representatives on the war powers of Congress. Southerners ought to know better, he said. As "slaveholding exterminators of Indians," as warmongers hungering for Indian lands and Mexican Texas, they ought to fully understand the war powers of Congress. Were they ready for war? "A Mexican war? . . . A general Indian war? A servile war? And, as an inevitable consequence of them all, a civil war?" Did they actually "imagine" that Congress had no constitutional authority over slavery in their states during the time of war? "From the instant that our slaveholding states become the theater of war, civil, servile, or foreign . . . the war powers of Congress extend to interference with the institution of slavery in every way by which it can be interfered with!"[26]

And so it went for over an hour. What are we to make of this tongue-lashing? It included a constitutional argument, to be sure. But to picture the irascible old man as simply a courageous defender of northern rights and the Constitution seems a bit far-fetched. There was obviously more to his anger than that. The old diplomat was hardly the peacemaker, the voice of moderation. He was clearly going out of his way to provoke the South and the Southwest. He knew very well that his logic would have no effect on congressional thinking. It would only infuriate hotheads like Joab Lawler of Alabama, Charles Haynes of Georgia, Waddy Thompson of South Carolina, and Henry Wise of Virginia. And when they responded with fury, he was hardly surprised.[27]

Noteworthy, too, were the small band of Whigs who voted with Adams. They were not typical Whigs of the Webster-Clay school. Most followed different drummers: one or two sympathized with the abolitionists; several were active in one of the great moral crusades of the age; most were former Antimasons; and all but one represented districts in which Antimasonry had run rampant. Like Adams, they too had castigated both Andrew Jackson and Henry Clay, along with other prominent Masons, for membership in a "vile conspiracy" which had corrupted local and state governments, and subverted the rule of law to the point where Masons could literally get away with murder. Especially suspicious of Jackson, who had scorned Antimasonry, they never doubted for a moment that Old Hickory and his followers were dishonest manipulators. And like Adams, they were quick to perceive a new evil, a monstrous "Slave Power," which threatened to fasten fetters upon the entire nation. Thus, unlike their fellow Whigs, they fought the

Slave Power on every issue, not only over all three of Pinckney's resolutions, but consistently for years to come.[28]

The other persistent myth about Adams is that he was virtually alone in his fight against the gag rule. That was never true. While only eight Congressmen joined him in opposing Pinckney's first resolution, virtually every northern Whig was on his side in opposition to the gag rule and the proposition that Congress "ought not" to interfere "in any way" with slavery in the nation's capital. It was the northern Democrats, not the northern Whigs, who supplied the needed votes to pass Pinckney's second and third resolutions. Indeed, less than 10 percent of the northern Whigs went along with the South, as compared to 80 percent of the northern Democrats. Here is a breakdown of the vote:

	For "no interference"	Against[29]
Northern Whigs	4	38
Northern Democrats	68	7
	For the "gag"	Against
Northern Whigs	1	46
Northern Democrats	59	15

This striking difference in party behavior, moreover, remained constant. Historians have sometimes argued that northern Democrats "sold out" in 1836 because Van Buren was running for President, and he desperately needed southern support.[30] While this might be true, they continued to vote with the South, roll call after roll call, for the next twenty-five years. Similarly, the eminent Gilbert Hobbs Barnes misled a generation of historians by arguing that the Whig vote changed from year to year, depending on whether the Whigs were a minority trying to make trouble for the Democratic majority, or a majority trying to legislate Whig programs.[31] In fact, at no time did northern Whigs support the gag, while northern Democrats supplied the crucial votes not only to pass the first gag but also to renew it at each session of the House until 1844.

This behavior, it is now clear, was part of a general pattern. After tabulating and analyzing all roll call votes in the House from 1836 to 1860, historian Thomas B. Alexander found that the two parties were remarkably "consistent" and "persistent" in the way they responded to the explosive slavery question. Beginning in 1836, wrote Alexander, the Whigs divided sectionally, North versus South, and the party never achieved any unity on the issue of slavery; meanwhile northern Democrats stood with their southern colleagues, and thus the party of Jackson always "clung together on the essentially southern side." There were times, to be sure, when northern Democrats did vote against the South, but even on these occasions they were outdone by northern Whigs. Year after year, the pattern remained the same: more Whigs than Democrats took a stand contrary to the South's.[32]

So Adams was never alone in battling the gag rule; nor was he the voice of moderation as he often claimed. The old myths have to be laid aside. A radical by the standards of his party, far more violent in his rhetoric, often in step with only Slade and other Antimasons, he still had the support of virtually every northern Whig in the struggle for "the sacred right of petition."

With half the North behind him, Adams made the most out of the controversy. Indeed, he thrived on it. When the vote was called on Pinckney's gag, he shouted: "I hold the resolution to be in direct violation of the Constitution of the United States, of the rules of the House, and of the rights of my constituents." The Speaker ignored him, the roll call continued, and the gag passed, 117 to 68.[33] But the new rule had to be renewed at each session of Congress, and thus there were other opportunities to savage southern slavemasters and northern Democrats on constitutional grounds, to excoriate them for denying his constituents the sacred right of petition. Adams loved it. The more he needled his opponents the better he felt. Calhoun called him "a mischievous, bad old man."[34] An unknown Congressman dubbed him "Old Man Eloquent." To Adams's delight the name stuck, and he became a new folk hero.

But the gag, it should be noted, also served the needs of his enemies. The Jacksonians desperately needed it to control the political agenda. The party's most cherished programs as well as slaveholder hegemony in national politics were at stake. How could Van Buren and other Democrats focus attention on such issues as bank and currency reform if Congress had to deal continually with the slavery question? Democrats thus expended an enormous amount of energy depicting the petition campaign as a conservative plot—indeed, a British plot—to divert attention from such pressing issues as money and banking. Pinckney, they thundered, was right: the gag was necessary "to arrest discussion" of the slavery question within the halls of Congress.[35]

That it undoubtedly did. The gag came when the American Anti-Slavery Society was at its peak. The society outwardly seemed to be rich and powerful, growing and dynamic, worth paying attention to. Its methods were purportedly the same as those British abolitionists used to force a reluctant Parliament to abolish slavery in the British West Indies. Its members were tireless. In 1837–38 alone, they bombarded Congress with over 130,000 petitions calling for the abolition of slavery and the slave trade in the District of Columbia, along with another 32,000 petitions for repeal of the gag rule; 22,000 against the admission of any new slave state; 21,000 for legislation barring slavery from western territories; and 23,000 for abolition of the interstate slave trade.[36] What if all these petitions, each signed by "fifteen hundred women," as one horrified Virginian put it, had reached the floor of Congress? And what if any one of them provoked a full-scale debate? Party leaders were not about to take any chances. They were certain that they would be faced with an uncontrollable donnybrook like the Missouri crisis.

As it was, the Speaker of the House had his hands full keeping Adams and his cohorts in line. There were two problems. First, because the original gag rule was a resolution, not a standing House rule, it expired at the end of the session. So at the beginning of the next session, Adams and others had a free rein until another gag was passed. And by December 1836, the "bad old man" had scores of petitions to present. What would the House do when he presented a memorial signed by 150 women of Dorchester? Or one from 228 women of South Weymouth? Or one sent by 50 men in Dover? Or petitions from groups in Weymouth, Duxbury, Kingston, Hanson, Scituate? Or from Braintree, his birthplace? He was eager to find out. Indeed, gone were the days when he was willing to sit back and let Slade be the "voice of freedom."[37]

His turn came on a cold day in early January. As on a normal petition day, he rose with the Dorchester petition and moved that it be read. Thomas Glascock of Georgia leapt to his feet and moved that it not be received at all. In opposition, Adams told his colleagues that they ought to listen carefully to these "pure and virtuous citizens" just as they would listen to their own mothers. For all these women wanted was "the greatest improvement that can be possibly be effected . . . the total abolition of slavery on earth." The petition was tabled without being read.

The old man then offered an identical petition, one from the women of South Weymouth, a town near his home. Again Glascock objected to its reception. But this time, over shouts of "Order," Adams started to read it. Despite interruptions, screaming and shouting, points of order following points of order, he continued until the Speaker finally commanded him to sit down. And then, while slowly taking his seat, he read faster and louder, trying to get in every last word. A furious debate followed over whether the ex-President had violated the rules of the House and the Speaker's call for brevity. Finally the petition was tabled. But the old man had another, exactly like the first two, from the men of Dover. This one generated a long debate over slavery before it too was finally tabled.[38]

Nine days later the gag rule was renewed. That was the middle of January, over a month after Congress had been in session. The gag's supporters knew they had to move more quickly in subsequent years, before Adams had a chance to present his stack of petitions. By 1838 they succeeded in imposing the gag on the first petition day of the session. Maine was called first, according to custom, and two antislavery memorials were presented. But next was New Hampshire, a Jacksonian stronghold, and a staunch New Hampshire Democrat, Charles G. Atherton, presented a gag and forced its immediate passage.[39]

In the next session, pro-gag men went a step further. They

instituted a more drastic gag, one that prohibited the *reception* of antislavery petitions, and also made this measure a standing House rule.[40] That completely changed the nature of the struggle. Before, pro-gag men had to find a way to impose a gag before Adams or Slade got the floor. Now, Adams and others had to revoke a standing rule.

Yet even after the gag rule was tightened the Speaker had his hands full coping with the second major problem, evasion. Once the gag was in place, as Adams put it, there were still "ways enough" to get at the forbidden subject of slavery.[41] It was really quite simple. All it took was his superior talent in using and abusing parliamentary rules, so as to hold his own position and to put his enemies in the wrong, and a willingness to keep throwing out bait until hotheads like Alabama's Joab Lawler or Virginia's Henry Wise took the hook. At times it was child's play.

There were days, in fact, when everything went right. One of the most memorable was February 6, 1837.[42] Adams had a whole stack of petitions, including one from "nine ladies of Fredericksburg, Virginia." He tried to present it, arguing that the women merely wanted the "prohibition" of the slave trade in the nation's capital, not the abolition of slavery. No matter, ruled the Speaker, the petition still fell under the gag and must be tabled. Well, said Adams, would the Speaker also rule on another piece of paper? It looked like a petition, but it was signed by scrawls and marks "purporting to come from slaves." Was it in order?

The question produced an immediate reaction. Was the old man suggesting that slaves had the right of petition? "I object," screamed Lawler of Alabama. "I want it to appear on the record that I objected!" It was astonishing, bellowed Charles Haynes of Georgia, that any "gentleman" would raise such a question. The ex-President, shouted Waddy Thompson of South Carolina, ought to be indicted by the Grand Jury of the District of Columbia for inciting slaves to rebellion. Yes, pontificated Dixon Hall Lewis of Alabama, "severe" punishment was in order. "Expel him! Expel him!" someone yelled. "Censure him!" roared another. Resolutions to censure or expel Adams were introduced. Amendments were added. Confusion reigned.

Amid the chaos, John M. Patton of Virginia decided to take a close look at the petition from "the nine ladies of Fredericksburg, Virginia." He had been raised there, and was curious to see who would sign such a document. On examining the names, he loudly accused Adams of misrepresentation. The women were not "ladies," he said; they were free Negroes or mulattoes; and one name he recognized was that of a mulatto woman of "infamous" reputation.

Adams, meanwhile, contented himself with needling his adversaries. At one point he suggested that they had better rewrite their resolutions if they hoped to censure him. He had only asked the Speaker a parliamentary question concerning a petition "purporting" to come from slaves. He had not presented the petition nor said that it was, in fact, from slaves. Then later he told them that it was indeed from slaves—twenty-two slaves who preferred slavery to abolition and wanted Congress *not* to tamper with slavery in any way.

That infuriated his opponents even more. The old man, screamed one southern spokesman after another, was trifling with the South, wasting the time of the House. Some demanded expulsion; others censure; but cooler heads finally called for a vote on three resolutions. The first branded sponsors of petitions from slaves as unfriendly to the South and the Union. The second said that slaves had no right of petition. And the third was preposterous. It said that Adams had "solemnly disclaimed all design of doing anything disrespectful to this House" and had "avowed his intention not to offer to present the petition" if the House so ruled—and thus no "further proceedings" against him were necessary.

Adams, who had made no such declarations or promises, now had his opportunity. Because the third resolution referred to him specifically by name, the House had the choice of granting him the "privilege" of defending himself in a "full hearing," or denying him the privilege and establishing a precedent that could be used against every other member. Once granted the right to defend himself, he could touch on the issue of slavery or any other issue that bore on his defense. And that he did. Posing as a champion of the right of petition, he ranged far and wide, attacking slavery and the morals of slaveholders.

He first scolded the House for even thinking of denying slaves the right of petition. That would be horrible: "No despot, of any age or clime, has ever denied this humble privilege to the poorest or the meanest of human creatures." Then he turned on Patton of Virginia. "The honorable gentleman makes it a crime because I presented a petition which he affirms to be from colored women, which women were of infamous character, as the honorable gentleman says—prostitutes, I think the gentleman said." Patton interrupted: "I did not say they were prostitutes. They are free mulattoes." Unruffled, Adams continued: "I thought the honorable gentleman had said they were 'infamous.' I shall forever entertain the proposition that the sacred right of petition, of begging for mercy, does not depend on character any more than it does on condition. It is a right that cannot be denied to the humblest, to the most wretched."

Again Patton interrupted, this time to make it clear to his colleagues that he was not personally acquainted with the women in question. Said Adams: "I am glad to hear the honorable gentleman disclaim any knowledge of them, for I had been going to ask, if they were infamous women, then who is it that made them infamous? Not their color, I believe, but their masters! I have heard it said in proof of that fact, and I am inclined to believe it is the case, that in the South there existed great resemblances between the progeny of the colored people and the white men who claim possession of them. Thus, perhaps, the charge of infamous might be retorted on those who made it, as originating from themselves." On he went, portraying slavemasters as moral lepers and creating "great agitation in the House!"

The agitation, of course, finally came to an end. But, to Adams's delight it took the House leaders five days to resolve the problem he ignited. The second resolution denying slaves the right of petition passed overwhelmingly, but the other two resolutions were voted down. The story of how Old Man Eloquent tricked the slaveholders was added to his growing legend, to be repeated down to this day.

In accusing slaveholders of sexual misconduct, Adams made good use of one of the standard themes in antislavery propaganda. On other occasions he highlighted another common theme, southern violence. He had reason to do so.

In 1837 the ex-President began receiving death threats. The first came from Pittsburgh, Pennsylvania, but most of the others bore southern postmarks. They were from men of substance, men who could read and write and had the money to pay exorbitant long-distance postal rates, rather than from backwoods ruffians. Some were vague: "I shall be constrained to put you out of the way." Others were specific: "On the first Day of May next I promise to cut your throat from ear to Ear." By early 1839 he was receiving roughly a dozen assassination letters a month. One Georgian wrote twice, threatening to shoot him down in the street, or to cut his "damned guts . . . out in the dark." Adams, said the Georgian, wanted to disgrace the country by putting "a Big Black, Thick lipped, Crack Heeled, Woolly headed, Skunk smelling, damned Negro . . . in Congress hall."[43]

Adams was not intimidated. The letters terrified his wife and troubled him, but he never gave serious thought to quitting Congress or toning down his language. He had no personal fear of southern Congressmen. They all treated him with respect, and "most of them with kindness and courtesy." They had a higher regard for him, he thought, than "northern members who truckled to them, such as John Randolph had nicknamed 'dough-faces.' " Such men "they generally held in contempt."[44] But they had one trait, at least, that he identified with the letter writers: whenever they were insulted, they too often took it as a reflection upon their honor and demanded satisfaction on the dueling grounds. He was tired of reading about their duels, listening to their challenges, and hearing them brand northern men cowards for refusing to duel.

Dueling had been a powerful force in politics for as long as Adams could remember. It first became fashionable during the American Revolution among officers in Washington's army. After the Revolution it subsided somewhat until the turn of the nineteenth century, when it enjoyed an enormous revival from New England to Georgia, among officers in the Mediterranean fleet as well as politicians on the mainland. Dueling gradually disappeared in the North but became well established in the South, where it was hailed as the touchstone of morality and essential to the southern gentry's superior way of life.[45]

Adams, accordingly, had dealt with duelists throughout his long career. In addition to such major historical figures as Alexander Hamilton, Aaron Burr, Henry Clay, and Andrew Jackson, the list included naval heroes such as Stephen Decatur and Oliver Hazard Perry, prominent New York newsmen such as William Leggett and James Watson Webb, and the "father of the Erie Canal," DeWitt Clinton. All three of Adams's opponents in the 1824 presidential election were duelists, as was his single opponent in 1828. Both of the major candidates in 1832 followed the code of honor. And in Congress Adams was literally surrounded by men who were celebrities in dueling circles. The most fabulous was South Carolina's James Hamilton, who in fourteen trips to the dueling grounds had always wounded but never killed his antagonist. That, in the eyes of his admirers, was perfection.

Most congressional duels were gentlemanly affairs, fought with pistols at ten paces, and often ending with two missed shots or a superficial wound, and then a reconcilition between the parties. But some were suicidal. After the 1816 election, which led to a dozen or more duels, local gossips goaded Senator Armistead T. Mason of Virginia into challenging his brother-in-law. The two men agreed on shotguns at four paces! Mason's gun caught in his jacket as he fired, and so he only blew off his brother-in-law's arm. Mason himself was blown to bits.

The possibility of a duel put a definite strain on Washington politics. Men of power always had to be on their guard, even in the drawing room or at the races, where the social code required easy familiarity. A man was expected to be relaxed, nonchalant, and cordial with all companions. Yet a jest that went too far or a witty retort might be taken as an affront— and then would come the inevitable challenge.

Adams was unusual in that he had no worries on this score.

His age and great prestige immunized him from the code of honor. Besides, everyone in Washington knew that he regarded dueling as barbarous, un-Christian, and stupid, and that he would ridicule anyone inane enough to challenge him. But his younger colleagues, with less status in Washington society, needed a delicate social touch. They were always vulnerable.

Adams was well aware of their predicament. During his Presidency, his son John had made the mistake of insulting a Washington newsman, Russell Jarvis, at a White House gathering. Later, after his son had refused to answer a letter from Jarvis demanding an explanation, Jarvis had accosted the young man at the Capitol Rotunda, and in accordance with the dueling code had yanked John's nose and slapped his face. Adams had tried to treat this incident as a simple assault, rather than a challenge to a duel, but that had failed to work. Half the country had branded his son a coward for not accepting the challenge, and his wife among others was certain that the nose pulling had ruined their son's career. So Adams had deep personal reasons, as well as moral reasons, for despising the code of honor.[46]

The issue came to a head in February 1838. A Washington correspondent of James Watson Webb's New York *Courier and Enquirer*, a Whig paper, charged an unnamed member of Congress with corruption. Virginia's Henry Wise, a staunch Whig, called for an investigation, and a freshman Jacksonian Congressman, Jonathan Cilley of Maine, ridiculed his suggestion, saying the charges emanated from a corrupt and partisan newspaper editor. In his retort Wise dismissed Cilley as a man "who won't hold himself personally accountable."[47] A few days later Webb got a young Whig Congressman, William Graves of Kentucky, to deliver a note to Cilley demanding an explanation. Cilley rejected Webb's note, and in so doing refused to acknowledge that the editor was a "gentleman." That incensed Graves's mentors. How could anyone imply that Graves, a man of honor, would bear a note from anyone but a gentleman?

So the young Kentuckian issued a challenge. Cilley, high-spirited and tired of being baited, accepted it and specified rifles at eighty yards. The duel, held just outside Washington, was bizarre. Usually the first exchange of fire satisfied all requirements of personal courage, but in this instance there was a second round, and then a third. While Cilley, an expert marksman, never came close to hitting Graves, on the third exchange Graves, a clumsy novice, shot his opponent through the stomach, killing him instantly.[48]

The news of Cilley's death sent shock waves through the country. Only southern Whigs seemed satisfied with the outcome; all others, including Andrew Jackson, expressed outrage. Pundits blamed the seconds, particularly Henry Wise, for failing to stop the duel after the first shot. Indeed, there was evidence that Wise had goaded on Graves and urged the two men to move closer. Democrats demanded punishment, and the Speaker appointed a seven-man committee to investigate the matter. Meanwhile Congress began receiving petitions, first just a few and then a flood, calling for the abolition of dueling in the nation's capital.

Adams was certain that the public outcry against the code of honor would have no effect. The slavemasters would never yield. Dueling, just like the "bullying letters" he received, was "an appendage of slavery." But the Jacksonians might try to single out Wise and Graves for punishment, and that he was against. He presented several petitions from Massachusetts residents, chiefly Methodist ministers and abolitionists, calling for the expulsion of Graves and Wise, and for an Act of Congress outlawing dueling among its members. But when the Cilley committee, dividing along party lines, called for the expulsion of Graves and the censure of Wise, he tore into the Jacksonian majority. How dare they turn this tragic killing into a partisan political measure? That, he snarled, was even more horrendous than the duel itself.[49]

After twenty days of debate, the Cilley committee's resolutions were tabled. But in the Senate, to Adams's surprise, Senator Samuel Prentiss of Vermont made headway with an antidueling billing. To suppress dueling in the nation's capital, the Vermont Whig recommended ten years' hard labor to anyone involved in a challenge, and death to the victor if his opponent should die. It was clear that Prentiss's measure would be watered down, but even with amendments it was better than nothing at all. So at the next session of Congress Adams introduced the

Senate bill to the House, made an impassioned speech for stiffer penalties, and demanded that the bill be expanded to cover the nation as a whole. He also introduced resolutions imploring the President to "call to account" former Speaker Andrew Stevenson, now minister to Great Britain, and naval captain Matthew Perry for their part in two recent duels.[50]

He knew very well, of course, that the House would never agree to such measures. But he wanted to rally public opinion to his side and fight from a position of strength. The tough stance, moreover, provided him with the opportunity to bludgeon his southern colleagues as they chipped away at the Prentiss bill with amendment after amendment.

The strategy worked. Amendments eliminated the death penalty and cut other penalties roughly in half, but in February 1839 Adams succeeded in getting the amended bill through the House. The new law never came close to suppressing dueling in the nation-at-large, nor even in the District of Columbia, where enforcement proved to be lax. But it infuriated Henry Wise and many other Southerners, who claimed that the code of honor was absolutely necessary to maintain proper behavior in the House. Congressmen, lamented Wise, were now free to call one another liars and cowards and never worry about the consequences. But that, as Adams realized, was not what really bothered the Virginian and other southern hotspurs. Far more irksome was the fact that antidueling legislation represented a triumph for New England morality over southern morality; symbolic maybe, but a triumph nevertheless. And in Adams's eyes, that alone made the whole effort worthwhile.[51]

Two years later, Adams further annoyed proslavery zealots by scoring another symbolic victory. In his first case before the United States Supreme Court since 1809, the old man in 1841 defended thirty-nine Africans who had seized the slave ship *Amistad*.

While sailing from one part of Spanish Cuba to another, the Africans had rebelled, killed the captain and cook, and taken their two Spanish masters prisoner. Led by the slave Cinqué, they had hoped to sail to Africa, but a clever ruse by the Spaniards led them instead into Long Island Sound, where they were captured and then taken to New Haven to await trial.[52]

News of their capture spread quickly and whetted the curiosity of many Americans. Newsmen began spreading wild yarns about African cannibalism, especially the man-eating capabilities of one captive with huge deformed teeth. As the strange story of their mutiny spread it became even odder and more barbarous with each telling. The jailer added to the circus atmosphere by putting his charges on exhibition at a New York shilling apiece. Phrenologists examined the size and shape of the captives' heads, the bumps and vales, and from that made predictions about their mental faculties. Among the many was Queen Victoria's private phrenologist, George Combe, who came to America the following year and made his own analysis.

Immediately upon hearing about the *Amistad* captives, Lewis Tappan and other abolitionists went to work. Here, they knew, was a chance to dramatize the fate of hundreds of thousands of victims of the slave trade. Tappan and his associates hired Yale divinity students to teach the prisoners the Gospel, roused churchgoers to support the cause, and then after a long search found a cabin boy on the New York docks who spoke the prisoners' dialect and would serve as their translator. The next step, finding able lawyers to defend the Africans in court, was easy. And then, in a complicated series of moves, the abolitionists had the Spanish slaveowners jailed on charges of assault, kidnapping, and false imprisonment.

That set off a furor. The Spanish Minister to the United States fired off an angry letter of some ten thousand words to the American Secretary of State. Northern newspapers denounced Tappan for involving the "whole United States" in hostilities with the Spanish government. Scores of outraged Southerners called for Tappan's arrest. But the whole chain of events captured the fancy of many prominent Northerners. Men who never before had a kind word for the abolitionists contributed money and polemics in behalf of the *Amistad* captives. Yale President Chauncey Goodrich contributed, and so did Jacksonian lawyer Robert Rantoul. Somehow the fate of these bewildered Africans, now lodged in a New Haven jail, touched them in a way that slavery in the South did not.

The *Amistad* case fell under the jurisdiction of Andrew T.

Judson of the District Court of Connecticut. A Van Buren appointee, Judge Judson was a staunch colonizationist, famous for his hostility toward blacks and abolitionists. In 1833 he had led the townfolk of Canterbury, Connecticut, in terrorizing Prudence Crandall until she abandoned her boarding school for black girls and left town.[53] But in 1840, to everyone's surprise, Judson ruled in favor of the Africans and ordered the United States government to transport them back to Africa. That infuriated President Van Buren, who was up for re-election and worried about his standing in the South. Van Buren ordered the prosecutor to appeal the decision, to the Supreme Court if necessary.

A year later, just before the case appeared before the Court, Tappan and his lawyer decided they needed additional legal help. Adams, they agreed, would be a real asset. Although he was not a first-class trial lawyer, he had followed their case with keen interest and had helped them by pushing through a House resolution that forced the State Department to publish its correspondence with the Spanish government, which among other things revealed that to satisfy Spanish demands the Van Buren administration even contemplated seizing the prisoners. Also, regardless of how faulty Adams's legal views might be, they knew that "his station, age, character, &c &c" would "give an importance to his services . . . not to be overlooked."[54]

Adams, as was his custom, hesitated before getting involved. He felt he was too old, too long out of legal practice; his eyes bothered him; his hands trembled like "an aspen leaf"; his memory deserted him "daily." But after some hesitation he took the case and worried for weeks over his argument.[55] His legal argument before the Court was not nearly as impressive as that of his associate, who systematically exposed the flaws in the government's case. But Adams's presence turned the Supreme Court into a "theater of great interest and attracted a crowded audience," and his nine-hour appeal for justice left its mark. Justice Joseph Story, in reporting to his wife, called it "extraordinary, for its power, for its bitter sarcasm, and its dealing with topics far beyond the record and points of discussion."[56]

Together, Adams and his associate easily won the case. The government's argument, declared Justice Story for the Court, was badly flawed. The Africans were never legally the property of the two Spaniards. Rather, "They were kidnapped Africans, who by the laws of Spain itself were entitled to their freedom." Therefore, there were no grounds for arguing that they were "pirates" and "robbers." Nor was there any reason for shipping them back to Africa. Instead, they were to be discharged at once, as any other free-born men and women.[57]

But that was not the end of it. Thanks to Adams's appearance before the Supreme Court, the abolitionists' victory in the *Amistad* case took on great symbolic importance. Tappan and his associates made the most of it by publishing the ex-President's oral argument as propaganda for their cause, and Adams added his measure by franking hundreds of copies to friends, every member of Congress, every member of the foreign service, and other prominent Americans. Fearful slavemasters, meanwhile, claimed that his well-publicized oratory in behalf of the "blood-thirsty" Africans would cause American slaves to rebel, slit their masters' throats, and free themselves. "Is your pride of abolition oratory not yet glutted?" wrote one Virginian. "Are you to spend the remainder of your days endeavoring to produce a civil and servile war? Do you like Aaron Burr wish to ruin your country because you failed in your election to the Presidency? May the lightning of heaven blast you, and may the great Eternal God in his wrath curse you at the last day and direct you to depart from his presence to the lowest regions of Hell!"[58]

Overcoming the abolitionist triumph, moreover, became a cause in itself. Thus, even though the Africans eventually went back to Africa as "missionaries," proslavery forces in the United States joined the Spanish government in keeping the issue alive. Responding to their complaints, President John Tyler, a Virginia slaveholder, called on the House Foreign Affairs committee in 1844 to review the entire case. The committee chairman, Representative Charles J. Ingersoll of Pennsylvania, submitted a report recommending indemnity payments of $70,000. The Supreme Court, he argued, had made the wrong decision. The evidence of "ignorant, half-civilized negroes" should not have been allowed, nor should have the testimony of British abolitionists. So once again Adams had to fight the *Amistad* case, this time on the floor of the House. Fortunately he had plenty of northern support, and the bill failed to pass.[59]

Two years later, however, the issue was again before the House. This time James Buchanan, the Secretary of State under James K. Polk, a Jacksonian stalwart and another slaveholding President, recommended paying the Spanish claim. An amendment was added to an appropriations bill, specifying $50,000 to Spain. And once again Adams, now ailing and pale, denounced the scheme as "robbery," and the House blocked the payment.[60] So it went, until long after Adams's death, as one President after another between 1844 and 1860 tried to satisfy the South and reverse the outcome of the *Amistad* case.

There was another small matter that also took on great symbolic importance during these years. In January 1842, Adams presented several petitions that so angered southern representatives that they tried to censure him. And that set off a furor that shook the nation.

The old man was in high spirits that January. He had just been appointed chairman of the Committee of Foreign Affairs, to the dismay of his old enemy Daniel Webster, some southern Whigs, and most Democrats, especially southern expansionists who wanted to annex independent Texas. He also had a large stack of petitions to present, including some that were bound to cause trouble. He was eager to get started, noted the abolitionist Theodore Dwight Weld, and at dinner "talked with as much energy and zeal as a Methodist at a camp meeting." Later, when his turn came to present petitions, he assured Weld that some would set the slavemasters "in a blaze."[61]

The next day the old incendiary presented a stack of antislavery petitions, all obnoxious to the South and quickly gagged, before he brought forth his fire-starter. The document was probably a hoax—indeed, it appeared to have been written on congressional stationery—but it purportedly came from citizens of Clarksville, Georgia. It called on Congress to remove Adams from his post as chairman of the Foreign Affairs committee on grounds of his abolitionism and "monomania" on all matters dealing with people as dark as Mexicans. In presenting their request Adams pretended to be just carrying out his duty, a reluctant but conscientious defender of the sacred right of petition.

His opponents were not fooled. Most realized immediately that he wanted to bait southern fire-eaters into calling for his removal, and that he intended to claim the floor, as a matter of personal privilege, to defend himself against the charges in the document. But knowing what was happening—and stopping it—were two different matters. And even though several Congressmen bolted out of their chairs and raised points of order to put a stop to the whole affair, Adams promptly raised the question of privilege, which overrode other parliamentary maneuvers, and succeeded in making his chairmanship part of the dispute.[62]

Weld, sitting in the gallery, watched in amazement. Never before, he later told his wife, had he witnessed "such a scene." In fighting for the privilege of defending himself, "the Old Nestor lifted up his voice like a trumpet; till slaveholding, slave trading, and slave breeding absolutely quailed and howled under his dissecting knife." The old man claimed that there was "an alliance between Southern slave traders and Northern democrats" to get rid of him as chairman of the Foreign Affairs committee. He accused slave traders of wanting to foment war against Great Britain for suppressing their business. He pointed to one of Henry Wise's recent letters to his constituents, in which the Virginian had raised the alarm against Adams, claiming that the old man would seek diplomatic recognition of the black regime in Haiti.

Throughout his tirade, noted Weld, scores of slaveholders tried to stop him by raising points of order, and "every now and then screaming at the top of their voices: 'That is false.' 'I *demand* Mr. Speaker that you *put him down*.' 'What are we to sit here and endure such insults.' 'I demand that you shut the mouth of that old harlequin.' " And gradually, half of the slaveholding members left their seats and gathered about Adams, heckling him. And Adams, in turn, fired back with sharp retorts. " 'I see where the shoe pinches, Mr. Speaker, it will pinch *more* yet.' 'I'll deal out to the gentlemen a diet that they'll find hard to digest.' 'If before I get through every slaveholder, slave-trader and slavebreeder on this floor does not get materials for better reflection it shall be no fault of mine.' "[63]

After a day and a half of sheer bedlam, the hullabaloo ended in something of a stalemate. The hopes of Wise and others to unseat Adams were thwarted, but five Southerners on the Foreign Affairs committee resigned rather than serve under him, and the Speaker had trouble finding five other Southerners to take their place. And the House, after several votes, finally refused to hear the "Old Nestor" further on the question of privilege.

But he still had the floor and petitions to present. Among others was a memorial from forty-six citizens of Haverhill, Massachusetts, calling on Congress to dissolve the Union, which they claimed was costing them too much. The South was a constant drain on their pocketbooks. Every year "a vast proportion of their resources" went to support the views and institutions of the South, and they got little in return—so they wanted out. In presenting their request Adams noted ambiguously that it was "not yet time" for such extreme measures, and moved instead that a committee be appointed to report an answer "showing the reasons why the prayer . . . should not be granted."[64]

Southern Representatives were beside themselves with vexation. For years they had been threatening disunion if men like Adams kept agitating the slavery question. Now suddenly the tables were turned and Northerners were calling for disunion. And instead of denouncing the petitioners, Adams was suggesting that they wait a little longer, that it was "not yet time" for such drastic action. Thus, as Weld put it, "all Babel broke loose" upon Adams. One Virginian asked if it was "in order to burn the petition in the presence of the House." Others wanted to reprimand the old man, to bring him before the bar of the House and censure him for misconduct. As usual, Adams encouraged them in their efforts, baiting them time and again, waiting for his opponents to make a fatal mistake.[65]

He did not have to wait long. On the first day of debate, Thomas Gilmer of Virginia offered a crisply worded resolution stating that Adams "had justly incurred the censure of the House" for presenting a petition calling for "the dissolution of the Union." That was much too simple and straightforward for Thomas Marshall of Kentucky, the nephew of the late Chief Justice John Marshall. So on the following day the Kentucky Whig offered a much longer and complex resolution, which among other things accused Adams of complicity in "perjury" and "high treason." Those words gave Adams the opportunity he needed. From that day forth he demanded the rights of a man accused of treason and turned the censure resolution into a "trial."

He needed additional help, however, to make certain that the "trial" lasted more than a few days. Henry Wise, as usual, aided the cause by fulminating for hours against British abolitionists and likening Adams to such well-known "traitors" as Aaron Burr and Benedict Arnold. Harangues by Gilmer and Marshall also played into Adams's hands, as did a well-publicized plan of Gilmer's to depose Adams as chairman of Foreign Affairs. But John Minor Botts, a Virginia Whig, and two other eminent Southerners spoke eloquently against the censure motion, and for a moment it appeared that they might muster enough votes to table the entire matter. To stop them Adams and a handful of northern Whigs cast their votes with the opposition.[66] With the failure of the tabling motion, Adams had the opportunity to speak for hours on end.

He was vicious and far-ranging in his attack. He accused slaveholders of trying to destroy trial by jury, the right of habeas corpus, freedom of the mails, of the press, of free speech, and of petition. Alluding to the southern practice of jailing free black seamen while their ships were in southern ports, he denounced the South for enslaving northern citizens in violation of their constitutional rights. He contrasted the schools, internal improvements, and general prosperity of New York State with the tumbled-down buildings, wretched roads, and cultural stagnation of Virginia, blaming the South's backwardness on slavery. He made much of the conspiracy to strip him of his chairmanship of Foreign Affairs. He challenged slaveholders and northern Democrats to expel him, defied them, even threatened them: "I have constituents to go to who will have something

to say if this House expels me. Nor will it be long before gentlemen see me here again!"

More savage still were his personal attacks. In the case of
Wise, he brought up the Cilley-Graves duel, pronounced Wise
totally unfit to be his judge, a criminal who three years before
had entered the House "with his hands and face dripping with
the blood of murder, the blotches of which were yet hanging
upon him." As for Marshall, Adams depicted him as a bibulous
young man in an alcoholic daze, an ignorant puppy with none
of his distinguished uncle's talents, who should go home to
Kentucky, study law, and "learn a little of the rights of the
citizens."

Amidst the invective Adams also scored points in his defense.
Why was he singled out for censure? Southern members had
been threatening disunion for years. Everyone in the House
knew, moreover, that Robert Barnwell Rhett of South Carolina
kept in his desk drawer a resolution urging Congress to consider
disunion, and that at least one member of the Cabinet, Abel
Upshur of Virginia, would advocate disunion if the government
ever stopped suppressing northern abolitionists. So what was
wrong with presenting the Haverhill petition? Were Northerners expected to be more loyal than Southerners? Was there a
double standard? Or was the "trial" the result of a "base conspiracy" to take away his chairmanship?

Two weeks passed before Adams, now fully in control, decided that "the House was tired of the whole subject, and that
to close it now would afford relief to all parties." He told the
Speaker on February 7 that he needed another week to complete
his defense, but he would stand aside if anyone wanted to table
the censure resolution "forever." Taking his cue, Botts of Virginia so moved, and this time the band of northern Whigs who
had helped earlier to prolong the debacle voted with the Virginian. The tabling motion passed, 106 to 93.[67] But Adams still
had petitions to present, and he brought forth two hundred
more before relinquishing the floor.

Historians once argued that public opinion decided the outcome.[68] That was not the case. News traveled too slowly for
public opinion to have much effect, and most southern Whigs
switched their votes early and favored tabling before Adams

had a chance to go on a rampage. And there was never any chance that northern Whigs, now some seventy strong and the dominant group in the House, would vote to censure. So Adams, rather than his prosecutors, was in control, and like a cat he played with his victims before the kill.

The old man's triumph had wide repercussions. Immediately the morale of antislavery forces in Washington skyrocketed. Weld wrote to his wife: "This is the first victory over the slaveholders *in a body* . . . since the foundation of the *government*, and from this date their downfall *takes its date*." Wrote antislavery Congressman Joshua Giddings to his daughter: "Well we have triumphed, the north has for once triumphed. . . . I am confident that the charm of the slavepower *is now broken*. I may be too sanguine—quite likely I am,—but such are my candid sentiments."[69]

Adams's triumph also caught the eye of William Lloyd Garrison in Boston. Hailing the event as "a signal victory for the cause of liberty and its advocates," the fiery editor of the *Liberator* took special note of the South's outrage. The old man, in presenting the disunion petition, had not only called the South's bluff but also frightened "the boastful South almost out of her wits, driving the slaveholding representatives to the wall." Following suit, Garrison placed a new motto on the masthead of his editorial calling for "Repeal of the Union." He soon began denouncing the Constitution as "a covenant with death and an agreement with hell." He also presented disunion resolutions to local antislavery societies, and within the year his followers adopted the rallying cry of "No Union with Slaveholders." Disunion thus became a new weapon in the antislavery arsenal.[70]

Adams's victory also left its mark on many slaveholders. Proslavery forces in Congress tried to ease the sting by censuring the less formidable, less articulate Joshua Giddings, who in March 1842 offered a series of resolutions denouncing the coastal trade in slaves and defending slaves who had mutinied aboard the *Creole*, an American brig sailing out of Hampton Roads, Virginia, for New Orleans. But after his censure, Giddings followed Adams's advice, resigned his seat, and took the issue to his Ohio constituents, who promptly re-elected him by an overwhelming margin of some three thousand votes. That, in turn, underscored the importance of Adams's victory.

The turn of events left lasting scars on House slaveholders. Representatives like Henry Wise, who deep down admired Adams and craved his respect, never got over the bitter "trial" and its aftermath. The "poisonous fangs" of "the hissing serpent of Braintree" had struck too often and too deep. Without question, Wise later noted, the old man was "the acutest, the astutest, the archest enemy of Southern slavery that ever existed."[71]

Adams meanwhile basked in glory. Never before had any member of his family received such public acclaim. In the summer of 1843 he made a trip to Niagara Falls with the widow of his son John and his oldest grandson. Crowds assembled along his train route, gave him three cheers, struggled to see and hear him.

Later that year he made another trip, this time to lay the cornerstone of the Cincinnati Observatory, a project he had pushed for six years. All along the Ohio Canal crowds gathered to pay him respect. At Akron a "very pretty" young woman kissed him on the cheek, and he in turn "returned the salute on the lip, and kissed every woman that followed, at which some made faces, but none refused." The adulation continued at Newark, Hebron, Columbus, Jefferson, Springfield, Dayton, Lebanon. In Cincinnati he encountered a huge banner across Sixth Street that read: "John Quincy Adams, the Defender of the Rights of Man."[72]

The acclaim gave Adams new energy to carry on the long fight against the gag. He sensed victory. The change enacted in 1840, making the gag a House rule and prohibiting the reception of antislavery petitions, never had the support of Pinckney's original gag. Now it was endangered by a new issue— an issue certain to make slavery the centerpiece of American politics—the "hell-born spirit" of slavemongers to acquire Texas and expand southern power.[73]

CHAPTER VI

Texas and "The Great Slave Power Conspiracy"

In one important way, the Jacksonians played into Adams's hands. For while they were most eager to silence Adams and the abolitionists, they were also insatiable land grabbers. And land hunger, more than anything else, brought slavery back into the political limelight. Indeed, there was no way the followers of Old Hickory could clamor for Indian and Mexican land and keep slavery off the political agenda.

The Jacksonians—not the Whigs—generally led the expansionist impulse. Although several prominent Whigs joined the Jacksonians in agitating for more land, the once popular notion that land hunger was bipartisan is largely myth. Careful studies of political opinion indicate that most Whigs had little appetite for acquiring huge chunks of additional land. Instead, they dwelt on the need to develop the vast country that the nation already possessed, to build a national network of roads and canals, to cultivate commerce and industry. The Jacksonians, in contrast, saw every acre of new territory as an additional guarantee for freedom and democracy.[1] "It is the exclusion of the people from the soil," declared the *Democratic Review*, that "oppresses England and destroys Ireland," that keeps people poor and makes famine endemic throughout Europe. Thus making certain that land was abundant and easy to acquire should always be democracy's primary goal.[2]

The parties generally practiced what they preached. Year after year, congressional Democrats fought Whig efforts to increase the price of government lands. Meanwhile a Jacksonian stalwart, Senator Thomas Hart Benton of Missouri, led the battle for squatters' rights, which resulted in a permanent act in 1841 that gave squatters on government lands the right to "preempt" up to 160 acres at the minimum price of $1.25 an acre. With less success, Benton also fought for severe price cuts on government lands that remained unsold, which eventually culminated in modest reductions in 1854. Simultaneously, George H. Evans in the *Working Man's Advocate* campaigned for free homesteads for eastern surplus labor. All the while, Democrats pushed for the acquisition of still more land.

In practice, Jacksonian expansionism always seemed to benefit the plantation South much more than the rest of the country. The tone was set in 1830, the year before Adams's arrival in Congress, when Jackson badgered the sharply divided Representatives into accepting his Indian Removal Act. The bill enabled the President to negotiate land exchanges with eastern tribes, whereby they would give up their eastern lands for acreage west of the Mississippi River. At the time most northern tribes had already been stripped of their potency, while in the South some 60,000 Cherokees, Creeks, Choctaws, and Chickasaws still possessed over 25 million acres, including pockets in western North Carolina and southern Tennessee, huge tracts in northwestern Georgia and eastern Alabama, and the northern two-thirds of Mississippi. The Choctaws in Mississippi alone outnumbered all the Indians of the Midwest. So the bill's greatest beneficiaries were white Southerners.

Was it intended that way? It was primarily happenstance according to most historians, but neither grateful Southerners nor suspicious Northerners believed that at the time—and certainly not Adams. Indeed, even before he set foot in Congress, he was certain that Jackson and his fellow slavemasters had made an unholy alliance with western land robbers to plunder the public domain. The Indians, he believed, were just the first victims. With Jackson's blessing "three or four southern states" were now free to nullify "all the Acts of Congress and all the Indian Treaties made for the last forty years" and "to exclude or exterminate all the Indians within their borders"; that the southern states would now do so was indisputable. The situation of the Indians was hopeless.[3]

But what about Jacksonian expansionism generally? Could it be stopped? Adams was pessimistic, but he went to Congress determined to stand in its way. At first only a few radical abolitionists and his fellow Antimasons agreed with his contention that Jackson's land policy was part of a Slave Power conspiracy. By the 1840s, however, this disquieting murmur would grow into a mighty roar.

Upon taking his seat in Congress, Adams's first line of attack was against the ongoing program of Indian removal. Even though he saw no hope in reversing Jackson's policies, he took every opportunity to savage the program and became one of its most formidable critics.[4]

The program was easy to attack. To carry out the mandate of the Indian Removal Act, the Jackson and Van Buren administrations had to negotiate at least seventy-nine treaties. While the bill did not authorize the use of force, this was the result. Force, fraud, bribery, and murder—all were necessary to get the desired treaties. And once the treaties were signed, force was often necessary to get unwilling Indians to move.

The upshot was one national disgrace after another. In 1832, at Bad Axe Creek, Illinois volunteers and federal troopers ignored attempts of Chief Black Hawk and his tribesmen to surrender, and shot and bayoneted some 150 men, women, and children. Three years later, in trying to round up the Seminoles in Florida, the army became embroiled in a war that lasted seven years and cost the lives of 1,500 federal troops—including Adams's nephew—and $20 million in expenses. In 1838 General T. S. Jesup resorted to treachery to capture the Seminole chief Osceola, arresting the young man under a flag of truce and throwing him into a military jail, where he died three months later. In the same year, General Winfield Scott herded 19,000 Cherokees out of Georgia to Oklahoma. Nearly one-fourth of the entire Cherokee nation died along the 800-mile "Trail of Tears."

So Adams had plenty of opportunities to attack Indian removal. He also had scores of allies. Indian removal was never as popular as Adams sourly anticipated in his diary, nor as historians later made out in textbooks. The original bill barely got through Congress, failing to pass the House on several test votes, and passing by a margin of 102 to 97 on the final vote. The vote was largely sectional, with two out of three Northerners voting against the bill, and four out of five Southerners voting in favor. Simultaneously, the vote also reflected party divisions, with the "nay" votes generally coming from areas that supported Adams in 1828, and the "aye" votes from areas that supported Jackson. Most enemies of Indian removal remained hostile to Old Hickory's policies, later opposing his Bank Veto and then joining the Whig party, while most supporters of Indian removal became diehard Jacksonians.[5]

In opposing Indian removal, then, Adams was in step with dozens of other politicians moving along the same political path. He first entered the fray four months after taking his seat in Congress, presenting petitions in favor of the Cherokees and against the state of Georgia, including one from New York City that was forty-seven yards long. Infuriated, the Jackson men tried to table the petitions, but lost a close vote, 91 to 92.[6] Thereafter, Adams regularly assailed the Jackson administration, Congress, and the southern states for the horrors growing out of Indian removal. Who was responsible for the suffering that accompanied Choctaw removal between 1831 and 1833? Who was at fault for the Indian wars? Who was to blame for the rapes, murders, and other crimes against the Cherokees in 1838? Adams left no doubt that the white man was to blame, and especially the southern white man.

In spite of his sharp tongue, Adams's voting record lagged behind that of other northern Whigs. While blaming the Indian wars on "slaveholding exterminators of Indians," he invariably voted to aid white victims of Indian raids. By 1838 he was the only Massachusetts Whig who voted funds to suppress Indian hostilities.[7] The government, he maintained, had an obligation to protect innocent citizens who were certain to suffer as a result of the government's previous actions.

Adams abandoned this line of reasoning in 1840, the fifth year of the Seminole War. After learning that the War Department was buying Cuban bloodhounds to run to ground Indians and runaway slaves in the Florida swamps, he introduced a sarcastic resolution demanding that the Secretary of War report the "martial history" of these particular bloodhounds and how they discriminated "between the blood of the freeman and the blood of the slave—between the blood of the armed warrior and that of women and children—between the blood of black, white, and colored men—between the blood of the savage Seminoles and that of Anglo-Saxon pious Christians." Four months later he launched a five-hour tirade against further expenditures on the Seminole War.[8]

Adams's tirades, like everything else he did, were widely reported and quickly won public acclaim in the North. Scores of concerned whites called on him to "save the poor Indians."[9] An outraged New Yorker, wanting to renounce his citizenship because of the government's Indian policies, also singled out Adams for help. So did Chief Big Kettle and other New York Senecas, John Ross and his Cherokee followers, and a host of other Indian leaders across the country.[10] As always, Adams thrived on the attention and especially the fact that underdogs regarded him as a champion of human rights. And, next to his battle for the right of petition, his denunciations of Indian removal probably added more than anything else to his reputation as the foremost defender of the rights of the oppressed.

But did he really care about the fate of the Indians? No, argued one Southerner after another. He was just another Yankee hypocrite—not as bad perhaps as Ralph Waldo Emerson, Daniel Webster, Caleb Cushing, and other New Englanders who denounced Indian removal one moment and speculated in Indian lands the next—but full of cant nevertheless. "Look at his record!" exclaimed Congressman Charles Haynes of Georgia. Was this not the same man who in 1802 gave a long speech justifying the Pilgrims' dispossession of the New England tribes? Was this not the same man who also justified Jackson's war against the Seminoles in 1819? Surely, his present sympathy for southern Indians was totally inconsistent with his previous record. Adams, snarled Haynes, was getting even with Georgia—and the South—for helping to drive both him and his father from the White House.[11]

The South's charge was powerful and perhaps irrefutable. But for the most part Adams ignored it. He just went about his way,[12] certain that the Pilgrims had served mankind in expanding the area of Anglo-Saxon freedom while the Jacksonians were utterly reprehensible in expanding the area of slavery. He enjoyed both the adulation of the North and East and the vituperation of the South and West. He still wanted no part of lost causes, however, and in 1841 refused to serve on the Committee of Indian Affairs either as the chairman or an ordinary member.[13] By then, the cause of the eastern tribes was as hopeless as he had always predicted.

A more hopeful cause, in Adams's mind, was that of Texas. Just as the Jacksonians coveted Indian lands, so too did they hunger for Mexican Texas. They had to proceed cautiously, however. The seizure of Texas was certain to provoke a full-scale debate in Congress over the expansion of slave territory and likely to drive Mexico to war.[14]

In trying to stop the Jackson men, Adams was again vulnerable because of his past record. Some critics distorted his record by claiming that he gave away Texas to get Florida in 1819. Others knew, however, that he had once been enthusiastic about Texas and westward expansion. Indeed, upon becoming President in 1825, he had instructed the State Department to buy as much of Texas as possible. And his Secretary of State, Henry Clay, had tried a number of desperate ploys to persuade Mexico to sell. But no Mexican government dared to sell, especially to its greedy northern neighbor; national pride was at stake.

When Jackson took office in 1829, he was anxious to succeed where Adams had failed. But it was hard to argue that Jackson's election brought a vast change in American policy. In time he was forced to replace the American minister to Mexico, and his choice was Anthony Butler, a fast-stepping South Carolinian who believed that loan-sharking, extortion, and bribery were the keys to successful negotiations. Yet, apart from the actors and the question of honest dealing, nothing changed: the goal was still to buy as much of Texas as possible.

In vain Adams tried to distinguish between his efforts to acquire Texas and Jackson's. The character of Texas, he contended, was vastly different when he was President. Texas was then a land of freedom, a land untainted by slavery and the

Slave Power. While it undoubtedly would have sympathized with the South because of its geographical proximity, he claimed, it would have been drawn to the North's political principles and pure spirit of freedom. It thus would have been an asset to all Americans, not just southern slavemasters. To his dismay, no one paid him much heed.

Mexico, however, made one change that Adams never let anyone forget. When he was President slavery was legal throughout Mexico, and therefore if American slaveholders had acquired Texas they would have simply brought their slaves to an area where slavery already legally existed—just as they were now doing in Choctaw and Cherokee country. But in 1829 Mexico abolished slavery, and hence if American slaveholders now took over Texas a vital historical process would be reversed. Indeed, said Adams, that was clearly the goal of Jackson, Calhoun, and other slavemasters.

The argument, while it sounded plausible to thousands of Northerners, struck southern Congressmen as just a lawyer's argument. The Mexican government had not enforced the 1829 emancipation decree in Texas, and Southerners knew that Adams was aware of this fact. Naïveté had never been one of his faults. He was, therefore, deliberately distorting and exaggerating Mexican "freedom." Moreover, if this argument had not been available, Southerners were certain that he would have conceived another for keeping Texas out of southern hands. As they saw it, he had no interest in black freedom; his primary motive was to make trouble for the Jacksonians and the South.

The southern indictment had two variants. While the Jacksonians hammered away on the old theme that the ex-President was a sore loser trying to get even, southern Whigs often took the opportunity to blast their Jacksonian adversaries by linking Adams's behavior to Democratic extremism. John Minor Botts of Virginia, for example, testified that Adams's actions were just a response to Calhoun and others who said that the "great object" in taking Texas was "the expansion of slave territory, and consequent increase and continuance of power of the *Democracy* of the South." "*I had it from his own lips,*" wrote Botts. They convinced him to "fight the devil with his own fire" and drove him "into the ranks of the Abolition party."[15]

Botts, of course, knew only part of the story. In fact, Adams began moving in this direction long before he met Botts and long before the Jacksonians came to power. As early as 1819, as we have already noted, Adams argued privately that northern Congressmen ought to waylay the Florida Treaty—which he himself had negotiated—and stop the expansion of slave territory. So the notion that he was just reacting to the extremism of Calhoun and other proslavery zealots of the 1830s and 1840s is far-fetched; their acts and proclamations only added fuel to the fire.

The Jacksonians, too, had a distorted view of reality. While there is no doubt that Adams wanted revenge and loved causing them trouble, there is also no doubt that he sincerely believed that an aggressive Slave Power directed the nation's expansionist impulse. He had the same view of the Slave Power that he had of Freemasonry. He was certain that both had too much power and that both poisoned the wellsprings of American liberty. And, like his fellow Antimasons, he moved freely from denouncing conspiring Masons to denouncing conspiring slave-masters.

Adams's notion of a Slave Power conspiracy, just like that of a Masonic conspiracy, has long been discredited by historians. The death blow probably came from the pen of Chauncey S. Boucher, who in 1921 relegated this fear to the dustbin of foolishness.[16] But since then, there have been scores of books and articles belittling the concept. The South, according to most of these accounts, simply lacked the singleness of purpose to carry out any sort of conspiratorial plot. The politicians were hopelessly disunited. Moreover, the southern Whigs represented the great slavemasters, and most southern Whigs were dead set against the annexation of Texas. Scholars today generally dismiss Slave Power imagery as just another manifestation of the mass paranoia of Jacksonian America.

In demolishing the conspiracy thesis, however, Boucher and other historians were frequently guilty of attacking straw men. They usually assumed, for example, that there was a common definition of Slave Power. That was never the case. In Adams's lifetime there were a bewildering number of complexities and variations in the definition of Slave Power. Did the term include all slaveholders or just wealthy planters? The border states as well as the Deep South? Southern Whigs as well as southern Democrats? Usually it was unclear. Adams's son Charles attempted precision when he said that the Slave Power consisted of 350,000 men controlling the political resources of fifteen states. And so did George Julian of Indiana when he said the Slave Power constituted no more than 4 percent of the white South and 1 percent of the nation as a whole.[17] But most men who used the term "Slave Power" were vague and elastic.

Adams, too, often used the term "Slave Power" loosely. Still, there was seldom any doubt whom he had in mind. In the 1830s, the expression always included the southern wing of the Democratic party, and oftentimes northern "doughfaces" who sided with southern Democrats. In the 1840s, another group was definitely added to the list—southern Whigs who identified with President Tyler. What about southern Whigs generally? He had no doubt that they would join forces with the Jacksonians in supporting slavery as the basis of the southern way of life, in gagging the abolitionists, and in upholding the three-fifths clause of the Constitution as a means of ensuring southern dominance in national politics. But he also recognized that they were not the driving force behind the expansion of slave territory. That was the passion of the Jacksonians and the Tyler Whigs. It was they he invariably had in mind when he lashed out against the "aggressive slaveocracy."

The temper of the times made it easy for Adams to adopt this rhetoric. People saw conspirators all about them. Some thought the "Monster Bank" planned to dominate the Republic; others worried about a takeover by the Pope and scheming Jesuits; still others pointed to the Mormons or British abolitionists. More important than this general atmosphere, however, was evidence linking Texas with the expansion of slavery. Some of this evidence was flimsy and circumstantial, some direct and substantial. In any case, there was more than enough to convince a suspicious Yankee like Adams that Jackson's and Tyler's Texas policies were part of a Slave Power conspiracy.

In arguing this thesis, Adams and others invariably began with the obvious fact that Mexico was vulnerable to the South's cupidity. Winning independence from Spain in 1821, Mexico inherited the vast northern territory of the Spanish empire which included present-day Texas, New Mexico, Colorado, Utah, Nevada, Arizona, and California. Apart from a scattering of Indian tribes, a few missions and military posts, the land was undeveloped and unpopulated. The new Mexican government, torn by poverty and chaos, was clearly unable to protect it.

In 1823, the leaders of independent Mexico decided to carry out a last-minute plan of the overthrown Spanish regime. To create a buffer zone between Mexico's interior and the United States, the government would encourage migration into Texas. Huge tracts of land would be given to big-time operators, Mexican and foreign alike, who promised to settle a certain number of colonists in Texas within a certain period.

Unfortunately for Mexico, land-hungry Americans from the southern and western states came in droves. The land was virtually free—only ten cents an acre as opposed to a minimum price of $1.25 an acre in the United States—and all colonists were exempt from taxes for seven years. The Americans soon outnumbered the Mexican population by two to one, then three to one. This produced alarm in Mexico City. To regain control, Mexican officials talked about settling large numbers of Germans and Swiss, Mexicans, and even convicts in Texas. But the first important act was the abolition of slavery in 1829, which was intended to discourage further immigration from the American South. More pointed still was an 1830 law explicitly forbidding future American migration into Texas and directing Americans already there, including slaveholders, to abide by Mexican law and custom. But nothing worked. The Mexican government was simply too weak to enforce its authority, and the new laws were openly defied as frontiersmen and planters streamed into Texas with their slaves. The Mexican government thus found it politic to make exceptions for Texas.

Then in 1834 General Santa Anna seized control of the Mexican government and established a dictatorship. When several Mexican states revolted in 1835, Texans joined the rebellion. The Texas revolt quickly became a war for independence, and in 1836 Santa Anna with 6,000 men stormed into Texas, burning villages and devastating fields, killing 188 Texans at the Alamo

in San Antonio, and butchering more than 300 defenders of
Goliad after they had surrendered. Soon Texas war cries—"Remember the Alamo!" and "Death to Santa Anna!"—rang through
the United States. Angry Southerners and Westerners raised
recruits and supplies, grabbed their rifles, and rushed to the
aid of Texas. Once independence was won, Texas appealed to
the United States to recognize its independence—or better yet
to annex it.

Adams, along with many Northerners, had little sympathy
for the Texas rebels. In his view, Santa Anna was just an excuse
for rebellion, not the cause of it. The Texans were not fighting
for liberty; quite the contrary, they were fighting to keep their
slaves in chains. But even more troubling were the actions of
the American government. While he could not prove it, he had
a gut feeling that the Texas revolution was a plot executed by
Jackson and other slavemasters to further southern interests.[18]

For one thing, the Texas commander-in-chief, General Sam
Houston, was a close comrade of Jackson's. He fought with
Jackson during the War of 1812 and suffered severe wounds at
the Battle of Horseshoe Bend, and then rose in Tennessee politics to become Governor in 1827. After his young wife deserted
him he took off to live with the Cherokees in the West. Twice
Houston visited Washington, dressed in buckskin and a blan-
ket, to speak in behalf of his tribesmen. On the second occasion,
after living with Jackson in the White House, he went to Texas.
The War Department claimed that he was sent to parley with
nomadic Indian tribes. Was that true? Or was he sent by Jackson
as part of a conspiracy?[19]

Also troubling was the government's behavior during the
rebellion. In defiance of existing neutrality agreements with
Mexico, the Jackson administration let the Texans enlist recruits
and raise money and supplies in the United States. Moreover,
on the pretext of protecting the United States against Indians,
Jackson ordered to the Texas border a large detachment of
soldiers under General E. P. Gaines, an ardent expansionist
who was anxious to help the Texas revolution and add Texas
to the United States. What were Gaines and Jackson up to?
Were the troops there, as the Mexicans claimed, to ensure the
success of the rebellion?[20]

For Adams there was never much doubt. He felt certain that Jackson and his cronies had engineered the Texas rebellion. But he was not about to level charges at Jackson on the basis of just intuition and Washington gossip. He needed facts. He had been so involved in other matters that he had missed half the developments in the Texas story. He needed those details, and more, before he took on a sitting President.[21]

In May 1836 the necessary facts unexpectedly turned up in Adams's mail. He received a bundle of newspapers containing four anti-Texas essays. The essays fascinated him: the author undoubtedly knew far more about Texas than he did, and the author's evidence substantiated his worst suspicions. But who was the author? The accompanying letter, signed by Benjamin Lundy, merely attested that the author's remarks were "strictly correct." Adams appealed to Lundy for more information and promised to make the facts known to the entire nation.[22]

The author, as it turned out, was Lundy. The 47-year-old Quaker had been following events in Texas for years. He had been involved in antislavery projects for some two decades, and one of his pet schemes was to establish a free-labor colony for ex-slaves in Texas. In pursuit of this dream he had been to Texas on three occasions in the early 1830s. From his travels he knew that Texas slaveholders, land speculators, and slave traders wanted no part of the Mexican emancipation law. They all saw slavery as central to their future profits, and they all thought their fortunes would skyrocket if Texas were free from Mexican authority. So at the first opportunity they rebelled.[23]

Lundy also knew that many prominent Americans expected to gain from the Texas rebellion. Moreover, he had been a newspaper editor for most of his adult life and had a vast collection of memorable quotes. Some were dynamite. Thomas Hart Benton of Missouri, for example, had been touting the annexation of Texas since the days of the Missouri Compromise. Among other reasons Benton cited, Texas would "add five or six more slaveholding states" to the Union and guarantee southern domination. Indeed, on one occasion Benton had waxed eloquent about the possibility of carving "NINE" more slave states out of Texas. And why were so many Virginians eager to acquire Texas? According to a speech delivered by Judge

Abel Upshur in 1829, the acquisition of Texas would drive up the price of Virginia slaves in the interstate slave trade. Three years later, in another speech, James Gholson of Virginia predicted the price would rise by "fifty per cent at least."

Lundy, moreover, knew that most of the original Texas land grants had been sold to joint-stock companies in New York, Nashville, and New Orleans. These firms, in turn, had marketed both stock in their enterprises and "scrip" entitling the bearer to certain Texas land. Now, after numerous transactions, much of the stock and scrip was in the hands of unscrupulous adventurers. Among the most infamous were the aged Aaron Burr, probably the most distrusted man in America, and his two protégés, the slippery Samuel Swartout (who later, while in charge of the New York City customhouse, stole one million dollars from the federal government) and the equally notorious Jane McManus. All three had a sizeable stake in the great Galveston Bay and Texas Land Company. That New York firm, in turn, was represented legally in Texas by none other than General Sam Houston. Burr and Swartout, moreover, had close ties with Andrew Jackson.[24]

Such facts, of course, did not prove conspiracy. But given Lundy's newspaper experience and his moral fervor, he had no trouble stringing his facts together in a convincing way. And by the winter of 1835-36 he knew that the Texas rebellion had destroyed his dream of an antislavery colony—so he took up his pen and wrote an exposé of the revolt. Fearing for his life, he published under the pseudonym "Columbus" in the Philadelphia *National Gazette*. He then sent several installments to Adams, on the chance that the old man might find in them something useful, but never expecting the former President to turn to him for help.[25]

Adams's request for more information thus exceeded all of Lundy's expectations. Lundy had never dreamed of having such influence. His kind had never had access to high places. So, after pledging Adams to keep his authorship of the "Columbus" essays a secret, Lundy bombarded Adams with further essays, pamphlets, maps, and scores of names, dates, organizations, and places. The details were especially helpful. Lundy took pains to be accurate, always adding phrases like "I believe" when there was any doubt, and thus eliminated Adams's fear of being tripped up on the "facts" and made to look the fool.[26]

Still, Adams was cautious. He first tested Lundy's material in late May 1836, just weeks after receiving the initial packet, in the memorable speech in which he attacked Pinckney's claim that Congress had no power whatsoever to interfere with slavery in the slaveholding states. In arguing the contrary, in insisting that Congress had unlimited power if those states ever became the theater of war, Adams turned time and again to the Texas war. He interspersed his argument with facts from Lundy, alluding for example to Benton's dream of "nine" new slave states, and virtually charged the Jackson administration and the slaveholding states with starting the Texas rebellion. But he was careful to hedge his accusations, even attributing key points to "public rumor" or using the expression "it is said."[27]

The hedge words went largely unnoticed, however. The central charge was too clear: "The war now raging in Texas is . . . a war for the re-establishment of slavery where it was abolished . . . and every possible effort has been made to drive us into the war, on the side of slavery." The venom was overpowering. Addressing Speaker Polk, Adams asked: "Do not you, an Anglo-Saxon, slave-holding exterminator of Indians, from the bottom of your soul, hate the Mexican-Spaniard-Indian emancipator of slaves and abolisher of slavery?" And what will be "your claim" in the upcoming war with Mexico? "Aggression, conquest, and the re-establishment of slavery where it has been abolished. In that war, Sir, the banners of *freedom* will be the banners of Mexico; and your banners, I blush to speak the word, will be the banners of slavery."

The hedge words, moreover, proved to be unnecessary. His stand against Texas was popular throughout much of the Northeast. Businessmen and industrialists, millhands, artisans, and abolitionists—all dreaded the prospect of acquiring a huge chunk of land on the southwest frontier. What good would it do them? It would probably mean more southern Congressmen to vote against the tariff, against national banks, against internal improvements, against antislavery petitions.[28] In addition, it was easy to raise doubts about the Jackson administration's posture.

What, after all, was Gaines doing on the Texas border? And why was Houston sent to Texas? Were the nomadic tribes in Texas really a threat to the United States? No self-respecting cynic ever believed that!

Events also played into Adams's hands. The Texas tribes never went on the warpath, and it soon became obvious that rumors of impending Indian attacks had been fabricated by Gaines and other expansionists. Then, after Sam Houston overwhelmed Santa Anna at the battle of San Jacinto, Gaines invaded Texas. That was hardly the act of a neutral nation, and even Jackson felt obliged to reprimand Gaines. But Old Hickory refused to take the next step and order Gaines out of Texas. Quite the contrary, citing the danger of Indian war and an old American boundary claim, which included land well inside Texas, Jackson approved Gaines's action.[29] The Mexican government claimed that Gaines was in Texas to protect Houston from a Mexican counterattack; that was the only explanation that made sense to suspicious Northerners.

Adams thus had little trouble raising a storm about Texas. His claim that the Texas revolution was a criminal act set off by slavemasters and land speculators had instant appeal throughout much of the Northeast. In some circles so did his charge that the whole affair was a wicked conspiracy plotted by Jackson and southern slavemasters, and aided by Van Buren and northern "doughfaces," to steal free soil from Mexico in order to bring in a covey of slave states so that the Slave Power would always dominate the Union.

Such reasoning, to be sure, appealed only to a minority, and it failed to stop Congress from passing resolutions in July 1836 calling for the formal recognition of Texan independence. But the conspiracy charge was formidable enough—and appealing enough—to assure Jackson that any attempt to annex Texas would touch off the whole explosive issue of slavery and southern domination.

So Jackson hesitated. Even though he publicly pretended to be neutral, he dearly wanted Texas and seriously considered fighting over it. But he hardly wanted to provoke a donnybrook in Congress. And at the time he was trying to engineer the election of his hand-picked successor, Martin Van Buren of New York, who was anxious to keep slavery out of the presidential campaign. Then, after Van Buren was safely elected, Jackson became deathly ill, and doctors drew nearly sixty ounces of blood out of his emaciated frame. His health shattered, he seemingly lost the will to fight, and in his December 1836 message to Congress he recommended extreme caution with regard to Texas. Then in February 1837, with the return of some of his old fire, Jackson lashed out against the Mexican government and even suggested that its conduct toward the United States justified war. But as the out-going President he had no time left to press for annexation. He could do no more than officially recognize Texan independence on the day before he left office.

The new President was more cautious than Jackson. Van Buren had fewer ties with the Texas revolutionaries and no desire whatsoever to push annexation. His cardinal rule was to maintain party harmony at all costs. The true policy of the party, he argued, was to avoid any issue that threatened the unity of northern and southern Democrats. The Texas question, just like antislavery petitions, thus had to be suppressed.[30]

That was easier said than done. In August 1837 the Texas minister to the United States presented a formal proposal for the annexation of his country. The Van Buren administration rejected it politely but firmly. The rejection, however, had virtually no effect on southern legislatures and politicians clamoring for immediate annexation. Nor did it have any effect on Adams, who was eager to agitate the issue. At a special session of Congress the old man demanded that the House call on the administration for all correspondence with Mexican and Texan officials. At one point he claimed that most Americans preferred dissolution of the Union to the admission of Texas. That threw the House into such a frenzy that Speaker Polk just barely restored order. To avoid further chaos, the House then passed a temporary rule confining debate in the special session to matters specifically mentioned in the President's message.[31]

At the opening of the regular session in December 1837, the temporary rule lapsed and again Adams had the opportunity to debate Texas. By this time, abolitionists had made Texas their prime issue. Of some 400,000 petitions sent to the House, over

180,000 opposed annexation. Anti-annexation petitions even outnumbered petitions denouncing slavery and the slave trade in the nation's capital. In Adams's home district and elsewhere in Massachusetts, factory owners joined forces with mill mechanics and artisans, the bone and sinew of the antislavery movement, to rail against the proposed acquisition of Texas.[32] With such support, and through several tricky parliamentary maneuvers, Adams blocked an attempt to table the Texas question. By forcing the issue to the floor, he not only could attack Texas but could also get around the gag rule and attack slavery itself. Seizing the opportunity, he filibustered against the expansion of slavery and the Slave Power for some three weeks, until Congress finally adjourned in July 1838.[33]

In a sense, Adams whipped a dead horse. The Van Buren administration had no intention of reversing its earlier decision against annexation. The risks were too great. Among others, as the Texas minister explained to his government, were "party trammels," the possibility of an unpopular war with Mexico, and the danger of disruption of the Union. At best, then, the avalanche of anti-annexation petitions and Adams's fulminations just stiffened the administration's resolve.[34]

Nonetheless, the filibuster added much to Adams's reputation. Hailed throughout the Northeast as his "great anti-Texas speech," fragments from it soon circulated in pamphlet form and were quoted as gospel by newsmen and politicians from Boston to Chicago. A few months later, when Texas finally withdrew its offer of annexation, friends and foes alike assumed that the old man had single-handedly crushed the proposed acquisition of Texas.

Once Texas withdrew its offer, Adams and his cohorts seemed to have the upper hand. The question of annexation went into abeyance. Sam Houston, the President of the new Lone Star Republic, pretended to be indifferent to the United States and for several years looked elsewhere for help.

The Texas Republic, with only seventy thousand people to Mexico's seven million, needed all the outside aid it could get. Diplomats were sent to Europe, loans were secured from London, and by 1840 the new Republic had treaties with France, Holland, Belgium, and Great Britain. Meanwhile Houston shrewdly played up the British connection, making sure every Anglophobe in Washington knew that the United States' former enemy backed an independent Texas as a buffer against American expansion, as an alternate source of cotton, and as a duty-free market for British industrial goods.

His strategy worked. The mere mention of British interest panicked American expansionists. Not only was Great Britian the most powerful country in the Atlantic world and the only one likely to stand in the expansionists' way, but it was widely regarded as the force behind the antislavery crusade. For years proslavery forces in the South and anti-abolitionists in the North had insisted that the American Anti-Slavery Society was an offshoot of a gigantic British plot to destroy the American Republic—just an instrument of British monarchists to sow seeds of dissension, slave rebellion, and disunion throughout the states.[35] Now, blared expansionists, the British obviously intended to seize Texas and then begin a flank attack on American institutions. Annexation was thus imperative.

The 1840 election, however, dashed the hopes of annexationists. The Whig candidate, William Henry Harrison, gained the presidency, and for the first time this party carried both houses of Congress. Annexation, it seemed, would have to wait until the Whigs were driven from power.

But the annexationists were lucky. Harrison died one month after he took office, and his successor, John Tyler of Virginia, was hardly a Whig at all. He had been given second place on the ticket only because his presence might win the support of Virginians, states' righters, and Democratic malcontents like himself. He had no use for the nationalistic and probusiness policies championed by the dominant voices of the party. True to his beliefs, he twice vetoed Whig bank bills on constitutional grounds. In disgust Whigs read him out of the party and denounced his few Whig followers as the "Corporal's Guard."

Deprived of party support, Tyler decided to push Texas to the fore. He hoped it would enable him to run for President in 1844 as the candidate of a new pro-Texas third party, or better yet as the Democratic nominee. A small band of loyal followers, aided by several Democrats, quietly did the groundwork.

The first glimmer of this underground campaign came in

April 1842, when one of the "Corporal's Guard," Henry Wise, delivered a fiery speech in the House calling for the annexation of Texas at all costs. The United States had to act now, declared Wise, or British emancipationists would soon get their way in Texas and endanger slavery in the American South. So be it if annexation led to war against Mexico and Great Britain; war would be good for the American soul. Indeed, he would be glad for the opportunity to rob Mexico's "bigotted priesthood" of its gold and extend slavery all the way to the Pacific. "Slavery should pour itself abroad without restraint, and find no limit but the Southern ocean."[36]

Wise, as usual, provided Adams with a golden opportunity to savage the South, and as usual, he took it. The old man pointed out that the Virginian's manifesto was proof positive of a Slave Power conspiracy. But, warned Adams, southern warmongers ought to think twice about getting into a war with Mexico or Great Britain. A war over Texas might do more to destroy slavery in the South than to protect it. A slave state might be invaded in retaliation, and that might set off slave rebellions, or even a massive slave insurrection in combination with a civil war and an Indian war. Were southern slavemasters ready for all that? And had they forgotten his earlier warning? Surely, they knew that once a slave state became a theater of war Congress would have "full and plenary power" over slavery within that state.

The hot exchange of words, however, had little immediate impact. Wise was always spouting off, always providing Adams with fodder. Few members took the Virginian seriously. Many regarded him as half-crazy and either listened in embarrassed silence or dismissed his remarks with laughter and catcalls. Adams likened him to a hapless fool masquerading as a great warlord, Tom Thumb trying to sound like Tamerlane or Genghis Khan.[37]

Adams, however, was more suspicious than most Congressmen. Back home in Braintree, he raised the issue again in a three-hour speech to his neighbors. He warned them of Tyler's plans to annex Texas and the danger of those schemes to the causes of freedom and peace. His speech was fully reported in the press and soon circulated as a pamphlet. But, overall, it too had little impact.[38]

That Wise had inside information finally became clear at the next session of Congress. In January 1843, another close friend of Tyler's, Thomas W. Gilmer of Virginia, published an elaborate argument for annexation. Reprinted in the *Madisonian*, the Tyler newspaper in Washington, it triggered a steady flow of supportive editorials. The administration's propaganda soon reached Andrew Jackson, now in retirement, who fired off a strong letter in support of Gilmer's arguments and called for immediate annexation before Texas fell into British hands. The Tyler men, not yet ready to move, decided to sit on the Old Hero's letter until the Texas campaign reached fever pitch.[39]

Meanwhile, the sudden outpouring of pro-Texas propaganda alarmed northern Whigs. The more cautious downplayed the slavery issue, arguing instead that the nation was in danger of overextending itself and that annexing a foreign nation was unconstitutional. In Massachusetts, this view was soon identified with Daniel Webster, who popularized it after stepping down as Tyler's Secretary of State.[40]

Taking a much tougher stance, Adams again blasted the Jacksonians for aiding Sam Houston during the Texas revolution and claimed that the purpose of the Texas intrigue was to increase the power of the slave states in Congress. Annexation, he concluded, would be identical to dissolution of the Union. To his surprise, twelve antislavery Whigs joined him in publishing these charges in "An Address to the People of the Free States," and after it was in print eight others added their names. Of the Massachusetts Congressmen, five Whigs signed it, four refused.[41]

Later, in a letter to his constituents, the old man insisted that the nation had become totally dominated by slave representation. "Your country is no longer a democracy, it is no longer even a republic—it is a government of 2 or 300,000 holders of slaves, to the utter exclusion of the remaining part, and all the population of the other States in the Union." The addition of Texas would thus make an impossible situation even worse. Again there were threats of disunion.[42]

In the past such threats would have worked. The mere prospect of a donnybrook over slavery would have caused Jackson and Van Buren to move cautiously. The Tyler men, however, were not to be deterred. Duff Green, a proslavery zealot and the administration's confidential agent in London, reported that Texas officials were busy negotiating with the British—indeed trying to float a loan to finance the compensated emancipation of Texas's 12,000 to 15,000 slaves—and that the British government had agreed to guarantee interest payments. Green was considered unreliable, and dispatches from the official American representative in London contained no hint of such negotiations. But the representative, Edward Everett, was from Massachusetts and the Tyler men were not about to trust a Yankee. Soon other reports from London added credence to Green's account. Tyler and his new Secretary of State, Abel Upshur of Virginia, decided they had to act swiftly before the British abolitionized Texas.[43]

They had some hard facts at their disposal. For years British politicians had made antislavery statements for home consumption, and by 1843 several high English officials were on record as favoring an independent Texas without slavery as well as the elimination of slavery throughout the world. In addition, American antislavery men clearly regarded the British as a potential ally. Adams, to the horror of many New Englanders, even justified England's 1840 opium war with China as a "branch" of England's worldwide crusade against slavery. He never trusted Britain's rulers, he said, but the English people had made the cause of human freedom the "hinge" upon which government policy must turn.[44]

American abolitionists, moreover, hoped to persuade the British government to buy out the slaveholding interests in Texas. The Texans, so it was argued, would gladly give up slavery in exchange for British gold, and the cost to the English government would be minimal because there were only about 12,000 slaves in Texas. Two abolitionists, Stephen Pearl Andrews and Lewis Tappan, approached Adams with such a scheme in early 1843. He told them it was a pipe dream, that the British government was insincere in its antislavery proclamations, but wished them "God speed."[45] They went off to the World Anti-Slavery

Convention in London, where they intrigued and talked openly about getting London bankers and British politicians to underwrite abolition in the Lone Star Republic.

Andrews also got Lord Broughton, an acerbic critic of the slave trade, to bring the Texas question before the House of Lords. What, asked Broughton, was Her Majesty's Government doing to stop the abominable trade in slaves between the United States and Texas—and the border war between Mexico and Texas? In response, Lord Aberdeen, the Foreign Secretary, assured Parliament that everyone in the world knew that Her Majesty's Government yearned for the end of slavery in Texas and elsewhere, and that the government would continue to use its good offices to bring peace to the Texas border.[46]

All this, of course, played into the hands of the Tyler men in Washington. Hoping to discredit Adams and other administration critics, Secretary of State Upshur began using this "evidence" in September 1843. Writing anonymously in the administration paper, the *Madisonian*, Upshur harped on the dangers of a British takeover in Texas. British monarchists, he claimed, hated and dreaded republicanism; their ultimate goal was to destroy the American Republic; and thus they had to be stopped before it was too late. Why, then, were Adams and others standing in the way? The old man, explained Upshur, had once been a patriot; he had played a leading role in the acquisition of Florida and as President had worked hard to acquire Texas. But since losing to Jackson, his patriotism had given way to extreme partisanship. Indeed, "treasonable practices" had become his "chief amusement and solace."[47]

So Adams's opponents tried to tar him with essentially the same charges he was hurling at them. He claimed that they were part of a conspiracy; they accused him of aiding and abetting a foreign conspiracy. Whom did the voters believe? In the South, the Tyler men had no trouble convincing most Democrats—and some Whigs—that Adams was a subversive. But in the North, at least twenty Whig Congressmen were solidly behind Adams, and many Van Buren Democrats were fearful. They knew that they would pay dearly at the polls if they were ever identified with the expansion of slavery and southern power. Only northern Democrats with little to lose—men with "safe"

seats or no hopes whatsoever—dared to ignore Adams's indictment. The others were hesitant.[48]

To win over the hesitant, the Tyler men fought desperately to
overcome Adams's arguments. The Old South, they explained,
would not gain from the addition of Texas. Cotton planters in
South Carolina and Georgia, in fact, would be hard pressed to
compete with the owners of fresh, fertile lands in Texas. Meanwhile northern manufacturers and merchants would have a
growing new market in which to sell their goods, and Boston
and New York entrepreneurs would have golden opportunities
to speculate in Texas lands and securities. Did Northerners want
to fatten their pocketbooks? Then they should ignore traitors
like Adams and join the crusade to acquire Texas. That was the
sure way to big money.[49]

Besides using blatant appeals to self-interest, the Tyler men
also tried to divert attention from Texas and slavery. That, in
turn, generated a call for the vast Oregon country, which stretched
from the Rockies to the Pacific and from the border of Mexican
California at the 42d parallel to Russian Alaska at 54° 40', and
which had been occupied jointly by the United States and Great
Britain since 1818. In the 1840s several thousand Americans
made the long trek across the Rockies to the fertile meadowland
of the Willamette Valley, and Democrats in the upper Mississippi Valley began agitating for a more aggressive Oregon policy. But there was no great popular demand for Oregon. The
Oregon plank was just window dressing to offset the charge
that the Tyler men were a prosouthern, proslavery party.[50]

Yet, despite the Oregon plank and constant appeals to northern greed, expansionists still faced an uphill struggle at the end
of 1843. Since the coming year was an election year, Tyler and
his supporters had to move quickly if they hoped to make
Texas—nay, Texas and Oregon—a sure road to the White House.
Somehow they had to convince frightened northern Democrats
that Adams's central theme—that annexation would not only
extend slavery but also increase southern power—was a red
herring. For help they turned to Senator Robert J. Walker of
Mississippi, the most active Democrat in Tyler's coterie of pro-
Texas zealots.

Walker was ideal for the job. Although he had made his career in Deep South politics, he had been born and raised in Pennsylvania, knew the North well, and was imaginative to say the least. He still harbored doubts about slavery and had freed his own slaves in the 1830s. But he was an incorrigible land speculator with an eye always on the main chance, and the mere thought of Texas lands and bonds had fired his imagination. Any hope of annexation, he realized, depended on northern Democrats. But how could he win their support? They generally hated both blacks and Englishmen with a passion, and some of them saw great riches in Texas acres and securities. But they dared not support annexation as long as it was identified with the growth of slavery and the Slave Power. In February 1844, Walker came up with an ingenious public letter. Thanks to a fund established by Texas land speculators and rich Southerners, it circulated widely in the North and created a sensation in the expansionist press.[51]

The letter dealt not only with northern fears. It also appealed to northern racism, as did African colonization, the old dream of ridding American society of both slavery and blacks. Slavery, argued Walker, was self-destructive. It ruined the soil, and the harsh dictates of economics would eventually force slaveowners to free their slaves. As it now stood, hundreds of thousands of freed blacks would soon flood northern cities, where they would live as a despised underclass of paupers and thieves. If Texas were annexed, however, millions of slaves would be drawn off from the worn-out lands of the Old South to the rich cotton lands of Texas. As a result, slavery would soon be contained in Texas, and then when Texas lands were depleted, the freed blacks would disappear over the border into Mexico and Central America, where the climate better suited them, and live happily among other "colored" people.[52]

Walker made some headway in the North against Adams, especially among wavering Democrats, and the Tyler men decided the time was ripe to release Jackson's pro-Texas letter of the previous year. The response worried northern Whigs, so much so that Horace Greeley repeatedly savaged Walker in the New York *Tribune*, and Adams's son Charles published a series of counterattacks in the Boston *Courier*. But Walker bore the burden of being associated with Tyler, a well-known proslavery zealot, a President without a party, and a much-hated man throughout the North. And Walker's reasoning was so clever, so specious, that he was often dismissed as a sophist.[53]

So, in the battle for northern minds, Adams remained supreme. His Texas argument survived a barrage of assaults, the best that the Tyler circle had to offer. It too was a mixture of fact and fiction, and historians have lambasted his entire notion of a Slave Power conspiracy. But to most northern Whigs and many northern Democrats in the spring of 1844, it seemed much nearer the truth than the propaganda emanating from the band of southern extremists clamoring for the immediate annexation of Texas.

If Adams had the more compelling argument in early 1844, events soon made it even more persuasive. And, again, he did nothing to shape the course of events.

A year before, the Tyler administration had begun negotiating secretly with Texas authorities for a treaty of annexation. In late February 1844, the secret negotiations were all but over when an explosion of a cannon on the warship *Princeton* killed the Secretary of State. To replace Upshur and complete negotiations, Tyler turned to slavery's foremost spokesman, John C. Calhoun of South Carolina. That sealed the link between slavery and Texas. After completing negotiations in April 1844, Calhoun sent the treaty to the Senate, along with a copy of a letter he had written to Richard Pakenham, the British minister to Washington.

The letter was a bombshell. Besides denouncing Pakenham's government for interfering in Texas and supporting abolition throughout the Atlantic world, Calhoun sang the praises of slavery and cited statistics to prove that blacks were better off as slaves than freedmen—and that southern slaves were better off than white workers in industrial England. More importantly, he justified annexation as a defense measure in behalf of slavery.[54] The annexation treaty was thus officially labeled a proslavery measure.

No one knows for certain what Calhoun intended, but historians have offered several educated guesses. Some suggest that he wanted to force southern Whig Senators, who generally opposed expansion, to rally around the cause of slavery. Others think that he hoped to make land-hungry northern Democrats acknowledge that slavery was a "positive good," or to provoke the British into an international incident and thus rally American patriotism to his side. And still others think that he had lost touch with reality—or was just plain stupid. Whatever the explanation, the consensus among historians is that Calhoun's indiscreet letter strengthened the hand of Adams and other antislavery Whigs.[55]

At the time, however, Adams hardly felt like a man who had suddenly been dealt a winning hand. The turn of events confused him. First, in violation of the Senate code of secrecy in diplomatic matters, a northern Democrat leaked a copy of Calhoun's letter to the New York *Evening Post*. Then, while the cry of "Slave Power Conspiracy" rang through the North, the nation's newspapers in just five days published letters from Henry Clay of Kentucky, Martin Van Buren of New York, and Thomas Hart Benton of Missouri. All three concurred that it was impolitic and unjust to annex Texas at that time.

Adams was dumbfounded. How could it be that the land-hungry Benton was suddenly against annexation? And why were two presidential hopefuls, Clay and Van Buren, so quick to go on record against annexation? Had Tyler forced their stand? Would he force himself on the Democratic party as its candidate for the Presidency? The Texas issue, thought Adams, was "Tyler's last card for a popular whirlwind to carry him through; and he has played it with equal intrepidity and address."[56]

The events of May added to Adams's gloom. As he feared, Van Buren's Texas letter raised a storm of protest among Democrats, especially in the southern and western states. Even Jackson turned on his former Vice-President and hand-picked successor. And at the Democratic convention held in nearby Baltimore, pro-Texas strategists rammed through a measure requiring a two-thirds majority for the presidential nomination. The strategy worked: Van Buren, who came to the convention with a majority of the delegates pledged to him, could not get two-thirds. Nor could his arch-rival, Lewis Cass of Michigan.

To break the deadlock, the party finally turned to James K. Polk, a Tennessee slaveholder whose hard-money views satisfied the Van Burenites, and whose zeal for expansion satisfied annexationists. The convention then adopted an expansionist platform calling for "the reoccupation of Oregon and the reannexation of Texas, at the earliest practicable moment." The Oregon plank would be used to divert attention from Texas and slavery.

So in late May 1844 Adams was sour and despondent. He complained bitterly in his diary about the "degeneracy" of the country and the "ruin" of its principles "under the transcendent power of slavery and slave-representation." He was virtually without hope.[57]

Then Whig Senators by an overwhelming vote slapped down Tyler's treaty. Of 22 Democrats who voted, 15 supported annexation; all but one of 28 Whigs voted against it; and thus annexation failed by a two-to-one margin. Adams was almost jubilant. He recorded each individual vote in his diary: the ayes first, then the nays, and finally the one absent member. He added: "I record this vote as a deliverance, I trust, by the special intervention of Almighty God, of my country and human liberty from a conspiracy comparable to that of Lucius Sergius Catilina."

But, as always, he saw the dark side. He had spent too many mornings reading Roman history to think that the Senate vote would put an end to the Texas conspiracy. He knew that while Cicero had foiled Catilina's conspiracy in 63 B. C., Cicero's triumph had been short-lived. The "fatally successful conspiracy of Julius Caesar" had quickly followed.

Would history repeat itself? He hoped not, but he had gone to the Senate and heard the wily Thomas Hart Benton introduce another bill for the annexation of Texas. He was pessimistic. "The annexation of Texas to this Union," he wrote, "is the first step to the conquest of all Mexico, of the West India Islands, of a maritime, colonizing, slave-tainted monarchy, and of extinguished freedom."[58] Was he at age seventy-seven ready for another battle? There would be, he was certain, yet another chapter in the Texas story.

CHAPTER VII

Mr. Polk's War

Adams had little time to ponder what the Slave Power would do next. As soon as the Senate rejected the Texas treaty, Tyler sent the House an urgent appeal for annexation by congressional act, which would require only a simple majority in both houses, rather than by treaty, which required approval by two-thirds of the Senate. Tyler seemed not to care whether it was legal to thus bypass the treaty process.

Secretary Calhoun insisted that time was of the essence, that if necessary a special session of Congress would be called in September, two months before the fall elections. But Congress was in no mood for such bullying. Weary after a long session, most members pushed for adjournment, wanting no part of the renegade President's scheme or Washington's summer heat. Still, by calling for immediate action, Tyler and Calhoun succeeded in making Texas even more prominent in the upcoming elections.

In Adams's mind the fall elections were indeed critical. He told one correspondent that the choices were clear; regardless of how Henry Clay equivocated on the Texas issue, annexation was less likely under Clay and the Whigs than under Polk and the Democrats.[1] And he campaigned hard while still pretending to be above it all. But instead of going after Polk, a lackluster politician who had twice failed to be re-elected Governor of Tennessee, he went after Polk's mentor, Andrew Jackson. His issue was Jackson's Texas letter, where among other things Old

Hickory had dredged up the old charge that in 1819 Adams had treacherously ceded Texas to Spain.

Speaking before a rally of the Young Men's Whig Club of Boston, Adams not only defended his good name but also savagely accused Jackson of fabricating this "fable" to justify the "robbery" of Texas from Mexico. In closing Adams called the young men to battle: "Your trial is approaching. The spirit of freedom and the spirit of slavery are drawing together for the deadly conflict of arms. The annexation of Texas to this Union is the blast of the trumpet for a foreign, civil, servile, and Indian war, of which the government of your country, fallen into faithless hands, have already twice given the signal—first by a shameless treaty, rejected by a virtuous Senate; and again by the glove of defiance, hurled by the apostle of nullification, at the avowed policy of the British empire peacefully to promote the extinction of slavery throughout the world. Young men of Boston: burnish your armor, prepare for the conflict, and I say to you, in the language of Galgacus to the ancient Britons, think of your forefathers! Think of your posterity!"[2]

The fiery call to arms had enormous impact. It quickly became a campaign document, circulating throughout New England and much of the North, reaching as far south as Baltimore. Jackson, in rebuttal, denounced Adams as a liar and "a traitor to his country." Every Whig, it seemed, wanted Adams's services. He was asked to preside over a Whig mass meeting in Brooklyn, to read his Boston address at the Broadway Tabernacle in New York, to speak to the Whigs of Sandwich on Cape Cod, to the Lyceum in nearby Roxbury, to the Young Men's Institute at Hartford, to the Young Men's Association at Albany. He was too old for so much speech-making, so much traveling, but loved the attention. He finally agreed to give another long speech, half at North Bridgewater, half at Weymouth Landing, two towns in his district. Again he tore into Jackson and the annexationists.[3]

The election, however, went badly. Adams added 1,400 votes to his previous victory margin, and the Whigs won a sweeping victory in Massachusetts, but nationally Polk edged out Clay. The national election turned on New York, which Clay lost by 5,000 votes, thanks partly to 16,000 antislavery voters who cast their ballots for an avowed abolitionist, James Gillespie Birney, who had no chance of winning. In fifteen of twenty-six states the election was extremely close, and overall Polk's margin of victory was a mere 1.4 percent.[4] But, as always, large blocs of electoral votes turned on a handful of popular votes, and in the electoral college Polk won easily, 170 to 105.

Adams called the election a "victory of the slavery element."[5] That was hardly an accurate appraisal of a contest that was close nationwide, especially one in which Polk lost his home state of Tennessee and several other slave states, and Clay's waffling on the Texas issue alienated many antislavery voters. Nor did it explain why foreign-born Catholics voted overwhelmingly against all Whig candidates.

But Adams was right in sensing the growing polarization between North and South. His own success in attacking both Democrats and Texas on antislavery grounds—along with similar successes scored by antislavery Whigs in upstate New York and Ohio—shocked both northern Democrats and southern Whigs. Was antisouthern sentiment about to sweep key constituencies in the North? What was in store for northern politicians who voted with the South? In many districts, the loss of just one vote out of every hundred meant defeat.

Rightly or wrongly, moreover, politicians of both parties had assumed throughout the campaign that a vote for Polk was a vote for Texas. So once the election was over, there was much talk of a mandate for annexation. Tyler and Calhoun insisted that the election amounted to a popular endorsement of *their* defeated treaty. That was too much for northern Democrats, who wanted no association with the renegade President or Calhoun's Pakenham letter, but they too interpreted the returns as a mandate for immediate annexation. And that, in turn, meant trouble. One Vermont Whig, upon seeing a Democratic victory banner flying over a Washington slave market, put it bluntly: "That flag means *Texas*, and *Texas* means *civil war*, before we have done with it."[6]

Adams, upon taking his seat in Congress that December, was primed for battle. He expected to put up a good fight and then lose. He was certain that in the end the "slave Democracy" would have its way. But on at least one key issue, victory was within his reach. He had come close to winning, indeed within an eyelash, the previous session.

The issue was the gag. Up until the previous session, his battle against the permanent gag rule imposed in 1840 had been almost as predictable as the calling of the roll. At the beginning of each session, one House member would move that the rules of the previous Congress be adopted as the rules of the coming session. Adams would then offer an amendment excepting the gag rule. While the usual speeches were made for and against the gag, southern Democrats would round up enough northern Democrats to block his amendment. They invariably succeeded, but usually with just three or four votes to spare.

The 1840 rule never had the support of Pinckney's original measure. The gag first proposed by Pinckney in 1836, which automatically tabled abolitionist memorials, always had the backing of two-thirds of the House. But the change southern hotspurs pushed through in 1840, making the gag a standing House rule and prohibiting the *reception* of antislavery petitions, was always far more controversial. It passed initially by just six votes, 114 to 108. Only 41 percent of the northern Democrats cast their votes for the 1840 rule, as compared to the 75 percent who had consistently voted for the Pinckney gag and its successors. A handful of southern Whigs also had reservations about the 1840 rule, and four or five consistently voted against it.[7] So southern Democrats, who supported the gag to the man, always had to work on their northern brethren to muster enough votes to keep the gag in force.

In the beginning, the trouble with the 1840 rule was largely constitutional. Many northern Democrats, such as Samuel Beardsley of New York and Hannibal Hamlin of Maine, found it impossible to justify. Tabling antislavery petitions was one thing; not receiving them at all was clearly another. Prohibiting the *reception* of abolitionist petitions, they argued, was tantamount to denying citizens the right of petition—and even some southern Whigs, including Speaker John White of Kentucky, were loathe to go that far.[8]

Besides the constitutional objection there was also a political argument. As time passed, more and more northern Democrats claimed that supporting the gag cost them votes on election day. Benjamin Bidlack of Pennsylvania, for example, argued that abolitionists in his district had no political clout whatsoever until the passage of the gag rule. They had been a despised minority. Townspeople had harassed them constantly, driving one speaker out of town without a hearing and riding a local abolitionist down the main street in broad daylight on a rail. But with the gag rule, everything changed. Abolitionists now called meetings to discuss the right of petition and talked about slavery for hours on end.

Moreover, complained Bidlack, he was troubled by the behavior of southern Whigs. He had originally gone along with the South because Southerners maintained that antislavery agitation would cause slaves to rebel and slit their masters' throats. How could he continue to justify this position when some southern Whigs refrained from voting—or voted against the gag? Their actions made him appear to be more proslavery than many Southerners.[9]

Other northern Democrats voiced similar complaints. William McCauslen of Ohio originally favored the 1840 rule but turned against it when he discovered how Whigs and other politicians rode this "hobby-horse" to his party's detriment. Alexander Duncan, another Ohio Democrat, thought the gag would eventually ruin the party in his district. The eminent Martin Van Buren reported that his New York followers were tired of hearing southern complaints about their lukewarm support of the gag. For the "truth" was that the party's southern principles were a liability in New York, and "every limb" of the state party had been hurt "often" and "severely" by their support of southern men and southern measures.[10]

What really hurt, in the eyes of many Van Buren men, was the constant pushing of Texas. That, as they saw it, violated the party's traditional policy of always striving to keep slavery out of politics. And yet southern Democrats not only pushed the issue but expected northern Democrats to endorse their schemes. What kind of party men were they? Were they trying to jeopardize the careers of their northern allies?

Such grumbling finally came to a head when Congress met in December 1843. The session began as usual, and Adams's amendment to eliminate the gag was voted down, 91 to 95. But then complications developed. Henry Wise, to the horror of his fellow Southerners, admitted defeat and proposed that a committee re-evaluate all the House rules. The House approved his suggestion, and Adams was appointed to the committee. In January, the old man reported that the committee recommended many changes, including the elimination of the gag rule. Wise, who by this time had sober second thoughts, submitted a minority report in favor of the gag. The House spent over a month arguing about the reports and suggesting amendments. In preliminary balloting, the gag failed by 86 to 106. But then, upon a motion to adopt the report as amended, the House tabled the whole subject by a vote of 88 to 87. So the gag, along with all the other old rules, was still in force.[11]

The gag might have limped along for years, perhaps even have regained some of its old vigor, if Van Buren had become the Democratic nominee that spring. But in blocking his nomination, pro-Texas men in effect dealt the gag a death blow. Some of Van Buren's followers wanted revenge. Others were stunned by the success antislavery propaganda had against Polk in parts of New England, New York, and northern Ohio during the fall elections. They decided it was time to distance themselves from the South.[12] The result was that Adams finally had the votes he needed—and then some—when Congress resumed in December 1844.

The end came quickly. On the second day of the session, Adams once again called for repeal of the gag rule. This time, without fanfare or debate, the House refused to table his resolution and then adopted it, 108 to 80. On his side, as always, were all the northern Whigs and four southern Whigs. Also on his side were 78 percent of the northern Democrats, much more than the usual 59 percent of recent years, and more than enough to kill the gag forever.[13]

Adams's nine-year battle against the gag was finally won. "Blessed, forever blessed, be the name of God!" he wrote in his diary.[14] Yet, as he wrote these words, he knew that his joy would soon turn to sorrow. The "hell-born spirit" of the slave-

mongers had already risen again in the shape of John Tyler and
Texas.

Immediately after the vote, the House turned to the President's
annual message. There were no surprises. Tyler, the lame-duck
President, was anxious to get Texas into the Union before he
left office. He wanted the credit.

The President, as usual, was obstinate. Ignoring the furor
caused by Calhoun's Pakenham letter, Tyler pretended that the
Senate's chief reason for rejecting his treaty was that "annexation had not been submitted to the ordeal of public opinion."
Now, he said, it had. The electorate had spoken. "A controlling
majority of the people and a large majority of the States have
declared in favor of immediate annexation." He thus called on
both houses of Congress to vindicate his rejected treaty by
passing a joint resolution that embodied its precise language.
There was no need, he maintained, for Congress to deal with
"collateral issues" such as the number of states to be carved
out of Texas. Such matters could best be decided by future
legislatures.[15]

Would Tyler's stubbornness prove fatal? The prospect worried Democrats, especially those who disliked the proslavery
taint of Tyler's treaty and the provision that the United States
assume Texas's inflated debt. A host of counterproposals soon
were in the making, nine in the House, six in the Senate.[16]

Not one was alike. At first, the only point of agreement was
that Texas's boundary disputes should be settled later by the
United States. Otherwise, annexationists seemed in hopeless
disagreement. Some wanted to admit all or part of Texas as a
state; others called for territorial status first. Even more troublesome was the number of states to be created out of Texas.
No one believed that the vast area would end up as just one
state. But how many states? Two? Three? Six? And would they
all become slave states as Adams feared? Some annexationists
obviously hoped so; others wanted Texas divided in two, half
slave, half free; while most called for a token limit on slavery,
barring it only in the northernmost tip, the small area lying
above the Missouri Compromise line. As for the debt, some

wanted no part of it, while others insisted that it be charged to the United States.[17]

The prospect of endless squabbling delighted Adams's associates. Joshua Giddings, the staunch anti-Texas Whig from Ohio, surmised that each plan would alienate at least forty Democrats, and thus not one measure had a chance of passing. But Adams was pessimistic. The Foreign Relations committee, he noted, had been stacked with pro-Texas men, and a revolution now raging in Mexico even seemed to be working in favor of the administration's "abominable purpose." And Giddings, he feared, had not sufficiently weighed "the despotism of party will."[18]

Whether it was his pessimism or his age, Adams found it hard to get into the fight. For nearly a month he sat and watched younger men carry his old torch. The Ohio men, led by Giddings and Edward S. Hamlin, matched his old ardor in savaging the Slave Power. But the major spokesman from his home state, Robert C. Winthrop of Boston, assured southern Whigs that the opposition in Massachusetts to annexation was based largely on constitutional grounds, that annexing a foreign nation was clearly unconstitutional, and that trying to do it by congressional act rather than by treaty was doubly wrong.[19] The speech satisfied Boston conservatives, but was much too cautious for Adams's taste.

Would Adams provide the fire that Winthrop's address lacked? He knew he should speak. The time to vote was rapidly approaching. He thought of nothing else, yet still made no progress in his preparations. Finally, on January 24, he set out for the House with numerous documents, determined to have his say.

It was not one of his better performances. He wasted too much time correcting earlier speakers, commenting on the Louisiana Purchase, justifying his past behavior; he had just reached the "threshold" of his speech when the one-hour time limit expired. Even worse, he left himself open to counterattack by saying that he "would go for Texas tomorrow" if slavery were forbidden there and Mexico's consent could be gained. Immediately the opposition jumped on those words, claiming that he had virtually admitted that Congress had the constitutional power to annex Texas. The next day he had to ask for time to explain that "the whole drift" of his speech "had been exactly the reverse."[20]

It made little difference. Because of Adams's earlier speeches, as well as those of other antislavery Whigs, some southern Whigs had already decided that they had to cover themselves. Southern Democrats had roasted them in the fall elections with the Texas issue, claiming that they were in league with British and northern abolitionists in opposing annexation. The charge probably cost them normally Whig Georgia. Anxious to avoid further losses at home, they offered a resolution of their own calling for the admission of Texas as a state. The debt would remain with Texas, four additional states might be formed, and slavery would be excluded only in the small area above the Missouri Compromise line. They had little zeal for acquiring Texas and probably hoped nothing would come of their resolution. But annexationists, eager to acquire their votes, quickly embraced their proposal.[21]

Thus, on the day after Adams's speech, all the proposals were successively defeated until that offered by the southern Whigs. It passed by 22 votes, with 111 Democrats and 9 southern Whigs in favor, 70 Whigs and 28 northern Democrats in opposition.[22] What happened to the forty Democrats who were certain to oppose each proposal? As Adams had anticipated, Giddings had been too optimistic in his count.

Now optimists in Adams's camp looked to the Senate. Surely the Senate would remain firm. It was, after all, the same Senate that had overwhelmingly rejected Tyler's treaty the previous spring; and the Whigs controlled it 28 to 24, which meant that annexationists had to win the support of every Democrat and at least three Whigs. To stiffen the resistance of Whigs and northern Democrats, the Massachusetts legislature passed a series of blistering resolutions denouncing annexation as unconstitutional and threatening trouble, perhaps even disunion, if Congress added any territory that in effect extended slavery and slave representation. The Boston *Atlas* published twelve letters, all addressed to Adams, bearing the same message.[23]

Adams, however, remained pessimistic. Neither the letters addressed to him nor the resolves of the Massachusetts legislature would have any effect. Nothing now would stop the annexation of Texas, for it was "written in the Book of Fate." Even the "insurmountable" argument that annexation amounted to the "perfidious robbery and dismemberment of Mexico" had lost its sting, as Mexico was now embroiled in civil war and anarchy, falling to pieces, unable to keep its identity. No constitutional objection would be of any use. "The Constitution is a menstruous rag, and the Union is sinking into a military monarchy, to be rent asunder like the empire of Alexander or the kingdoms of Ephraim and Judah."[24]

Adams's pessimism was borne out. With the help of an amendment and much arm-twisting, the annexationists succeeded in getting the votes they needed—and no more—in the last week of the session. The bill passed 27 to 25. The next day the House agreed to the amendment. Tyler signed the following day, March 1, 1845, just three days before leaving office. Noted Adams: "It is a signal triumph of the slave representation in the Constitution of the United States . . . the heaviest calamity that ever befell myself and my country . . . ."[25]

Adams expected even gloomier days under Tyler's successor. Like other believers in a Slave Power conspiracy,[26] he had no doubt what Polk would do. As a southern Democrat, to whom slavery was all-important, Polk would further the dreams of the slavemongers. That meant he would "flinch" on the Oregon question and push aggressively for more land south and west.

Adams began pushing in the opposite direction shortly before Polk took office. The lame-duck Tyler administration, in its zeal to acquire Texas, had let the Oregon issue drift. To keep the issue before Congress, Adams ushered through a resolution calling on the President for the diplomatic correspondence with Great Britain concerning Oregon.[27] In his view, the only way to neutralize the Slave Power's gains in the Texas bill was to make sure the Democrats honored the other half of their campaign pledge and took "all Oregon." With Oregon, moreover, there would be no "perfidious robbery" of another "civilized" nation, no act of conquest, as neither Great Britain nor any other foreign nation had clear title to Oregon. The area was a virtual no-man's-land, peopled largely by wandering "savages," open to any "civilized" people who adhered to God's command to "be fruitful and multiply, and replenish the earth and subdue it."[28]

Adams was certain, however, that the new administration would find some way to renege on its pledge. The overriding problem, as he saw it, was the southern Democrats. They hungered after Mexico and Cuba, new slave country, not Oregon. Indeed, they had everything to lose from the acquisition of Oregon, which would cancel out the "signal triumph" of slave representation in the Texas bill by creating a vast new area for the expansion of free states. For this reason, Adams paid no heed to Polk's bellicose proclamations. On taking office Polk said: "Our title to the country of the Oregon is 'clear and unquestionable,' and already are our people preparing to perfect that title by occupying it with their wives and children." Soon war headlines appeared on both sides of the Atlantic, and for the first time the American people caught the "Oregon fever."[29] But not Adams: he was certain that the new President would find some excuse for backing down.

The best excuse, in fact, was of Adams's own making. As Secretary of State and President, he had offered repeatedly to split the vast Oregon country with Great Britain along the 49th parallel. Others had made the same offer. In the 1844 election campaign virtually every Whig had adopted his old proposal while blasting the Democrats "All Oregon" program as not only extravagant but also a menace to peace. In addition, there was widespread speculation that the British were now ready to accept the 49th parallel, even though they had steadfastly rejected it in the past. And many were convinced that the land north of the 49th parallel was some sort of iceberg or desert, fit only for a penal colony, hardly a Garden of Eden. So why fight for it?

Polk did the expected. In July 1845, while Congress was out of session, he told the British minister in Washington, Richard Pakenham, that in deference to earlier presidential offers he would settle at the 49th parallel. But Pakenham, to the dismay of his superiors, rejected the offer out of hand; and when the British government tried to make amends, Polk refused to negotiate. Instead he took the matter to Congress in December, explaining in his first annual address what had happened, and assuring Congress that he was no longer willing to compromise. He called on Congress to serve "notice" on England of the termination of the joint occupancy of Oregon which had been in effect since 1818. His belligerent tone again produced war cries on both sides of the Atlantic. Again, Adams thought it was just bluff.

On what grounds could Adams insist on "All Oregon" when he had done so much to prejudice the case against it? How could he justify his sharp about-face? His answer was that times had changed, that he had made his original offer nearly thirty years before with the understanding that it would be turned down, but that its effect would be to keep the peace and post-pone the Oregon question until the United States was in a position to maintain its Oregon claims "by an appeal, if nec-essary, to arms."[30] Did this mean that he was now willing to fight Great Britain for "All Oregon"? Not necessarily, but he was certainly willing to use the threat of force at the bargaining table and push the British to the brink of war. And that was one thing that most of his fellow Whigs, as well as most south-ern Democrats, were unwilling to do.

Adams thus broke with the representatives of conservative Boston in the long debate over serving the British "notice." While they denounced Polk's saber rattling for endangering the peace, he sided with antislavery Whigs and expansionist Dem-ocrats from the Midwest who clamored for "Fifty-Four Forty or Fight." Initially he was quiet about it, keeping a low profile in the first month of debate.

Then a Georgia Whig asked him a direct question: Did he really believe that the United States had a clear claim to the entire Oregon country? In response Adams asked the clerk to read the passage from the Bible commanding man to "be fruitful and multiply, and replenish the earth and subdue it." That, he argued, "is the foundation not only of our title to the territory of Oregon, but the foundation of all human title to all human possessions." In comparison, exploration and discovery gave very poor titles. "We claim that country—for what?" he asked. "To make the wilderness blossom as the rose, to establish laws,

to increase, multiply, and subdue the earth, which we are commanded to do by the first behest of God Almighty." In contrast,
the British wanted Oregon only "to keep it open for navigation,
for hunters to hunt the wild beasts . . . for the buffaloes, braves
and savages of the desert."[31]

His position enraged pacifists on both sides of the Atlantic.
In Parliament Lord George Bentinck denounced him for "im-
piously and blasphemously" calling to aid "the Word of God
as a justification for lighting up the firebrand and unleashing
the hell-dogs of war." A leading English Quaker charged him
with inflaming his countrymen to war. Adams objected. If war
came, he argued, the blood of all its victims would be on England's head, for Britain had "no honest purpose" for wanting
Oregon. All England wanted was "to stunt our natural growth
. . . to prevent the conversion of . . . a wilderness of savage
hunters to a cultivated land of civilized Christian men . . . to
prolong the dominion of the buffalo and the bear. . . ."[32]

In Congress the "notice" debate lasted until April 1846.
Then, as Adams anticipated, the voices of conciliation got their
way. Realizing that Britain was eager to compromise, a coalition
of southern Democrats and conservative Whigs pushed through
a notice that was couched in friendly terms. Outraged "All
Oregon" Democrats turned to Polk for help, but the wily President had been quietly courting war with Mexico—and now
was anxious to settle with England. He sent the notice to London. The British responded with an offer to partition the Oregon
country along the 49th parallel with Britain keeping all of Van-
couver Island. In June, Polk laid the British proposal before the
Senate, which ratified it, 41 to 14.

The turn of events infuriated many of Adams's allies, especially "All Oregon" Democrats who had staked their political
careers on Polk's promises. Their cries of anguish, however,
had no effect on Adams. He had assumed all along that Polk
would follow the dictates of Slave Power politics and abandon
the Oregon men. They were fools to think otherwise.

If Adams thought it was easy to predict the outcome of the
Oregon crisis, he was even more confident about his view of

the Mexican war. He never doubted for a moment that Polk started the war. More importantly, he acted on this assumption and thus put his reputation at risk.

Again, as in the Oregon crisis, Adams was an exception. Although he was hardly privy to inside information, knew few of the details that lay behind the President's war message, and was clearly guessing about much of what happened, he still had no second thoughts. As he saw it, the South was bent on expanding slavery's domain, and in keeping the President had used his power in foreign affairs and prerogatives as commander-in-chief to create a situation with Mexico that virtually guaranteed war. And through numerous distortions and falsehoods, Polk steamrolled a reluctant Congress into supporting his war. He thereby set a horrendous example for all future Presidents and made Congress's constitutionally delegated power to declare war virtually meaningless.

The old diplomat did not guess entirely right. Polk, it is now clear, was never a member of any Slave Power conspiracy. Nor were Mexican leaders innocently sitting on their hands. Some were clearly warhawks, working the Mexican people into war fever, promising that they would hoist the Mexican flag over the American White House before they gave up their claim to Texas. Most scholars, over the years, have blamed the war on multiple causes or abstractions such as "Manifest Destiny" or "American Nationalism." Blaming Mexico has never been popular; nor has blaming the South and Polk.[33]

Still, when Senator Robert Kennedy proclaimed in the 1960s that the Mexican war was a national disgrace, few historians challenged his statement. For despite many books proving that neither side was exclusively to blame, many historians have long believed that the United States was at fault. While they have dismissed Adams's notion of a conspiring Slave Power as nonsense, they have generally agreed with his contention that Polk lied to the country and was the aggressor—and that the example that Polk set for later Presidents was indeed dangerous.

Polk, as historians now see him, was an incredibly hard-driving, aggressive President who was always willing to compromise the Oregon question but never the Mexican question.

He wanted as much of northern Mexico as he could get, particularly California with its three magnificent harbors, and he deliberately courted war with Mexico to get it.[34]

Mexico, moreover, was an easy mark. Since 1829 coup and counter-coup, revolution and counter-revolution, had been the order of the day. No regime could survive and give in to the United States, especially to its bullying and bribing. To recognize Texan independence was also certain to topple any regime. Thus, once the United States annexed Texas, Mexico broke off diplomatic relations with Washington.

At the same time, men on both sides hoped to find some quiet way of solving the Texas problem. The solution would obviously have to allow Mexican leaders to save face. One concern was the southern boundary of Texas, which many Americans acknowledged was the Nueces River, and not the Rio Grande farther south as Texans claimed. Peace would come, argued many Whigs, as soon as Texas gave up its preposterous claim to the Rio Grande.[35]

At first the Polk administration gave some attention to the Mexican government's need to save face. The American minister to Mexico was even reprimanded for being unnecessarily tactless and ordered home. But the concern for tact soon passed, as Polk supported Texas's boundary claim to the hilt, and in response to a Mexican overture to negotiate sent John Slidell of Louisiana to Mexico City to buy California and New Mexico, to establish the Texas boundary at the Rio Grande, and to settle a host of American debt claims against the Mexican government. News of Slidell's mission reached Mexico City before he did, and soon after his arrival the Mexican government was overthrown by General Mariano Paredes and some 7,000 soldiers. The new military regime refused to have anything to do with Slidell and reasserted Mexico's claim to all Texas. In the meantime Polk ordered General Zachary Taylor and 1,500 men into the disputed area between the Nueces River and the Rio Grande.

In April 1846 Polk decided to regard the rebuff of Slidell as cause for war. But before drafting his war message, he waited several weeks until Congress approved the conciliatory Oregon "notice," thus ending the crisis with England. Then, just as he was about to send his war message to Congress, news arrived in Washington that Taylor's dragoons had suffered sixteen casualties in a skirmish with Mexican troops near the Rio Grande. Hastily revising his call for war, Polk told Congress that Mexico "has invaded our territory, and shed American blood upon American soil," and thus war already "exists by the act of Mexico herself."

Was it really "American soil"? At issue was Texas's true border. For if it were not the Rio Grande, then Polk had ordered the invasion of Mexican soil. In fact, Polk's case for the Rio Grande was shaky at best. When Adams was Secretary of State and in heated negotiations with Spain during the Florida crisis of 1819, he had used the Rio Grande border for Texas in early bargaining, but had quickly backed away from this position. Several Presidents before Polk had recognized the Nueces, some 150 miles to the north, as the true border. For years Mexican citizens had inhabited and controlled the desert area between the two rivers.

So Adams, in accusing Polk of starting the war, had little trouble making a case. He also had plenty of support in Congress. Nearly every Whig was against the war, and so was John C. Calhoun and many of his supporters. Even the "All Oregon" wing of the President's own party questioned his Mexican policy.[36] "Why," demanded a Chicago Democrat, "should we not compromise our difficulties with Mexico as well as with Great Britain? The same doctrine that our southern friends preach about surrendering Oregon to the 49th would apply to the surrendering of all Texas to the Nueces. If it be wicked to go to war with England for disputed territory, it is not only wicked but cowardly to go to war with Mexico for the same reason."[37]

Yet, while the majority in Congress questioned Polk's Mexican policy, only a handful agreed with Adams's contention that Polk's primary aim was the extension of slavery. To southern Whigs that charge was just another of the old man's irresponsible attacks on the South. To many northern Whigs it endangered northern business connections with the cotton states and was totally illogical to boot. How could anyone ignore the fact, they demanded, that such staunch slaveholders as John C. Calhoun opposed "Mr. Polk's war"? Or the fact that many of the most rabid warhawks were the sensationalist penny papers of Boston, New York, and Philadelphia?[38]

To most antiwar men, it made better sense to see the President as taking the "cowardly" way, expanding at the expense of Mexico rather than England. Slogans like "All of Oregon or Nothing" and "Fifty-four Forty or Fight" might be good to stir the hearts of patriots at election time, but actually fighting England was obviously another matter. Great Britain was powerful, Mexico weak, and like any ordinary bully Polk chose to pick on the weak.[39]

But what really distinguished Adams from most Congressmen was his nerve. Many disliked the idea of war with Mexico. Several dozen undoubtedly thought Polk's explanation of the events leading to the initial fighting was a pack of lies. A sizable majority was convinced that Polk had started the war. But they all realized that they would be branded "traitors" if they were wrong and Polk was telling the truth—or if American troops were overwhelmed and butchered by an invading Mexican army. How many would vote against the war and risk all-out attacks on their patriotism? How many would dare to be branded traitors? That, in the end, was the pivotal question.

At the time, moreover, the risk seemed enormous. News that a Mexican patrol had ambushed Taylor's dragoons reached Washington on a weekend. Within hours the administration's newspaper was on the streets, clamoring for war against Mexico, claiming that Taylor's men needed aid immediately or they might be destroyed. On Monday an excited Congress received Polk's war message and a war bill authorizing the President to call out 50,000 men and appropriating $10 million. Insisting that time was of the essence, the Democratic leadership limited debate to just two hours in the House and one day in the Senate. In the House, three-fourths of this time was consumed by the clerk repeating various portions of the President's war message and reading parts of accompanying documents. Then, in the closing minutes of debate, the Polk forces sprang on the House an addition to the war bill—a preamble that endorsed the President's interpretation of events on the Rio Grande.[40]

About one-third of the House voted against this addition, and even Democrats objected vehemently to the strong-arm tactics. But few could resist the war juggernaut. Just before the final vote, Garrett Davis of Kentucky told the House: "It is our own President who began this war." But even he lacked the nerve to vote against the war bill. The call for war thus passed by an overwhelming majority, 174 to 14 in the House, and 40 to 2 in the Senate.[41]

Adams headed the fourteen House members who dared to vote against the war. He was proud of the young men who stood with him, who refused to be intimidated by the charges of disloyalty and treason hurled at them by Polk's supporters. All were northern Whigs, and most were Yankees, either representing districts in New England or New England settlements in the West. Five were from Massachusetts, five from Ohio. Most shared his notion of a Slave Power conspiracy; all blamed Polk for the war. He told one of them that he hoped American officers would resign their commissions, and the soldiers would desert, rather than fight in such an "unrighteous" war.[42] Few Congressmen had the nerve to go so far.

Once war became a reality, Adams continued to vote with the dissidents. But he said little in debate. His views, well known, hardly needed repeating, and he was weary, feeling his age, no longer fit for battle.[43]

That summer, two days after his eightieth birthday, he tried to renew one of his old habits. He went to the Potomac for a morning swim. It took him a full half-hour to get there on foot, as compared to eighteen minutes in his heyday. Finding a group of young men occupying his favorite swimming rock, he chose a spot upstream. On his third morning out the sun was bright and the temperature 74 degrees, but a brisk breeze gave him a chill.[44] It was just another reminder, he knew, that he would never be young again. All he could do was encourage younger men to carry on his old ways, men like Joshua Giddings of Ohio, William Seward of New York, Charles Sumner of Massachusetts, and especially his own son Charles.[45]

Charles was now carrying on the old Adams tradition of infuriating the Boston elite. Convinced that the Whig party was impotent in the face of southern aggression, the younger Adams and several other "Conscience" Whigs had taken on the regular

Whigs in Massachusetts with the hope of driving them out of power. Charles had taken over a financially strapped Boston newspaper and blasted the "regulars" who voted for Polk's war bill. The preamble, he argued, was obviously a lie, the war a crime. Why then did Congressman Robert C. Winthrop of Boston vote for such an abomination? The editorials created a sensation on State Street and Beacon Hill. To his son Adams wrote: "Proceed-Persevere-Never despair—don't give up the ship."[46]

The squabble among Massachusetts Whigs, however, soon caused both Adamses much grief. Nationally the Whigs won the fall elections of 1846, and the following year Winthrop became their candidate for Speaker of the House. Charles became part of a "Conscience" movement to withhold a few key votes from the Boston Representative. The elder Adams, however, feared that this action would lead to the election of a Democratic Speaker. He also felt a special obligation to the Winthrop family because the father had stood behind him during "hard times" in the past. So he backed Winthrop to the hilt, voted for him on all three ballots, tried to persuade one of Charles's cohorts to vote for him, and even administered the oath of office to him.[47]

The news of the old man's actions created a sensation in Boston. It was proof positive, declared the "regulars," that the great Adams regarded his son's schemes as wicked and misguided. Charles was so upset that he begged his mother to keep the old man on a tight leash and make sure that he did no further damage. Equally upset, John Quincy Adams tried to make amends by assuring everyone that philosophically he agreed with his son and the "Conscience Whigs." The damage, however, could not be undone.[48]

Nationally the Whigs were also divided into two camps. Adams belonged to the smaller, more militant faction, known variously as "radicals," "ultras," "Conscience Whigs," or "Young Whigs." He was the spiritual leader of the group, and its only "name" politician, but because of his age and health not its chief spokesman. That task fell largely to Joshua Giddings. The "ultras" had a small political base, with strength in only a few congressional districts, no ties whatsoever to the South and few to the Senate. Most of the great names in the Whig party,

including Daniel Webster and Robert C. Winthrop of Massachusetts, belonged to the larger, more conservative faction, which
had a national following and strength in both houses.

The two factions differed more in words than in voting behavior. In general, Whigs opposed the war, and all northern
Whigs opposed the expansion of slavery. The "ultras" were
simply bolder in their proclamations. Aiming their appeal strictly
at Northerners, the "ultras" insisted that the war was a scheme
of the Slave Power to extend slavery and southern power. They
were also quick to denounce the supporters of the war as crim-
inals and murderers. The conservatives meanwhile maintained
that all talk about a conspiring Slave Power was nonsense, and
that agitating the slavery issue would only destroy the Whig
party and the Union. In effect, they accused the "ultras" of
promoting disunion and civil war. The "ultras," in turn, accused them of sacrificing morality for political expediency.

This fight loomed large, however, only in Whig strongholds
like Massachusetts. Elsewhere, where Democrats were serious
rivals for power, party differences were paramount. In these
genuine two-party districts it was easy to see that the Democrats
were the war party while Whigs of all stripes generally reflected
the strong undercurrent of antiwar sentiment that pervaded
most of New England, much of the Midwest, and portions of
the South.

This antiwar feeling ran so deep that it survived even the
war's success. On the front line, the war went extremely well,
costing relatively few lives and making heroes by the dozens,
as one army under General Zachary Taylor routed superior
Mexican forces at Buena Vista, another army led by General
Winfield Scott captured Mexico City, and still another under
Colonel Stephen Kearney seized Santa Fe and then California.
Zealous Democrats clamored incessantly about expanding from
"the arctic to the tropic" and the great penny papers of New
York, Philadelphia, Baltimore, and Boston whipped up support
for taking "all Mexico." Yet neither the battlefield victories nor
the expansionist hoopla did much for Polk and his party. The
President was never very popular, his war policy was always
criticized, and his party suffered heavy losses in the 1846
congressional elections.

Whigs in Congress, however, were caught in a trap. They could denounce the war, treat the President as a war criminal, and even call him "The Father of Lies," as Horace Greeley did in the New York *Tribune*. But they could not with impunity abandon the men they had called to the battlefield. That was widely regarded as treason, and those who voted against bills for war supplies and reinforcements were branded "traitors." And even if Congress refused to give the President the money and men necessary to sustain the war, that was no guarantee that Mexico would stop fighting. Mexico's hatred for the United States was so great that even if Polk were forced to withdraw American troops it seemed possible that Mexico might pursue and try to conquer Texas. To most Whigs the war was thus like a raging house fire: Polk might have started it, but as good citizens they had to man the buckets and help put it out as quickly as possible.[49]

This logic bothered Adams. He found it "most remarkable" that an overwhelming majority of both houses could sustain the war while "professing to disapprove its existence and pronouncing it unnecessary and unjust." He was somewhat taken with the argument of his colleague Giddings, who claimed that antiwar men ought to follow the example of the great British Whigs of 1776 who refused to vote supplies for an unjust and oppressive British war against the thirteen American colonies. That was the only way, said Giddings, to force Polk out of Mexico.[50]

Yet Adams had trouble following this advice. He was a radical, to be sure. He was one of only four House members to support the proposal of Massachusetts Congressman Charles Hudson that American troops be pulled out of Mexico and that peace be negotiated without any demands for territorial concessions or reparations.[51] He voted regularly against measures to reward, honor, and decorate the war's participants. Still, he ended up voting for one appropriations bill after another, even though he recognized the inconsistency of doing so.

Adams was more consistent than most Whigs, however, when it came to taking land from Mexico. He regarded any dismemberment of Mexico as stealing. That position had wide Whig support at the beginning of the war, but once American troops occupied vast portions of northern Mexico opinions began to vary. Conservative Whigs from the commercial Northeast—and even some "ultras"—were willing to forget the golden rule when it came to California. The port of San Francisco alone, noted Daniel Webster, was twenty times as valuable as Texas.

Still, Whigs of all stripes supported "no territory" amendments to war bill after war bill. In some cases it was largely for tactical reasons. "No territory" provided all Whigs, including those who secretly hankered for California, with a strong initial position to counter Polk's desire to acquire all of northern Mexico. Many hoped to use "no territory" as a bargaining chip to force the expansionist President to back down or modify his demands. "No territory" also provided all Whigs with a sure-fire way to make political capital out of the war. With the amendment on the floor, they were able to savage Polk for waging a war of conquest while at the same time extolling the heroics of Whig generals and lauding the "boys on the front line."

Furthermore, "no territory" was neutral on the slavery question. It had the same practical result as the call for "no more slave territory" without the nasty side effects. It satisfied a basic demand of all northern Whigs without alienating southern Whigs. To men like Daniel Webster and Henry Clay, who loved their party dearly and wanted to avoid a sectional crisis, it seemed at times like a godsend. It allowed them to at least cope with the most ominous issue of the day.

Keeping slavery out of politics, however, proved impossible. While Adams and the "ultras" raised it as soon as the war began, a band of dissident Democrats succeeded in making it the paramount issue of the war.

As early as February 1845, more than a year before the war began, Van Buren had warned his followers that the Democrats must not lead the country into a war in which "the opposition shall be able to charge with plausibility, if not truth, that it is waged for the extension of slavery."[52] As soon as it became clear that Polk was anxious to fight for a larger Texas—but not a larger Oregon—northern Democrats knew from experience that northern Whigs were going to roast them with the proslavery, prosouthern charge. And this time they might make it stick.

Polk did nothing to combat this uneasiness. Instead, he convinced many northern Democrats that the Oregon men were right in saying that he was not to be trusted. His handling of federal patronage left the Van Burenites with the impression that he was trying to weaken their position in New York politics and strengthen a "rival" Hunker faction. They were also furious at being dragooned into supporting the Mexican war bill. Pennsylvania Democrats meanwhile felt that Polk's low tariff policies had jeopardized their chances of re-election. Midwestern Democrats were beside themselves when he vetoed a bill designed to improve rivers and harbors along the Great Lakes.[53]

Still, northern Democrats were slow to push the slavery issue. Not until the last days of the congressional session, in August 1846, did a small band of northern Democrats decide to take a stand. They had been in session for nine months, and were just about to go home, when Polk sprang on them a last-minute request for two million dollars to negotiate the acquisition of California and New Mexico. During a two-hour recess they decided to amend the bill so as to prohibit slavery in any land obtained by virtue of the appropriation. To present this amendment they chose David Wilmot, an obscure Pennsylvania Democrat who was friendly with the South but in trouble with his constituents for his vote on the tariff, and angry at Polk for his handling of federal patronage.[54]

When Wilmot offered this proviso it created only a minor stir. As always, the closing hours of the session were chaotic, with debate limited to ten minutes per speaker and two hours altogether. Half the members clearly had their minds on catching a train to Baltimore and going home. Others took Wilmot's proviso as just a tactic to derail the Two Million Bill, rather than a serious attack on slavery. And some Southerners, while secretly fuming, refrained from attacking the proviso to avoid giving it prominence. Even antislavery Whigs failed to jump into the fray. Giddings, their chief spokesman, was already on his way home to Ohio, while several others were of two minds about the proviso. Much as they liked its antislavery character, it was clearly expansionist in tone, acknowledging the propriety of taking land from Mexico, and they were vehemently against any conquest of Mexico.[55]

Adams was one of the few who spoke on the amendment. He said that he favored the amendment in principle but thought it was unnecessary. Slavery was unlawful in Mexico and would remain so in any ceded area. Indeed, the only way slavery could be established in the ceded area was if "it was made an article of the treaty itself" or Congress passed positive legislation after the land was acquired. It might even be argued that the proviso was a step backward, since it seemed to imply that the legal status of slavery would be in doubt.[56]

Despite his initial reaction, Adams voted for the proviso at every opportunity and eventually changed his mind about its importance.[57] The first round of voting proved beyond doubt that the proviso had bite. It split both parties along sectional lines. The ayes and nays were not generally recorded that hot August night, but in the one case they were, Southerners were in opposition, 67 to 2, and Northerners in favor, 83 to 12. Eight northern Whigs placed their antiexpansionist feelings first and voted against the proviso. The others all joined Adams in voting for the amendment he had labeled superfluous. So too did northern Democrats, including those who supported Polk's Oregon compromise, his tariff policies, and his rivers-and-harbors veto. Only four northern Democrats and two southern Whigs truly crossed sectional lines and voted with the other side.[58]

The proviso never became law. Although it passed the House attached to Polk's Two Million Bill by a four-to-three margin, the package had little chance of getting through the Senate in the few minutes before adjournment. And to make sure that both died, John Davis, a Massachusetts Whig who had voted against the war, filibustered until the hour of adjournment arrived. The outcome delighted many antislavery Whigs, who reported to Giddings that he had missed a glorious event, and that it would have been "worth another weeks board" for him to have remained in Washington and had a hand in the President's defeat. But in Massachusetts the "Conscience" Whigs were unhappy. Led by Charles's newspaper, they took Davis to task, claiming that he had prevented an antislavery triumph by talking the bill to death.[59]

When John Quincy Adams arrived home that summer, he knew that the proviso was not dead. Polk still needed a special appropriation, and as soon as he asked for one the proviso could be conveniently attached. But Adams was hardly looking forward to another battle. Glad to be home after nine months in Washington, he was certain that his faculties were declining "from day to day into mere helpless impotence."[60]

He still tried, however, to lead a vigorous life. He took long walks and partook in a groundbreaking ceremony in nearby Wayland for an aqueduct to Boston. Even though he suffered through a sleepless night, a sore throat, and an attack of palsy so severe he could barely write, he found enough strength several days later to preside over a meeting at Faneuil Hall. Its purpose was to protest the rendition of a slave who had escaped from New Orleans as a stowaway on a Massachusetts vessel and landed at South Boston. The meeting, he noted, closed by giving him a vote of thanks but "not without opposition." He also stood for re-election and won handily by a two-to-one margin. The victory, he claimed, proved that his constituents endorsed his views on Oregon and the Mexican war.[61]

But death was now stalking him. On November 20, while visiting his son in Boston, he rose as usual at about four o'clock, rubbed himself with a horsehair strap and mitten, and after breakfast went for a walk with a friend. Suddenly he collapsed, and only with help staggered back to his son's house. He had suffered a cerebral hemorrhage and was in a stupor for days. It took him weeks to recover. Afterwards, he wrote his last will and testament, leaving the bulk of his estate to his wife, his only surviving son, Charles, and the wife and daughter of his deceased son John. Ten pages long, the will showed that he still had a gift for detail. He also wrote a "posthumous memoir" which he attached to his diary. It too was full of detail. In it he wrote of his collapse: "From that hour I date my decease, and consider myself, for every useful purpose, dead."[62]

* * *

But the old man was not as dead as he fancied. He was up and about by New Year's Day and walking the streets of Boston in late January. On February 8 he was off to Congress, taking the train to Springfield, switching to another train to New Haven, catching the steamer to New York City, and traveling by a series of trains to Philadelphia, Baltimore, and finally Washington.[63]

By the time he arrived in Washington, Congress had been in session for over two months. At the outset, Polk had delayed renewing his request for money to negotiate with Mexico, and hence for at time there was no legislation to which the Wilmot Proviso could be readily attached. But in January there had been a major flare-up over slavery when the House took up a bill organizing the Oregon Territory. To a clause barring slavery from the territory, Armistead Burt of South Carolina proposed adding the phrase, "inasmuch as the whole of said territory lies north of 36°30' north latitude."

Congress, Burt had argued, had no constitutional right to prohibit slavery anywhere, but as a basis for sectional peace he was willing to see the Missouri Compromise line extended to the Pacific. By that he had clearly meant that the free states could have Oregon only if they let the slave states have the vast area below 36°30'. It had also become clear that Burt was not speaking just for himself. Other southern firebrands had raised the same points; one Calhounite after another had stressed that Congress had no legal right to bar slavery in the territories, that the Missouri Compromise was in fact unconstitutional, that slavery followed the flag, and that the South was making a concession to the North in allowing Congress to outlaw slavery in the Oregon Territory. When the House had refused to accept Burt's "compromise," Shelton F. Leake of Virginia had issued a threat, first accusing the House members of being "a magnificent abolition society," and then promising them that the South would not submit to the subjugation that the House apparently planned for it.[64]

So when Adams entered the House to a standing ovation that February, the members were primed for battle. The Calhounites had already shown their weapons, proven that they would attack not only the proviso but also Adams's contention that the Mexican territories would be free unless Congress enacted positive legislation establishing slavery. Some northern Democrats had shown signs of deserting the proviso in the face of administration pressure, perhaps even voting with the South on key ballots. But antislavery Whigs were eager to take up the slack, to push the proviso at every opportunity.

Adams, in fact, arrived just at the moment of decision. Several days before, Polk's men had introduced a bill to provide the administration with three million dollars to cover "extraordinary expenses" in making peace with Mexico. To this bill Wilmot and his supporters had tried to add a tougher version of the proviso, one that would bar slavery in "any territory on the continent of America which shall hereafter be acquired." Debate had been heated and long, but they had run into a series of parliamentary roadblocks and had failed to formally get their amendment on the floor.[65]

In the past, Adams could have helped Wilmot and his supporters overcome these technical barriers. He had long been a master in parliamentary maneuver, in using the rules of the House to his own advantage. But no one turned to the tottering old man for help. Because of his health, he was excused from all committee assignments except that of the Library of Congress. And because of his feeble voice, the other members could not hear him, and few of his remarks were recorded. He said little, if anything, on most issues before the House, only insisting on being heard when a last-minute attempt was made to pay a $50,000 indemnity to the Spanish owners of the slave ship *Amistad*. To pay this indemnity, he insisted, "would be a perfect robbery committed on the people of the United States. Neither these slave dealers, nor the Spanish government on their behalf, has any claim to this money whatever." Yet while the House followed his advice and defeated the appropriation, 28 to 94, few members could hear what he said.[66]

So Adams's only weapons this session were his great prestige and his vote. The latter was immediately needed. On February 15, two days after his arrival, Wilmot and his supporters finally overcame the parliamentary barriers and formally presented the proviso. To derail it, opposition forces twice tried to substitute amendments extending the Missouri Compromise line. Supporters of the proviso beat back both attempts and brought up

their own measure for a vote. Thanks partly to administration
pressure, eighteen northern Democrats joined the South in opposition. But every northern Whig except one voted for the
proviso, and the proviso and the appropriation bill both passed
the House by identical votes of 115 to 106.[67]

Four days later in the Senate, Calhoun responded with a set
of resolutions echoing the southern stance in the debate over
the Burt amendment. The passage of the proviso, he ranted,
would give the North overwhelming power in the future, and
such a destruction of sectional balance would mean "political
revolution, anarchy, civil war, and widespread disaster." As a
southern man, a cotton planter, a slaveholder, he would never
acknowledge inferiority. "The surrender of life is nothing to
sinking down into acknowledged inferiority."[68]

Shortly thereafter, the Senate rejected the proviso and passed
its own Three Million Bill without any mention of slavery. The
Senate bill came before the House on March 3, the last day of
the session. If the bill passed as it was, then Polk would have
his three million and the proviso would be dead. To prevent
this, antislavery forces again tried to attach the proviso, and
again Adams voted in its favor. But the administration worked
hard to kill the proviso, and six northern Democrats switched
their votes, while several others absented themselves from the
proceedings. As a result, while every northern Whig now supported the proviso, a total of twenty-two northern Democrats
now voted with the South. The proviso was thus defeated, 97
to 102, and Polk obtained his three million with no strings
attached.[69]

So once again the bitter taste of defeat accompanied Adams on
his long train ride back to Quincy. In Massachusetts he was
treated like a dying man and no longer regarded as the head
of his own family. He was now completely overshadowed by
Charles, who was being wined and dined by "regular" Whigs.
The "regulars" had split into two camps, and in a struggle for
power each faction sought the support of Charles and other
"Conscience" men. At the same time, however, "Conscience"
Whigs still had their own agenda and hoped to make all-out
support of the Wilmot Proviso the test of party loyalty, whereas

many "regulars" wanted to avoid further fights with southern Whigs, bury the proviso, and adopt the battle cry of "no territory" whatsoever.[70]

Adams took a fatherly interest in his son's career, but neither his son nor any of the warring factions paid him much heed. His summer at Quincy was thus a quiet one, except for his grandchildren, who had the full run of the house, hung about his library and ransacked his desk, played with his sword-cane and traveling pistols, and knocked over a row of tumblers that he had swiped from his wife to cover caterpillars, which he hoped would change into butterflies or moths, but never did. His interest in science was still strong, and when he got the chance he made a special trip to see Harvard's new observatory. He also took a keen interest in the celebration of his fiftieth wedding anniversary, a quiet family affair that occurred in July.[71]

By then, Adams was convinced that he could return to Congress in December, although he doubted that he would be much use in debate. He was still pessimistic. He told one correspondent that while he hoped to see a blow struck against slavery, "the consummation is not to bless my eyes nor to delight my years." He told another, who sought his advice on writing a history of the Mexican war, that "there was no aspect of right or wrong of which we can claim the benefit in the controversy."[72] Yet even though he had little hope of changing the nation's course in this "most unrighteous" war, he still needed to be in public life. He would die, he told his wife, the minute he gave it up.[73]

So once again the old President and his wife made their way back to Washington. The nation's capital was buzzing about the conquest of Mexico. The only issue now in doubt, boasted Democrats, was how much land Mexico would be forced to relinquish at the peace table. In early December, Adams had a long conversation with the zealous expansionist Robert Walker, now Polk's Secretary of the Treasury. He felt weak and afterwards, he wrote, decided to "consider every word henceforth issuing from my lips as my last words and dying speech." On December 10 he turned down the opportunity to give the ceremonial address at the laying of the cornerstone of the Washington monument.[74]

Ten days later, however, he insisted on presenting two petitions calling for peace with Mexico on generous terms.[75] By
January 1848, he seemed much better. Some of his old feistiness
returned. Indeed, by the middle of the month he was on his
feet questioning Polk's right to withhold certain documents
from Congress: "I think this House ought to sustain, in the
strongest manner, their right to call for information upon questions in which war and peace are concerned. They ought to
maintain their right, and maintain it in a very distinct manner,
against this assertion on the part of the President. . . . I should
say more, Sir, if I had the power."[76] Several weeks later he
seemed hale and hearty to those who saw him, challenging a
House attempt to dispense with the reading of the previous
day's minutes, attending a reception for the Mayor of Washington, participating in a floor measure to provide relief for the
heirs of Revolutionary hero John Paul Jones, serving on the
library committee, and holding open house for scores of visitors.

Two days after the open house, on February 21, 1848, Adams
was early in his seat. He had no idea that the President had
just received a treaty of peace, a harsh one by Adams's standards that took from Mexico one-third of its territory and added
over one million square miles to the United States, including
California and most of what is now the American Southwest.
The House had under consideration a more mundane matter,
a resolution to tender thanks and decorations to various generals for their gallant actions in 1847. When the Speaker called
for ayes and noes, Adams replied with a firm "No."

A few minutes later, an antislavery reporter noticed a deep
color tinging the old man's temples. The ex-President seemed
to be trying to say something, trying to rise, when his right
hand grabbed convulsively for the corner of his desk and he
slumped over to his left. His neighbor caught him before he
hit the floor. Another called out: "Mr. Adams is dying!" Quickly
colleagues brought in a sofa and laid him on it. In this fashion,
they moved him first into the Rotunda, then the East Portico,
and finally into the Speaker's room. Reviving slightly, Adams
called for his old rival and associate Henry Clay, who hurried
in to pay his last respects and left weeping. At one point the
dying man tried to say: "Thank the officers of the House." Later

he apparently murmured: "This is the end of earth, but I am composed." Then he slipped into a coma, and when his wife arrived he was unable to recognize her. Two days later, at twenty minutes after seven o'clock in the evening, the old warrior died.[77]

The funeral ceremonies in Washington and Massachusetts took on the air of a national pageant, with frequent cannon salutes, tolling of bells, marching military companies, funeral bands, tons of crepe paper, and long lines of mourners. Nearly every politician in the country, it seemed, gave a funeral discourse. Particularly noteworthy were Adams's old enemies who called him "a great man," "a sage," "a patriarch," "a Cicero." Even the Boston elite, who had never taken to him in his lifetime, paid him great tribute in a grand ceremony at Faneuil Hall. None other than Daniel Webster wrote the inscription on the casket. So for a season the irascible old man was forgotten and Adams was remembered as a saint by friend and foe alike.[78]

But the world soon returned to normal. Just as Adams's body was finally being laid to rest in Quincy, the Virginia legislature in a strict party vote tabled a resolution to honor the illustrious ex-President from Massachusetts.[79] The passions that John Quincy Adams aroused thus lived on, shattering the national political parties, tearing apart the bonds of union, and soon splitting the country itself into two warring nations. They would not be buried until hundreds of thousands of other Americans joined him in the grave.

Notes

The following abbreviations are used in the notes:

JQA John Quincy Adams
LCA Louisa Catherine Adams, wife of JQA
GWA George Washington Adams, eldest son of JQA and LCA
JA2d John Adams, second son
CFA Charles Francis Adams, youngest son

Unless otherwise noted, all diaries, records, and correspondence of the Adamses appear in the Adams Papers, Microfilms (Massachusetts Historical Society). This collection consists of 608 reels and is available in research libraries throughout the United States.

Chapter I. The Road to Seat No. 203

1. See JQA Diary, Dec. 5, 1831; *Memoirs of John Quincy Adams, Comprising Portions of His Diary from 1795 to 1848* (ed. by Charles Francis Adams; 12 vols., Philadelphia, 1874–77), 8, p. 431.
2. JQA Diary, June 18–Aug. 3, 1829.
3. *Journals of Ralph Waldo Emerson* (ed. by E. W. Emerson and W. E. Forbes; 10 vols., Boston, 1909–14), 6, pp. 349–50.
4. *Diary of Charles Francis Adams* (vols. 1 and 2 ed. by Aida DiPace Donald and David Donald, vols. 3–6 ed. by Marc Friedlaender and L. H. Butterfield; Cambridge, Mass., 1964–), 1, p. 315 (Sept. 6, 1824).
5. JQA to GWA, Jan. 1, 1828.
6. CFA, *Diary*, 3, pp. 328–29 (Sept. 28–29, 1830).
7. LCA to Mrs. JA2d, Nov. 28, 1830; LCA to JA2d, Oct. 1, 30, 1830.

8. JQA to JA2d, Oct. 27, 1830; LCA to JA2d, Nov. 14, 1830.

9. JQA to CFA, Nov. 27, 1831.

10. LCA to JA2d, Nov. 14, 1830; LCA entry 1836, in LCA Diary, Verse Compositions, &c., 1835–41.

11. JQA Diary, Nov. 18, 1830; JQA, *Memoirs*, 8, pp. 239–40. Solomon Lincoln, Jr., to John Blazer Davis, Oct. 1, 6, 13, 1830, "Letters of John Brazer Davis, 1819–1831," *Massachusetts Historical Society Proceedings* 49 (1915–16): 234–38; Handbill, signed by Seth Sprague and Artemas Hale (Chairman and Secretary of National Republican District Convention), ca. Oct. 15, 1830, Adams Papers; *Boston Daily Advertiser*, Oct. 25, 1830.

12. JQA, *Memoirs*, 8, p. 247 (Nov. 7, 1830).

13. JQA Diary, June 25, 1830; JQA to James Barbour, April 4, 1829; JQA to the Rev. Charles W. Upham, Feb. 2, 1837, as quoted in Henry Adams, *The Degradation of Democratic Dogma* (New York, 1969), pp. 24–25; see also Edward H. Tatum, Jr., ed., "Ten Unpublished Letters of John Quincy Adams, 1796–1837," *Huntington Library Quarterly* 4 (April 1941): 381–84; Henry Adams, ed., *Documents Relating to New England Federalism* (Boston, 1877), p. 140.

14. See, for example, Frederick Jackson Turner, *Rise of the New West, 1819–1829* (New York, 1906); Charles and Mary Beard, *The Rise of American Civilization* (2 vols; New York, 1927), 1, chap. 12; Arthur Schlesinger, Jr., *The Age of Jackson* (Boston, 1945); Richard Hofstadter, *The American Political Tradition* (New York, 1948), chap. 3; Lee Benson, *The Concept of Jacksonian Democracy* (Princeton, 1961); Robert Remini, *The Election of Andrew Jackson* (Philadelphia, 1963).

15. Richard H. Brown, "The Missouri Crisis, Slavery, and the Politics of Jacksonianism," *South Atlantic Quarterly* (Winter 1966): 55–72; William J. Cooper, Jr., *The South and the Politics of Slavery, 1828–1856* (Baton Rouge, 1978), chap. 1.

16. Albert F. Simpson, "The Political Significance of Slave Representation, 1787–1821," *Journal of Southern History* 7 (Aug. 1941): 315–42; William Plumer, Jr., *Life of William Plumer* (Boston, 1857), pp. 265, 304; H. C. Lodge, *Life and Letters of George Cabot* (Boston, 1877), pp. 344–46; "Boreas" [Sereno E. Dwight], *Slave Representation* (n.p., 1812), p. 21. See also Worthington C. Ford, ed., *Writings of John Quincy Adams* (7 vols.; New York, 1913–17), 3, p. 71.

17. Norman J. Risjord, *The Old Republicans: Southern Conservatism in the Age of Jefferson* (New York, 1965), pp. 258ff; Lynwood M. Dent, "The Virginia Democratic Party, 1824–1847" (Unpub. Ph.D. diss., Louisiana State University, 1974), pp. 23ff.

18. JQA, "First Annual Message, December 6, 1825," in James D. Richardson, ed., *Messages and Papers of the Presidents, 1787–1897* (20 vols.; New York, 1897), 2, pp. 865–83.

19. Dec. 8, 1825.

20. Risjord, *The Old Republicans*, pp. 164–65, 245–48, 269; *Annals of Congress*, 14th Cong., 1st Sess. (1815–16), 842.

21. Ulrich B. Phillips, "Georgia and States' Rights . . .," *American Historical Association, Annual Report for . . . 1901* (Washington, 1902), 2, pp. 48–72; Annie Heloise Abel, "The History of Events Resulting in Indian Consolidation West of the Mississippi," *American Historical Association Annual Report for . . . 1906* (Washington, 1908), 1, pp. 335–57.

22. Dent, "The Virginia Democratic Party," p. 75.

23. JQA to the Rev. Charles W. Upham, Feb. 2, 1837, as quoted in Henry Adams, *The Degradation of Democratic Dogma*, pp. 24–25.

24. LCA, "Record of a Life, or My Story," begun July 23, 1825, and "Adventures of a Nobody," begun July 1, 1840, in LCA Miscellany, Adams Papers. LCA also wrote many plays and poems, which perhaps illustrate another side of her character; here the women are generally strong and noble, the men weak and emotional.

25. LCA to CFA, Aug. 19, 1827.

26. JQA Diary, July 26, 1811.

27. LCA, "Record of a Life."

28. GWA to Thomas O. Bracket, Sept. 25, 1817.

29. Correspondence between JQA, GWA, LCA, and CFA, 1825–29; CFA, *Diary*, 2, p. 376 (May 13, 1829). The Adams Papers include only a fraction of George's writings; the more sensitive documents were destroyed by his brother Charles. See CFA, *Diary*, 2, pp. 372, 376, 3, pp. 213, 219, 347, 4, pp. 101–3 (May 3, 4, 13, 1829; April 14, 24, Oct. 26, 1830).

30. JQA Diary, entries May, June 13–14, 1829; *Boston Daily Advertiser*, May 4, 1829.

31. JQA Diary, May 4–7, 1829; LCA to CFA, May 7, July 5, 1829; JQA to LCA, June 13, 15, 1829; notebook of LCA, undated; statement of LCA, April 12, 1847, Adams Papers.

32. *Report of a Trial: Miles Farmer, versus Dr. David Humphrey Storer . . . Relative to the Transactions between Miss Eliza Dolph and George Washington Adams . . . .* (Boston, 1831).

33. Samuel Flagg Bemis, *John Quincy Adams and the Union* (New York, 1950), p. 211.

34. I am indebted to Professor Ronald Story, University of Massachusetts, Amherst, for most of the information in this paragraph.

Details on estates come from Norfolk County Probate Court, File
No. 115 (1826) and File No. 121 (1846).

35. JQA Memorandum Book, with drafts of his will and statements
of his estate, 1829–32, Adams Papers.

36. JQA Diary, May 14, 1830.

37. CFA, *Diary*, 3 and 4 *passim* (1829–32); LCA to JA2d, Aug. 29, Oct.
20, 1832; JQA and JA2d, correspondence 1829–33.

38. JQA to CFA, March 3, 23, 1837; JQA to Antoine Giusta, June 21,
1839; CFA, Diary, July 1, 29, Nov. 18, 1836, July 28, 1840, April
22, 1844.

39. On Adams's district, I have culled much information from census
returns and town histories, which are very uneven in quality, and
from John P. Bigelow, *Statistical Tables: Exhibiting the Condition of
Industry in Massachusetts, 1837* (Boston, 1837) and Louis McLane,
*Report of the Secretary of the Treasury, 1832: Documents Relative to the
Manufactures in the United States* (Washington, 1833).

40. Computed from Returns of [Massachusetts] Votes, 1780–1884 (Boston: Secretary of the Commonwealth, Archives Division, 1964),
microfilm.

41. *Ibid.* See also Paul Goodman, "The Politics of Industralism: Massachusetts, 1830–1870," in Richard L. Bushman et al., *Uprooted
Americans: Essays To Honor Oscar Handlin* (Boston, 1979), pp. 163–
207.

42. Ronald P. Formisano, *The Transformation of Political Culture: Massachusetts Parties, 1790s–1840s* (New York, 1983), chaps. 8, 12, and
passim.

Chapter II. Adams and Democracy

1. For the vast literature on Jacksonian Democracy, see Charles G.
Sellers, Jr., "Andrew Jackson versus the Historians," *Mississippi
Valley Historical Review* 44 (March 1958): 615–34, and Ronald P.
Formisano, "Towards a Reorientation of Jacksonian Politics: A Re-
view of the Literature, 1959–1975," *Journal of American History* 63
(June 1976): 42–65.

2. For Jackson's position in Tennessee politics, see Thomas Perkins
Abernathy, *From Frontier to Plantation in Tennessee* (Chapel Hill,
1932), and Charles G. Sellers, *James K. Polk, Jacksonian, 1795–1843*
(Princeton, 1957).

3. *Argus of Western America* (Frankfort, Ky.), March 18, 1829, as quoted
in Schlesinger, *Age of Jackson*, p. 6.

4. The generally accepted portraits of Jackson and Adams, found in

textbooks and repeated on political platforms, reflect largely the work of the Progressive historians. Put forth in the early 20th century by Frederick Jackson Turner and Charles A. Beard in many of their writings, the stereotypes were popularized further by Claude Bowers, *The Party Battles of the Jackson Period* (Boston, 1922); Vernon L. Parrington, *The Romantic Revolution* (New York, 1927); Marquis James, *The Life of Andrew Jackson* (2 vols.; Indianapolis, 1933, 1937); and Wilfred E. Binkley, *American Political Parties: Their Natural History* (New York, 1943).

5. The style-of-living controversy is detailed in Edwin Miles, "President Adams' Billiard Table," *The New England Quarterly* 45 (March 1972): 31–43. An accurate account of Adams's actual style of living can be found in George Dangerfield, *Era of Good Feelings* (New York, 1952), pp. 384–85.

6. JQA, *Memoirs*, 8, p. 433 (Dec. 11, 1831), 9, pp. 251, 255 (Aug. 11, 18, 1835), 8, pp. 268–70 (Jan. 10, 1831), 9, p. 345 (April 8, 1837). See also George A. Lipsky, *John Quincy Adams: His Theories and Ideas* (New York, 1950), pp. 124–27.

7. JQA, "Observations Upon the Operation of the French Constitution . . . ," Oct. 4, 1797, Adams Papers; JQA to George Bancroft, March 31, 1838, "Letters of John Adams and John Quincy Adams," *New York Public Library Bulletin* 10 (April 1906): 249f; JQA, *Memoirs*, 4, p. 120 (July 28, 1818), 8, p. 433 (Dec. 11, 1831), 10, p. 468 (April 28, 1841); Lipsky, *JQA's Theories and Ideas*, pp. 170–75.

8. JQA to George Bancroft, Oct. 25, 1835; Lipsky, *JQA's Theories and Ideas*, pp. 112–13.

9. Cf. JQA, *Life in a New England Town, 1787, 1788* (Boston, 1903); JQA, *An Oration Addressed to the Citizens of the Town of Quincy on the Fourth of July, 1831* (Boston, 1831); JQA to George Bancroft, Oct. 25, 1835; JQA, *Parties in the United States* (New York, 1841); JQA, *The Social Compact, Exemplified in the Constitution of the Commonwealth of Massachusetts . . .* (Providence, 1842).

10. *Ibid.*

11. George Wilson Pierson, *Tocqueville and Beaumont in America* (New York, 1938), pp. 418–20.

12. See n. 13, Chapter I.

13. JQA Diary, *passim*; CFA, *Diary, passim*.

14. Stephen Higginson to Timothy Pickering, Jan. 12, 1800, Feb. 15, 1804, in J. F. Jameson, ed., "Letters of Stephen Higginson, 1783–1804," *American Historical Association, Annual Report for . . . 1896* (Washington, 1897), 1, pp. 833, 839f.

15. Greenfield *Gazette*, May 16, 1808; Salem *Gazette*, Jan. 22, April 15,

May 10, 1808; Hampshire *Gazette*, April 20, 1808, as quoted in Samuel Flagg Bemis, *John Quincy Adams and the Foundations of American Foreign Policy* (New York, 1949), p. 148; W. C. Ford, "The Recall of John Quincy Adams in 1808," *Massachusetts Historical Society, Proceedings* 65 (Jan. 1912): 354–75.

16. Shaw Livermore, Jr., *The Twilight of Federalism: The Disintegration of the Federalist Party, 1815–1830* (Princeton, 1962), pp. 117–19; Richard McCormick, *The Second American Party System: Party Formation in the Jacksonian Era* (Chapel Hill, 1966), pp. 41–43.

17. Bemis, *JQA and the Union*, pp. 163–64; Henry Adams, ed., *Documents Relating to New England Federalism, 1800–1815* (Boston, 1877), pp. 1–13.

18. CFA to JQA, Dec. 17, 1828; Henry Adams, *New England Federalism*, pp. 23–26.

19. *Boston Daily Advertiser*, Nov. 18, 1828.

20. Claude M. Fuess, *Daniel Webster* (2 vols.; Boston, 1930), 1, pp. 173–74; Josiah H. Benton, *A Notable Libel Case* (Boston, 1904), pp. 93–94.

21. Henry Adams, *New England Federalism*, pp. 43–92.

22. JQA to CFA, Nov. 26, 1828; William Plumer to JQA, Dec. 20, 1828, Jan. 16, 1829; JQA to William Plumer, Dec. 31, 1828, Jan. 26, 1829; Henry Adams, *New England Federalism*, pp. 144–46.

23. Henry Adams, *New England Federalism*, pp. 107–329; JQA to CFA, Dec. 31, 1828, Feb. 20, 1829; JQA to GWA, Jan. 19, Feb. 22, 1829.

24. Henry Adams, *New England Federalism*, p. vii.

25. JQA, *Memoirs*, 9, p. 263 (Nov. 23, 1835).

26. John Taylor of Caroline to James Monroe, Nov. 8, 1809, in William E. Dodd, "John Taylor of Caroline: Prophet of Secession," *John P. Branch Historical Papers*, 2 (June 1908), p. 302.

27. JQA, *Memoirs*, 6, p. 170 (Aug. 9, 1823).

28. Following the McCarthy era, most studies of Antimasonry owed something to Richard Hofstadter's *The Paranoid Style in American Politics* (New York, 1965). Implicitly linking Antimasonry to mental disorder, these studies tended to be dismissive. See, for example, Lorman Ratner, *Antimasonry: The Crusade and the Party* (Englewood Cliffs, N.J., 1969) and Seymour M. Lipset and Earl Raab, *The Politics of Unreason: Right Wing Extremism in America, 1790–1970* (New York, 1970).

29. Charles McCarthy's study appears in the *American Historical Association Report for . . . 1902* (Washington, 1903), pp. 367–574. It was finally superceded by William Preston Vaughn, *The Antimasonic Party in the United States, 1826–1843* (Lexington, Ky., 1983),

which I have relied on repeatedly for details in the following pages. I have also relied on Michael F. Holt, "The Antimasonic and Know Nothing Parties," in Arthur M. Schlesinger, Jr., ed., *History of U.S. Political Parties* (New York, 1973), 1, pp. 575–93, and on James S. Chase, *Emergence of the Presidential Nominating Convention, 1789–1832* (Urbana, Ill., 1973), pp. 121–81.

30. Dorothy Ann Lipson, *Freemasonry in Federalist Connecticut* (Princeton, 1977); Kathleen Smith Kutolowski, "The Janus Face of New York's Local Parties: Genessee County, 1821–1827," *New York History* 59 (April 1978): 159–72.

31. Vernon Stauffer, *New England Federalism and the Bavarian Illuminati* (New York, 1918).

32. Contemporary accounts of Morgan's abduction include *A Narrative of the Facts Relating to the Kidnapping and Presumed Murder of William Morgan* (Batavia, N.Y., 1827); [John C. Spencer], *Report of the Special Counsel on the Subject of the Morgan Abduction, Jan. 27, 1830* (n.d.); Samuel D. Greene, *The Broken Seal; or Personal Reminiscences of the Morgan Abduction and Murder* (Boston, 1870). More recent is Robert Daniel Burns, "The Abduction of William Morgan," *Rochester Historical Society, Publication* (Rochester, N.Y., 1927), 6, pp. 219–30.

33. The most detailed account of these events is in Elder David Bernard, *Light on Masonry: A Collection of the Most Important Documents on the Subject of Speculative Freemasonry . . . in Relation to the Abduction of William Morgan . . .* (Utica, N.Y., 1829).

34. Holt, "The Antimasonic and Know Nothing Parties," pp. 580f, and Leland M. Griffin, "The Antimasonic Persuasion: A Study of Public Address in the Antimasonic Movement, 1826–1838," (Unpub. Ph.D. diss., Cornell University, 1950).

35. Jabbez D. Hammond, *The History of Political Parties in the State of New York* (2 vols.; Cooperstown, N.Y., 1844), 2, p. 382.

36. Whitney Cross, *The Burned-Over District* (Ithaca, N.Y., 1950), pp. 116–20; Glyndon G. Van Deusen, *Thurlow Weed: Wizard of the Lobby* (Boston, 1947), pp. 38–69; Van Deusen, *William H. Seward* (New York, 1967), pp. 12ff; Fawn M. Brodie, *Thaddeus Stevens: Scourge of the South* (New York, 1959), pp. 38–40, 56–60; David Ludlum, *Social Ferment in Vermont, 1791–1850* (New York, 1939), pp. 86–133; Vaughn, *The Antimasonic Party*, p. 187.

37. *Doings of the Plymouth County Antimasonic Convention Held at Abington* [*March 10, 1828*] (n.p., n.d.); Moses Thatcher, *An Address Delivered Before the Antimasonic Convention . . . for Plymouth County . . . Dec. 9, 1829* (Boston, 1830); *Abstract for the Proceedings of the Antimasonic State Convention of Massachusetts, Held in Faneuil Hall, Boston, Decem-*

ber 30 and 31, 1829, and January 1, 1830 (Boston, 1830); [Moses Thatcher], *Address to the People of Massachusetts, from the Antimasonic Convention, Held in Faneuil Hall, December 30 and 31, 1829, and January 1, 1830* (Boston, 1830); *An Abstract of the Proceedings of the State Convention of Massachusetts, Held in Faneuil Hall, Boston, May 19 and 20, 1831* (Boston, n.d.).

38. JQA Diary, June 24, 1829.

39. JQA to Stephen Bates, July 16, 1830.

40. JQA Diary, Nov. 12, 15, 28, 1830; JQA to Richard Rush, June 17, 1831.

41. JQA, *Memoirs*, 8, pp. 232, 261–62, 400 (June 22, 1830; Jan. 2, Aug. 25, 1831). Antimasonic strength was computed largely from Return of [Massachusetts] Votes, the official returns by towns for statewide and national elections, and from various newspaper reports of town and assembly elections. The newspaper reports, which generally include unofficial and often incomplete returns, indicate that Antimasonry took hold locally about 1½ years before it became a force in statewide or national elections.

42. JQA, *Memoirs*, 7, p. 345 (Oct. 25, 1827); Richard Rush to JQA, May 11, 1831; JQA to Richard Rush, May 23, 1831; JQA Diary, May 20, 1831; JQA, *Memoirs*, 8, pp. 364–68 (May 31, June 2, 6, 10, 1831); Stephen Bates to JQA, Aug. 17, 1831; JQA to Stephen Bates, Aug. 22, 1831; JQA, *Memoirs*, 8, 403–4 (Aug. 27, 1831); JQA to Edward Ingersoll, Sept. 21, 1831, in JQA, *Letters on the Masonic Institution* (Boston, 1847), p. 14.

43. JQA, *Memoirs*, 8, pp. 363, 379 (May 20, July 11, 1831).

44. Edward Ingersoll to JQA, Sept. 14, 1831; JQA, *Letters on the Masonic Institution*, pp. 2–24.

45. Edward Ingersoll to JQA, Oct. 19, 1831; William Leete Stone to JQA, June 17, 1832; Stone, *Letters on Masonry and Antimasonry Addressed to the Hon. John Quincy Adams* (New York, 1832); JQA, *Letters on the Masonic Institution*, pp. 47–95.

46. *National Intelligencer* (Washington), April 22, 1830.

47. *Letters of John Quincy Adams to Edward Livingston* (Boston, 1833).

48. Quotes in this paragraph and following paragraphs come from JQA's pamphlets: *Letters on the Masonic Institution* and *Letters to Edward Livingston*. (The two documents are often bound together, under one title.)

49. Chase, *Presidential Nominating Conventions*, p. 167; Vaughn, *The Antimasonic Party*, pp. 57–58.

50. JQA, *Memoirs*, 8, pp. 414–15 (Oct. 5, 1831), 9, pp. 6–15 (July 10, 30, Sept. 14, 20, 1833); *Fourth Antimasonic State Convention . . .*

Boston, Sept. 11, 12, and 13, 1833 . . . (Boston, 1833); Boston *Advocate*, Sept. 13, 14, 17, 1833.

51. JQA, *Memoirs*, 9, pp. 16, 20 (Sept. 23, Oct. 5, 1833); JQA to Richard Rush, Oct. 1, 1833; Boston *Advocate*, Sept. 18, 19, Oct. 25, Nov. 11, 22, 1833.

52. Computed from official returns, Nov. 12, 1833.

53. JQA to CFA, Nov. 19–21, 26, 1833; JQA, *Memoirs*, 9, pp. 58, 64–65 (Dec. 22, 1833; Jan. 2, 1834); Boston *Advocate*, Jan. 2, 9, 10, 1834.

54. Computed from Return of [Massachusetts] Votes.

55. JQA, *Memoirs*, 8, p. 364 (June 2, 1831); *Proceedings, Grand Lodge of Massachusetts, 1826–1844* (Boston, n.d.), *passim*; [E. H. Cobb], "A Reminiscence of the Dark Days of Anti-Masonry," *Philadelphia Keystone* 11 (July 21, 1877): *passim*; Erik McKinley Eriksson, "Effects of Antimasonry on the Masonic Fraternity, 1826–1856," *Builder* 13 (1927): 72–73; Boston *Advocate*, 1831–36, *passim*.

56. JQA, *Memoirs*, 9, pp. 64–66, 70–72, 74–75, 103–4 (Jan. 2, 7, 13, Feb. 28, 1834); *An Investigation into Freemasonry by a Joint Committee of the Legislature of Massachusetts* (Boston, 1834); [Cobb], "A Reminiscence of the Dark Days of Anti-Masonry," p. 21.

57. Charles Grandison Finney, *The Character, Claims and Practical Workings of Freemasonry* (Cincinnati, 1869), p. v.

58. JQA, *Memoirs*, 9, pp. 114–15 (March 27, 1834).

59. JQA, *Memoirs*, 9, pp. 64–66, 70–72, 74–75, 103–4, 184 (Jan. 2, 7, 13, Feb. 28, Sept. 6, 1834); Boston *Advocate*, Jan.–Oct. 1834. On efforts to heal the breach, see 1833–34 correspondence, Caleb Cushing Papers, Library of Congress; Edward Everett Papers, Massachusetts Historical Society; Levi Lincoln Papers, Massachusetts Historical Society; and John Davis Papers, American Antiquarian Society.

60. Daniel Webster to Jeremiah Mason, Jan. 1, 10, 25, 1835, in J. W. McIntyre, ed., *Writings and Speeches of Daniel Webster* (18 vols.; Boston, 1903), 16, pp. 245–49.

61. JQA to CFA, March 5, 31, April 4, 1835; CFA to JQA, March 17–18, 1835; CFA, *Diary*, 6, pp. 73, 79, 81 (Feb. 11, 18, 20, 1835).

62. Boston *Advocate*, May 14, June 23–Aug., Nov. 1, 1835; CFA, *Diary*, 6, p. 147 (May 29, 1835); Martin B. Duberman, "Charles Francis Adams, Antimasonry and the Presidential Election of 1836," *Mid-America* 43 (April 1961): 114–26.

63. JQA to Benjamin F. Hallett, March 7, 1835; JQA to CFA, March 5, 1835, May 24, 1836. The Boston *Atlas* claimed that Adams hoped to destroy the Webster party in Massachusetts and the Jacksonians nationally (June 9, 1836).

64. Computed from Return of [Massachusetts] Votes.
65. *Ibid.*

Chapter III. Guardian of the Future

1. JQA, *Memoirs*, 9, p. 78 (Jan. 17, 1834).
2. For information on voting behavior I am heavily dependent on recent research, particularly Thomas B. Alexander, *Sectional Stress and Party Strength: A Study of Roll-Call Voting Patterns in the . . . House of Representatives, 1836–1860* (Nashville, 1967); Alvin W. Lynn, "Party Formation and Operation in the House of Representatives, 1824–1837" (Unpub. Ph.D. diss., Rutgers University, 1972); David J. Russo, "The Major Political Issues of the Jacksonian Period and the Development of Party Loyalty in Congress, 1830–1840," *Transactions of the American Philosophical Society, New Series* 62 (May 1972): 3–51; and Joel Silbey, *The Shrine of Party: Congressional Voting Behavior, 1841–1852* (Pittsburgh, 1967).
3. For further details on the turnover rate and the internal workings of Congress, see Lynn, "Party Formation," pp. 340–97, 489–95.
4. JQA, *Memoirs*, 8, pp. 433–34, 436–37 (Dec. 12, 13, 1831).
5. My understanding of Adams's economic thinking has been influenced not only by his own writings but also by the work of many scholars, especially Harold J. Callahan, "The Political Economy of John Quincy Adams" (Unpub. Ph.D. diss., Boston University, 1975); Joseph Dorfman, *The Economic Mind in American Civilization, 1606–1865* (2 vols.; New York, 1946); Carter Goodrich, *Government Promotion of American Canals and Railroads, 1800–1890* (New York, 1960); Lipsky, *JQA's Theories and Ideas*; Harry E. Miller, *Banking Theories in the United States before 1860* (Cambridge, Mass., 1927); Joseph J. Spengler, "The Political Economy of Jefferson, Madison, and Adams," in David K. Jackson, ed., *American Studies in Honor of William Kenneth Boyd* (Durham, N.C., 1940), pp. 3–59; William Appleman Williams, "The Age of Mercantilism: An Interpretation of the American Political Economy, 1763–1828," *William and Mary Quarterly* 15 (Oct. 1958): 419–37.
6. JQA to Edward Cross, April 22, 1822; JQA to Peter S. DuPonceau, Aug. 7, 1837; JQA, *Memoirs*, 4, pp. 325, 370 (April 5, May 14, 1819), 5, p. 128 (May 22, 1820); *Niles' Weekly Register*, 52, pp. 293–94, 358 (July 8, Aug. 5, 1837); *Washington Globe*, Aug. 1, 1837.
7. Charles F. Adams, ed., *Works of John Adams* (10 vols.; Boston, 1856), 9, p. 610.

8. "Report of Mr. Adams," *Register of Debates*, 22d Cong., 1st Sess. (1831–32), Appendix, 70.

9. JQA to Thomas Boylston Adams, July 20–Aug. 3, 1800.

10. For the concentration of wealth in Massachusetts, cf. James Henretta, "Economic Development and Social Structure in Colonial Boston," *William and Mary Quarterly* 22 (Jan. 1965): 75–92; Alice Hanson Jones, "Wealth Estimates for the New England Colonies about 1770," *Journal of Economic History* 32 (March 1972): 98–127; Edward Pessen, "The Egalitarian Myth and the American Social Reality . . . ," *American Historical Review* 76 (Oct. 1971): 989–1034; Horace Wadlin, *Twenty-Fifth Annual Report of Massachusetts Bureau of Statistics of Labor* (Boston, 1885), pp. 264–67; Richard Eddy Sykes, "Massachusetts Unitarianism and Social Change" (Unpub. Ph.D., diss., University of Minnesota, 1967); Frederick C. Jaher, *The Urban Establishment: Upper Strata in Boston, New York, Charleston, Chicago, and Los Angeles* (Urbana, Ill., 1982), pp. 115–56.

11. Indispensable on the new order's problems are Norman Ware, *The Industrial Worker, 1840–1860* (Boston, 1924); Oscar Handlin, *Boston's Immigrants* (Cambridge, Mass., 1941); Alan Dawley, *Class and Community: The Industrial Revolution in Lynn* (Cambridge, Mass., 1976).

12. JQA to Daniel Schnelby, June 15, 1824; JQA to Charles W. Upham, Feb. 2, 1837.

13. JQA, "First Annual Message, December 6, 1825," in Richardson, *Messages and Papers of the Presidents*, 2, p. 871; JQA to Charles W. Upham, Feb. 2, 1837.

14. JQA, *Memoirs*, 7, pp. 187–88 (Nov. 27, 1826).

15. JQA to Benjamin Waterhouse, Oct. 20, 1813.

16. "Report of the Secretary of the Treasury on the State of Finances, 1827," *American State Papers* (38 vols; Washington, 1832–61), 5, p. 638; JQA, *Memoirs*, 7, p. 347 (Oct. 30, 1827).

17. Thomas LeDuc, "History and Appraisal of U.S. Land Policy to 1862," in Howard W. Ottoson, ed., *Land Use Policy in the United States* (Lincoln, Neb., 1963), pp. 3–27; LeDuc, "Public Policy, Private Investment, and Land Use in American Agriculture, 1825–1875," *Agricultural History* 37 (Jan. 1963): 3–9; Paul W. Gates, "An Overview of American Land Policy," *Agricultural History* 50 (Jan. 1976): 213–29; Gates, ed., *Public Land Policies: Management and Disposal* (New York, 1979).

18. JQA, "Inaugural Address, March 4, 1825," in Richardson, *Messages and Papers of the Presidents*, 2, pp. 864–65; JQA, "First Annual Message, December 6, 1825," in Richardson, 2, pp. 871ff; JQA to Charles W. Upham, Feb. 2, 1837.

19. "Report of the Committee of Manufactures," *Register of Debates*, 22d Cong., 1st Sess. (1831–32), Appendix, 85.
20. JQA, *Memoirs*, 8, p. 229 (May 22, 1830).
21. JQA, *Memoirs*, 8, p. 447 (Dec. 28, 1831). For the day-to-day details of Adams's congressional battles in his first two years as a Representative, the most helpful source is John Macoll, "Congressman John Quincy Adams, 1831–1833" (Unpub. Ph.D. diss., Indiana University, 1973).
22. *Register of Debates*, 22d Cong., 1st Sess. (1831–32), 1763–65; *Niles' Weekly Register*, 42 (April 21, 1832), pp. 134–47.
23. JQA, *Memoirs*, 8, pp. 443, 445–48 (Dec. 26, 28, 1831).
24. JQA, *Memoirs*, 8, pp. 444, 439 (Dec. 27, 20, 1831); see also John A. Munroe, *Louis McLane: Federalist and Jacksonian* (New Brunswick, N.J., 1973), pp. 339–50 *passim*.
25. JQA to J. H. Pleasants, June 25, 1824; JQA to John Bailey, March 30, 1835; JQA, "Inaugural Address, March 4, 1825," in Richardson, *Messages and Papers of the Presidents*, 2, pp. 864–65; "Report on Manufacturers," *Register of Debates*, 22d Cong., 1st Sess. (1831–32), Appendix, 85ff; "Minority Report of the Committee of Manufactures," *Register of Debates*, 22d Cong., 2d Sess. (1832–33), Appendix, 43ff; JQA, *Memoirs*, 6, pp. 22, 451–52 (June 16, 1822; Dec. 22, 1824), 7, p. 80 (Dec. 14, 1825), 8, p. 273 (June 1830).
26. *The Transportation Revolution, 1815–1860* (New York, 1951), pp. 20–21.
27. "Minority Report of the Committee of Manufactures," *Register of Debates*, 22d Cong., 2d Sess. (1832–33), Appendix, 45–46; JQA to John Bailey, March 30, 1835.
28. "Report of the Secretary of the Treasury, on the Adjustment of the Tariff Duties on Imports, April 27, 1832," *House Executive Document* 222 (Serial 220), 22d Cong., 1st Sess. (1831–32).
29. Quoted in John D. Macoll, "Congressman John Quincy Adams, 1831–1833," p. 65.
30. JQA, "Rubbish I," May 1–23, 1832.
31. "Report on Manufactures," *Register of Debates*, 22d Cong., 1st Sess. (1831–32), Appendix, 79–92; *House Report* 481, 22d Cong., 1st Sess. (1831–32).
32. JQA to CFA, June 6, 1832; JQA to LCA, June 11, 1832.
33. *Register of Debates*, 22d Cong., 1st Sess. (1831–32), 3830–31; JQA to LCA, June 29, 1832; JQA, "Rubbish I," July 1, 8, 1832.
34. Benjamin Waterhouse to JQA, July 2, 1833; LCA to JA2d, July 30, 1832.

35. JQA to CFA, Nov. 25, Dec. 11, 1832; JQA to Richard Rush, Nov. 30, 1832.

36. JQA, *Memoirs*, 8, p. 503 (Dec. 5, 1832).

37. CFA to JQA, Dec. 17, 1832; JQA to CFA, Dec. 11, 1832; JQA to George Sullivan, Dec. 11, 1832; JQA to Benjamin F. Hallett, Dec. 17, 1832; JQA to Samuel Southard, Dec. 19, 1832.

38. JQA to CFA, Dec. 25, 1832, March 3, 13, 1833; JQA to William Plumer, Jr., April 6, 1833; JQA, *Memoirs*, 8, pp. 504–7, 513–14 (Dec. 10, 14, 17, 19, 27, 28, 1832).

39. "Minority Report of the Committee of Manufactures," *Register of Debates*, 22d Cong., 2d Sess. (1832–33), Appendix, 46.

40. *Democracy in America* (ed. by Phillips Bradley; 2 vols., New York, 1958), 1, pp. 429–30.

41. *Register of Debates*, 22d Cong., 2d Sess. (1832–33), 1564–68, 1609–16, 1640–53 (Feb. 1, 4, 7, 1833), Appendix, 41–61; JQA to CFA, March 26, 1833; JQA, *Memoirs*, 8, p. 510 (Dec. 24, 1832).

42. JQA, *Memoirs*, 8, p. 510 (Dec. 24, 1832).

43. *Register of Debates*, 22d Cong., 1st Sess., Appendix, 54–73; *Speech [Suppressed by the Previous Question] of Mr. John Quincy Adams, of Massachusetts, on the Removal of Public Deposites, and Its Reasons* (Washington, 1834).

44. In addition to the many town histories pertaining to the Plymouth district, information on banking can be found in Vera Shlakman, *Economic History of a Factory Town* (Northampton, Mass., 1935), pp. 243–47; Fritz Redlich, *The Molding of American Banking, 1781–1840* (New York, 1951); D. R. Whitney, *The Suffolk Bank* (Cambridge, Mass., 1878); Jean Alexander Wilburn, *Biddle's Bank: The Crucial Years* (New York, 1967), pp. 77–78; John M. McFaul, *The Politics of Jacksonian Finance* (Ithaca, N.Y., 1972), p. 27; Oscar and Mary Handlin, *Commonwealth: A Study of the Role of Government in the American Economy: Massachusetts, 1774–1861* (New York, 1947), pp. 177–78.

45. Thomas P. Govan, *Nicholas Biddle: Nationalist and Public Banker, 1786–1844* (Chicago, 1959), pp. 107, 111.

46. JQA to Nicholas Biddle, Dec. 3, 1831; Biddle to JQA, Dec. 12, 1831; JQA, *Memoirs*, 8, p. 425 (Nov. 9, 1831).

47. Reginald C. McCrane, ed., *The Correspondence of Nicholas Biddle* (Boston, 1919), pp. 155–56, 169–70; JQA, *Memoirs*, 8, p. 457 (Jan. 14, 1832).

48. John Williams to JQA, Dec. 14, 1831; William Plumer, Jr., to JQA, Jan. 28, Feb. 10, 1832.

49. Thomas Hart Benton, *Thirty Years View* (2 vols.; New York, 1854–

56), 1, pp. 235–42; JQA, *Memoirs*, 8, pp. 470, 480 (Feb. 11, 23, 1832); *Register of Debates*, 22d Cong., 1st Sess. (1831–32), 1874ff.

50. JQA, *Memoirs*, 8, pp. 482–83, 494–96 (March 1, 14, 1832); Nicholas Biddle to JQA, March 4, 1832; JQA to Biddle, March 7, 1832; *Register of Debates*, 22d Cong., 1st Sess. (1831–32), 2160 (March 14, 1832).

51. May 12, 1832.

52. McDuffie would have signed Adams's report, too, if Adams had not interspersed it with remarks in favor of the tariff and internal improvements. See JQA to Nicholas Biddle, May 15, 1832; JQA to Robert Walsh, May 28, 1832.

53. *House Report* 460, 22d Cong., 1st Sess. (1831–32), 379–80; *Register of Debates*, 22d Cong., 1st Sess. (1831–32), Appendix, 54–73.

54. Bray Hammond, *Banks and Politics in America from the Revolution to the Civil War* (Princeton, 1957).

55. See, in particular, McFaul, *The Politics of Jacksonian Finance*; Wilburn, *Biddle's Bank*; and Frank Gatell, "Sober Second Thoughts on Van Buren, the Albany Regency, and the Wall Street Conspiracy," *Journal of American History* 54 (June 1966): 19–40.

56. Nicholas Biddle to John G. Watmough, May 11, 1832, *Correspondence of Biddle*, p. 190; Richmond *Enquirer*, quoted in *National Intelligencer*, May 30, 1832; Boston *Courier*, May–July, 1832; JQA to LCA, June 11, July 3, 11, 1832; JQA, "Rubbish I," June 16, July 5, 7, 8, 10, 11, 13–16, 1832; *House Journal*, 22d Cong., 1st Sess. (1831–32), 1069–76, 1082, 1097 (July 3, 4, 6, 1832).

57. JQA, *Memoirs*, 8, pp. 531–32 (March 2, 1833).

58. JQA, *Memoirs*, 9, pp. 121–24, 127–28 (April 4–6, 12–14, 1834); J. Gales, Jr., to JQA, April 13, 1834; Nicholas Biddle to JQA, April 14, 1834; Joseph Hopkinson to JQA, April 21, 1834; *National Intelligencer*, April 12, 1834; *Speech Suppressed by the Previous Question*.

59. *Speech Suppressed by the Previous Question*; *National Intelligencer*, April 12, 1834; *Register of Debates*, 23d Cong., 1st Sess. (1833–34), 3477–515.

60. For the controversy over the selection of "pet banks," see Harry N. Scheiber, "The Pet Banks in Jacksonian Politics and Finance, 1833–1841," *Journal of Economic History* 23 (June 1963): 196–214; Frank Gatell, "Spoils of the Bank War: Political Bias in the Selection of Pet Banks," *American Historical Review* 70 (Oct. 1964): 35–58; and Gatell, "Secretary Taney and the Baltimore Pets: A Study of Banking and Politics," *Business History Review* 39 (Spring 1965): 205–27.

61. *National Intelligencer*, April 12, 1834; *Register of Debates*, 23d Cong., 1st Sess. (1833–34), 3490; JQA to John Bailey, Dec. 17, 1833.

62. JQA, *Memoirs*, 9, pp. 311–12 (Nov. 11, 1836).

63. The pathbreaking reinterpretation that challenged many sacred cows, including the widely held assumption that Jackson's policies somehow ruined the American economy, is Peter Temin's *The Jacksonian Economy* (New York, 1969). Also important are Hugh Rockoff, "Money, Prices, and Banks in the Jacksonian Era," in Robert Fogel and Stanley Engerman, *The Reinterpretation of American Economic History* (New York, 1972), and Marie Sushka, "The Antebellum Money Market and the Economic Impact of the Bank War," *Journal of Economic History* 36 (Dec. 1976), pp. 809–35.

64. Important treatments of the later years of the "Bank War" include McFaul, *Politics of Jacksonian Finance*; William G. Slade, *Banks or No Banks: The Money Issue in Western Politics, 1832–1865* (Detroit, 1972); James R. Sharp, *The Jacksonians Versus the Banks: Politics in the States After the Panic of 1837* (New York, 1970).

65. JQA to Alexander H. Everett, Nov. 7, 1837; JQA to Peter Du-Ponceau, Aug. 7, 1837; JQA to Charles A. Davis, July 25, 1837; JQA to George Bancroft, March 31, 1838, *New York Public Library Bulletin* 10 (April 1906): 250.

66. JQA to Charles A. Davis, July 25, 1837; JQA, *Memoirs*, 10, p. 40 (Nov. 10, 1838).

67. *Ibid.*

Chapter IV. The Rise of Organized Antislavery

1. JQA, *Memoirs*, 8, pp. 433–34 (Dec. 12, 1831).

2. Sept. 1, 1835.

3. Leonard L. Richards, *"Gentlemen of Property and Standing": Anti-Abolition Mobs in Jacksonian America* (New York, 1970), pp. 65–71, and *passim*.

4. For recent general histories of the abolitionists, see Merton L. Dillon, *The Abolitionists: The Growth of a Dissenting Minority* (DeKalb, Ill., 1974), and James Brewer Stewart, *Holy Warriors: The Abolitionists and American Slavery* (New York, 1976).

5. Richards, *"Gentlemen of Property and Standing"*, pp. 21–22.

6. Richard D. Birdsall, *Berkshire County: A Cultural History* (New Haven, 1959), chap. 7.

7. Page Smith, *John Adams* (2 vols.; Garden City, N.Y., 1962), 2, pp. 657–58; JQA, *Memoirs*, 1, p. 81 (Feb. 23, 1795); *JQA to the Inhabitants of the Twelfth Congressional District . . . March 3, 1837*; JQA to Sarah M. Grimké, April 24, 1837; JQA to Anna Quincy Thaxter, July 31, 1838; JQA to John Greenleaf Whittier, Oct. 28, 1839; JQA, *Memoirs*, 11, pp. 285–86 (Jan. 3, 1843).

8. JQA, *Memoirs*, 3, pp. 27–28, 39–42 (Sept. 1, 23, 25, 1814), 7, p. 90 (Dec. 22, 1825); JQA to Sherlock S. Gregory, Nov. 23, 1837; JQA, "The Progress of Society from Hunter State to That of Civilization," *American Review* 2 (July 1845): 80–89. A recent study of Adams's attitude toward Indians is Lynn Hudson Parsons, " 'A Perpetual Harrow Upon My Feelings': John Quincy Adams and the American Indian," *The New England Quarterly* 46 (Sept. 1973): 339–79.

9. Smith, *John Adams*, 2, p. 926.

10. JQA's letterbook, Nov. 5, 1835; JQA to George Parkman, Nov. 19, Dec. 31, 1835; F. A. Kemble, *Journal of a Residence on a Georgia Plantation, 1838–1839* (New York, 1863), p. 66; [JQA], "Misconceptions of Shakespeare upon the Stage," *New England Magazine* 9 (Dec. 1835): 435–40; [JQA], "The Character of Desdemona," *American Monthly Magazine* 7 (March 1836): 209–17.

11. [Benjamin Watkins Leigh], *The Letters of Algernon Sidney in Defense of Civil Liberty . . .* (Richmond, Va., 1830), pp. 22ff. For a modern update of Leigh's censure, see Richard Drinnon, *Facing West: The Metaphysics of Indian-Hating and Empire Building* (New York, 1980), pp. 108–11.

12. For Adams's justification of Jackson, see his dispatch to British minister George William Erving, Nov. 18, 1818, in *The Writings of John Quincy Adams* (ed. by Worthington C. Ford; 7 vols., New York, 1913–17), 6, pp. 474–502.

13. For the race question and party behavior in various northern states, see James T. Adams, "Disfranchisement of Negroes in New England," *American Historical Review* 30 (Dec. 1925): 543–47; Dixon Ryan Fox, "The Negro Vote in Old New York," *Political Science Quarterly* 32 (June 1917): 252–75; Marion T. Wright, "Negro Suffrage in New Jersey, 1776–1875," *Journal of Negro History* 32 (April 1948): 168–224; Edward R. Turner, *The Negro in Pennsylvania* (Washington, 1911); John L. Stanley, "Majority Tyranny in Tocqueville's America: The Failure of Negro Suffrage in 1846," *Political Science Quarterly* 84 (Sept. 1969): 412–35; Phyllis T. Fields, "Republicans and Black Suffrage in New York State: The Grass Roots Response," *Civil War History* 21 (June 1975): 136–47; Ronald P. Formisano, "The Edge of Caste: Colored Suffrage in Michigan, 1827–1861," *Michigan History* 56 (Spring 1972): 19–41.

14. JQA's introduction to Joseph C. and Owen Lovejoy, *Memoirs of Elijah P. Lovejoy* (New York, 1838), pp. 3–4; "The Letters Addressed by JQA to His Son on the Study of the Bible," Appendix to Abigail Adams, *Letters of Mrs. Adams, the Wife of John Adams, with an Introductory Memoir by Her Grandson, Charles Francis Adams* (4th edition;

Boston, 1848), pp. 432–35 and *passim*; JQA, *Memoirs*, 5, pp. 11–12 (March 2, 1820).

15. JQA to George Bancroft, Oct. 25, 1835. See also JQA to Elizur Wright, Jr., April 16, 1837; JQA to D. Jenkins and Others, Committee of the People of Colour of Columbus, Ohio, April 14, 1841.

16. JQA, *Memoirs*, 5, p. 191 (Oct. 22, 1820), 7, p. 465 (March 7, 1828).

17. William Jay, *Miscellaneous Writings on Slavery* (Boston, 1853), pp. 247ff; Donald L. Robinson, *Slavery in the Structure of American Politics, 1765–1820* (New York, 1971), pp. 347–61; Samuel Flagg Bemis, *John Quincy Adams and the Foundations of American Foreign Policy* (New York, 1949), pp. 231–32, 293, 416.

18. Everett S. Brown, "The Senate Debate on the Breckinridge Bill for the Government of Louisiana, 1804," *American Historical Review*, 22 (Jan. 1917): 340–64; Brown, ed., *William Plumer's Memorandum of Proceedings of the United States Senate, 1803–1807* (New York, 1923), pp. 75–76, 103–4, 143–49, 353–54.

19. Hugh G. Soulsby, *The Right of Search and the Slave Trade in Anglo-American Relations, 1814–1862* (Baltimore, 1933), pp. 13–38; Betty Fladeland, *Men and Brothers: Anglo-American Antislavery Cooperation* (Urbana, Ill., 1972), pp. 113–44; Bemis, *JQA and Foreign Policy*, pp. 412–35.

20. Brown, "Senate Debate on Breckinridge Bill," pp. 340–64.

21. *Letter of the Hon. John Quincy Adams, in a Reply to a Letter of the Hon. Alexander Smyth, to His Constituents* (Washington, 1823).

22. JQA, *Memoirs*, 5, p. 54 (March 31, 1820).

23. JQA, *Memoirs*, 5, p. 10 (March 3, 1820).

24. JQA, *Memoirs*, 4, pp. 529, 502 (Feb. 20, Jan. 10, 1820).

25. JQA, *Memoirs*, 4, p. 531 (Feb. 24, 1820); 5, pp. 11–12 (March 3, 1820).

26. JQA, *Memoirs*, 4, p. 530 (Feb. 23, 1820); Everett S. Brown, ed., *The Missouri Compromise and Presidential Politics, 1820–1825, from the Letters of William Plumer, Jr., Representative from New Hampshire* (St. Louis, 1926), pp. 15–17, 117–19.

27. JQA, *Memoirs*, 5, pp. 10–12 (March 3, 1820).

28. JQA, *Memoirs*, 5, pp. 205–11 (Nov. 24–29, 1820).

29. Philip Hamer, "Great Britain, the United States, and the Negro Seamen Acts, 1822–1848," *Journal of Southern History* 1 (Feb. 1935), pp. 3–28; William W. Freehling, *Prelude to Civil War: The Nullification Controversy in South Carolina* (New York, 1965), pp. 111–16.

30. JQA to Moses Brown, Dec. 9, 1833. Of the abolitionist leaders, William Lloyd Garrison and James Gillespie Birney were particularly critical of Adams. See Wendell P. and Francis J. Garrison,

William Lloyd Garrison (4 vols.; New York, 1885–89), 3, pp. 97–98; *Liberator*, June 16, 1848; Dwight L. Dumond, ed., *Letters of James Gillespie Birney, 1831–1857* (2 vols., New York, 1938), 2, pp. 671–72, 767–73.

31. Data on antislavery societies in Adams's district came from many sources, but especially New England Anti-Slavery Society, *First and Second Annual Reports* (Boston 1833–34), and American Anti-Slavery Society, *Second through Fifth Annual Reports* (New York, 1835–38).

32. *Emancipator*, Aug. 30, 1837.

33. JQA, *Memoirs*, 4, pp. 292–94 (March 12, 1819).

34. JQA, *Memoirs*, 4, pp. 354–56, 475–77 (April 29, 30, Dec. 10, 1819); 8, pp. 286–87, 309 (Jan. 20, Feb. 2, 1831), 9, pp. 437–38 (Nov. 20, 1837).

35. For further details see Richards, *"Gentlemen of Property and Standing"*, pp. 30–46 and *passim*.

36. *Liberator*, Feb. 5, 1831, July 19, 1834; *Emancipator*, Jan. 14, Aug. 19, 1834; *Antislavery Record*, 1 (Jan. 1835), pp. 7–8; American Anti-Slavery Society, *Sixth Annual Report*, p. 87; Avery Craven, *Growth of Southern Nationalism, 1848–1861* (Baton Rouge, 1953), pp. 188f.

37. Cf. Smith, *John Adams*, 2, p. 646, with JQA to Dr. George Parkman, Dec. 31, 1835; JQA, "Misconceptions of Shakespeare," pp. 438–39. For a recent study of Adams's racial attitudes, which appeared too late to be of aid to me, see William Jerry MacLean, "Othello Scorned: The Racial Thought of John Quincy Adams," *Journal of the Early Republic* 4 (Summer 1984): 143–60.

38. JQA, *Memoirs*, 4, p. 531 (Feb. 24, 1820), 10, p. 483 (Aug. 19, 1839). In the matter of temperament, it is worth noting that Adams was able to discuss the issue with abolitionist acquaintances in an "animated but good humored" fashion, and that Adams expressed interest in a mulatto correspondent's contention that the growth of the mulatto population was due to "the frequent sexual union sought by the white man with the Negro woman." Those were two things that Northern anti-abolitionists were simply incapable of doing; such issues drove them to fits of name-calling and violence. Cf. JQA, *Memoirs*, 10, pp. 129–30 (Aug. 19, 1839); JQA to Thomas Gaillard, Feb. 21, 1837; with Richards, *"Gentlemen of Property and Standing"*, *passim*.

39. JQA, *Memoirs*, 10, p. 483 (June 21, 1841), 11, pp. 477–78 (Jan. 6, 1844).

40. JQA, *Memoirs*, 11, pp. 155, 162, 294, 502 (May 16, 26, 1842; Jan. 14, 1843; Feb. 5, 1844).

41. JQA to Dr. Benjamin Waterhouse, Oct. 15, 1835.

42. JQA, *Memoirs*, 5, pp. 210, 11–12 (Nov. 29, March 3, 1820).

43. Boston *Atlas*, Aug. 25, 1835.

44. These letters appeared later in pamphlet form: *Letters Against the Immediate Abolition of Slavery* (Boston, 1835).

45. CFA, *Diary*, 6, p. 200 (Aug. 20, 1835); JQA, *Memoirs*, 9, pp. 251–59 (Aug. 11–22, 1835).

46. *Ibid.*

Chapter V. The New Folk Hero

1. *Resolves of the General Court . . . of Massachusetts, 1836* (Boston, 1838), pp. 296–98.

2. Richardson, *Messages and Papers of the Presidents*, 3, pp. 1394–95; cf. Jackson to Amos Kendall, Aug. 9, 1835, Jackson Papers, Library of Congress; *Congressional Globe*, 24th Cong., 1st Sess. (1835–36), Appendix, 6–10.

3. Richards, "*Gentlemen of Property and Standing*", pp. 73–74.

4. Clement Eaton, "Censorship of the Southern Mails," *American Historical Review* 48 (Jan. 1943): 266–80; W. Sherman Savage, *Controversy Over the Distribution of Abolition Literature* (n.p., 1938).

5. *The Works of John C. Calhoun* (ed. by Richard Crallé; 6 vols., New York, 1853–57), 5, pp. 196–97.

6. *Register of Debates*, 24th Cong., 1st Sess. (1835–36), 1103–8, 1136–71, 1721–37, and *passim*.

7. *Congressional Globe*, 24th Cong., 1st Sess. (1835–36), 24–35 (Dec. 16–18, 1835); *Register of Debates*, 24th Cong., 1st Sess. (1835–36), 1966ff (Dec. 18, 1835). For concise summaries of the debates, see Robert P. Ludlum, "The Antislavery 'Gag Rule': History and Argument," *Journal of Negro History* 26 (April 1941): 203–43; and George C. Cable, "Slavery, Politics, and the South: The Gag Rule as a Case Study," *Captiol Studies* 3 (Fall 1975): 69–87.

8. Cable, "Slavery, Politics, and the South," p. 70 n. 3.

9. See, e.g., *Acts of the General Assembly of Virginia, 1835–1836* (Richmond, 1836), pp. 395–96; *Acts of the General Assembly . . . of Georgia . . . in November and December 1835* (Milledgeville, 1836), pp. 297–300; *Acts of the General Assembly of Kentucky . . . 1835–1836* (Frankfort, 1836), pp. 683–87; *Laws of the State of Mississippi, 1836* (Jackson, 1836), pp. 101–3. See also "An Alabama Protest Against Abolitionism in 1835," *Gulf States Historical Magazine* 2 (July 1903): pp. 26–34.

10. Richards, "*Gentlemen of Property and Standing*", pp. 88–92.

11. *Register of Debates*, 24th Cong., 1st Sess. (1835–36), 1971, 1975, 1979–80 (Dec. 18, 1835), and *passim*.
12. *Register of Debates*, 24th Cong., 1st Sess. (1835–36), 2024–34 (Dec. 22, 1835), and *passim*.
13. For the vehemence of the southern response, see *Niles' Weekly Register* 49 (Dec. 1835–Jan. 1836), *passim*, as well as *Register of Debates*, 24th Cong., 1st Sess. (1835–36), *passim*. Some House speeches were also published as pamphlets; see, e.g., *Speech of Mr. [Francis] Pickens, of South Carolina . . . January 21, 1836 . . .* (Washington, 1836) and *Remarks of Mr. [John Henry] Hammond of South Carolina . . . February, 1836* (Washington, 1836).
14. JQA to CFA, Dec. 15–19, 1835.
15. *Register of Debates*, 24th Cong., 1st Sess. (1835–36), 2042ff (Dec. 23, 1835).
16. JQA, *Memoirs*, 9, pp. 266–74 (Jan. 4–18, 1836).
17. JQA, *Memoirs*, 9, pp. 274–76 (Jan. 18, 1836).
18. *Register of Debates*, 24th Cong., 1st Sess. (1835–36), 2482f (Feb. 4, 1836).
19. For Pinckney's troubles, see Charles Wiltse, *John C. Calhoun: Nullifier, 1829–1839* (Indianapolis, 1949), pp. 283f; William W. Freehling, *Prelude to Civil War* (New York, 1965), pp. 350f.
20. *Register of Debates*, 24th Cong., 1st Sess. (1835–36), 2491–2502 (Feb. 8, 1836); JQA to Solomon Lincoln, April 4, 1836.
21. For Polk's motives, see James K. Polk to William R. Rucker, Feb. 22, 1836, in *Correspondence of James K. Polk* (ed. by Herbert Weaver and Kermit L. Hall; Nashville, 1975), 3, pp. 511–13. Cf. Charles G. Sellers, Jr., *James K. Polk: Jacksonian, 1795–1843* (Princeton, 1957), pp. 313–14, and Wiltse, *John C. Calhoun: Nullifier*, pp. 284–85.
22. *Register of Debates*, 24th Cong., 1st Sess. (1835–36), 3758ff (May 18–26, 1836); Appendix, 104–14.
23. For Adams's account of these events, see his letters to Rufus Freeman, May 18, 1836; S. Sampson, May 21, 1836; Benjamin Lundy, June 2, 1836; Robert Walsh, June 3, 1836; Nicholas Biddle, June 10, 1836; Dr. George Parkman, June 22, 1836; Friend E. P. Atlee, June 25, 1836. See also JQA, *Memoirs*, 9, pp. 282–88 (May 18–26, 1836).
24. JQA, *Memoirs*, 12, p. 171 (Feb. 19, 1845).
25. *House Journal*, 24th Cong., 1st Sess. (1835–36), 876; *Register of Debates*, 24th Cong., 1st Sess. (1835–36), 4027ff (May 25, 1836).
26. *Register of Debates*, 24th Cong., 1st Sess. (1835–36), 4046ff (May 25, 1836).
27. JQA, *Memoirs* 9, pp. 287, 298 (May 25, June 19, 1836). For further references, see Charles Francis Adams, ed., "John Quincy Adams

and Martial Law," *Massachusetts Historical Society, Proceedings*, Second Series, 15 (Jan. 1902): 436–78.

28. This paragraph is based on career-line studies of the eight Congressmen.

29. Computed from *House Journal*, 24th Cong., 1st Sess. (1835–36), 881, 884. I used several sources in determining party affiliation, but mainly the *Biographical Directory of the American Congress, 1774–1971* (Washington, 1971).

30. See, e.g., John M. McFaul, "Expediency vs. Morality: Jacksonian Politics and Slavery," *Journal of American History* 62 (June 1975): 24–39.

31. Gilbert Hobbs Barnes, *Antislavery Impulse, 1830–1844* (Washington, 1933), chaps. 11–18.

32. Alexander, *Sectional Stress and Party Strength, passim.*

33. *Congressional Globe*, 24th Cong., 1st Sess. (1835–36), 406 (May 26, 1836).

34. J. Franklin Jameson, ed., "Correspondence of John C. Calhoun," *American Historical Association, Annual Report . . . 1899* (Washington, 1900), 2, p. 513.

35. For the Democratic treatment of antislavery politics, cf. Richard H. Brown, "The Missouri Crisis, Slavery, and the Politics of Jacksonianism," *South Atlantic Quarterly* 65 (Winter 1966): 55–72; McFaul, "Expediency vs. Morality," pp. 24–39; Joel H. Silbey, " 'There are Other Questions Beside That of Slavery Merely': The Democratic Party and Antislavery Politics," in Alan M. Kraut, ed., *Crusaders and Compromisers* (Westport, Conn., 1983), pp. 143–75; and Leonard L. Richards, "The Jacksonians and Slavery," in Lewis Perry and Michael Fellman, eds., *Antislavery Reconsidered* (Baton Rouge, 1979), pp. 99–118.

36. American Anti-Slavery Society, *Fifth Annual Report*, p. 48.

37. JQA to Messrs. Greene and Osborne, Editors of the Quincy Patriot, Jan. 14, 1837; JQA to Allen Danforth, Editor of the Plymouth Old Colony Memorial, Jan. 17, 1837; JQA to the Petitioners for the Abolition of Slavery and the Slave Trade in the District of Columbia, from the Twelfth Congressional District . . ., Jan. 21, 1837; *Letters from John Quincy Adams to His Constituents of the Twelfth Congressional District in Massachusetts* (Boston, 1837).

38. *Register of Debates*, 24th Cong., 2d Sess. (1836–37), 1314–39.

39. *Congressional Globe*, 25th Cong., 3d Sess. (1838–39), 23–25, 27–28 (Dec. 11–12, 1838).

40. *Congressional Globe*, 26th Cong., 1st Sess. (1839–40), 150–51 (Jan. 28, 1840).

41. *Congressional Globe*, 26th Cong., 1st Sess. (1839–40), Appendix, 746.

42. The following account is taken primarily from *Register of Debates*, 24th Cong., 2d Sess. (1836–37), 1586–1735 (Feb. 6–11, 1837); *Congressional Globe*, 24th Cong., 2d Sess. (1836–37), 162–75 (Feb. 6–11, 1837); *Letters from JQA to His Constituents*.

43. "Dirk Hatteraik" to JQA, Feb. 10, 1837; A Friend of Slavery to JQA, Jan. 25, 1839; Peter Longate to JQA, Feb. 27, 1839; Richard Rinald to JQA, Jan. 15, Feb. 15, 1839.

44. JQA, *Memoirs*, 10, p. 41 (Nov. 12, 1838).

45. Most books on dueling, unfortunately, are just a collection of anecdotes. To understand more about dueling's rise and fall, I assembled data from the *Dictionary of American Biography*, which reports 46 duels. For brief comments on the significance of dueling, see Daniel J. Boorstin, *The Americans: The National Experience* (New York, 1965), pp. 206–12; John Hope Franklin, *The Militant South* (Cambridge, Mass., 1956), pp. 44–62; and David Brion Davis, *Homicide in American Fiction* (Ithaca, N.Y., 1957), pp. 266–83.

46. Samuel F. Bemis, "The Scuffle in the Rotunda," *Massachusetts Historical Society, Proceedings* 71 (1953–57): 156–66; *Report on the Assault by Russell Jarvis*, House Report No. 260, 20th Cong., 1st Sess. (1827–28); LCA "To My Children," May 1, 1828; LCA to CFA, Dec. 16, 27, 1835.

47. *National Intelligencer*, Feb. 16, 1838.

48. Accounts of the duel are found in Don Seitz, *Famous American Duels* (New York, 1929), pp. 251–83; Myra L. Spaulding, "Dueling in the District of Columbia," *Records of the Columbia Historical Society* 29–30 (1928), pp. 186–210.

49. JQA, *Memoirs*, 9, pp. 500, 502–3 (March 4, 6, 7, 1838); JQA to CFA, March 19, 1838; JQA to Dr. Benjamin Waterhouse, May 14, 1838.

50. JQA, *Memoirs*, 10, pp. 50–52, 56 (Dec. 4–6, 1838); *Congressional Globe*, 25th Cong., 3d Sess. (1838–39), p. 18 (Dec. 6, 1838).

51. JQA, *Memoirs*, 10, pp. 68–69 (Dec. 19, 1838); Spaulding, "Dueling in the District of Columbia," pp. 197–201.

52. Of the various accounts of the *Amistad* affair, I have relied mostly on John W. Barber, *A History of the Amistad Captives . . .* (New Haven, 1840); William A. Owens, *Slave Mutiny: The Revolt of the Schooner Amistad* (New York, 1953); Mary Cable, *Black Odyssey: The Case of the Slave Ship Amistad* (New York, 1971); Bertram Wyatt-Brown, *Lewis Tappan and the Evangelical War Against Slavery* (New York, 1971), chap. 11.

53. Richards, *"Gentlemen of Property and Standing"*, pp. 38–39.

54. Lewis Tappan to Roger Sherman Baldwin, Oct. 16, 28, 1840, Baldwin Papers, Yale University Library.

55. JQA, *Memoirs*, 10, p. 358 (Oct. 27, 1840); JQA, Diary, Nov. 11, 1840

56. Quotes taken from Charles Warren, *The Supreme Court in United States History* (2 vols.; Boston, 1937), pp. 72–76.

57. 15 *Peters U.S. Reports*, pp. 587–98.

58. Anonymous to JQA, Dumfries, Virginia, June 15, 1841.

59. *Address of Hon. John Quincy Adams to His Constituents, April 3, 1845* (n.p., 1845).

60. *Congressional Globe*, 29th Cong., 2d Sess. (1846–47), Appendix, 437–38 (March 2, 1847).

61. Theodore Dwight Weld to Angelina G. Weld and Sarah Grimké, Jan. 9, 23, 1842, *Letters to Theodore Dwight Weld, Angelina Grimké Weld, and Sarah Grimké* (ed. by Gilbert H. Barnes and Dwight L. Dumond; 2 vols., Washington, 1934), 2, pp. 889, 899.

62. *Congressional Globe*, 27th Cong., 2d Sess. (1841–42), 157–67, 207; JQA, *Memoirs*, 11, pp. 67–70, 98–99 (Jan. 21, 22, 24, Feb. 23, 1842).

63. Theodore Dwight Weld to Angelina G. Weld and Sarah Grimké, Jan. 23, 1842, *Weld-Grimké Letters*, 2, p. 899–900.

64. My principal sources for the Haverhill petition controversy are the *Congressional Globe*, 27th Cong., 2d Sess. (1841–42), 168–215, and the *National Intelligencer*, Feb. 11–15, 1842. Also useful is Lynn H. Parsons, "Censuring Old Man Eloquent: Foreign Policy and Disunion, 1842," *Capitol Studies* 3 (Fall 1975): 89–106, which includes a breakdown of the vote, although somewhat misinterpreted, and makes much of the attempt to remove Adams as chairman of Foreign Affairs. For Adams's account, see *Memoirs*, 11, pp. 70–88 (Jan. 24–Feb. 7, 1842).

65. Theodore Dwight Weld to Angelina G. Weld and Sarah Grimké, Jan. 23, 1842, *Weld-Grimké Letters*, 2, p. 901.

66. Based on analysis of the roll call, *Congressional Globe*, 27th Cong., 2d Sess. (1841–42), pp. 200–1 (Feb. 2, 1842).

67. JQA, *Memoirs*, 11, pp. 87–88 (Feb. 7, 1842); *Congressional Globe*, 27th Cong., 2d Sess. (1841–42), 214–15 (Feb. 7, 1842).

68. Bemis, *JQA and the Union*, p. 435.

69. Theodore Dwight Weld to Angelina G. Weld, Feb. 6, 1842, *Weld-Grimké Letters*, 2, p. 913; Joshua Giddings to his daughter, Feb. 8, 1842, Joshua R. Giddings, George W. Julian Manuscripts, Library of Congress.

70. William Lloyd Garrison to Richard D. Webb, Feb. 27, 1842, Garrison Papers, Boston Public Library; *Liberator*, Feb. 25–May 13, 1842; Aileen S. Kraditor, *Means and Ends in American Abolitionism: Garrison*

and His Critics on Strategy and Tactics, 1834–1850 (New York, 1967), pp. 196–217.

71. Quotations from Craig Simpson, "A Good Southerner: The Life of Henry A. Wise of Virginia" (Unpublished Ms.), pp. 98–99. Professor Simpson was good enough to send me a copy of his manuscript. See also Barton H. Wise, *The Life of Henry A. Wise of Virginia, 1806–1876* (New York, 1899), pp. 61f.

72. JQA, *Memoirs*, 11, p. 419 (Nov. 2, 1843).

73. JQA to William H. Seward and Christopher Morgan, Aug. 8, 1844.

Chapter VI. Texas and "The Great Slave Power Conspiracy"

1. Cf. Albert K. Weinberg, *Manifest Destiny* (Baltimore, 1935); Richard W. Van Alstyne, *The Rising American Empire* (New York, 1960); Frederick Merk, *Manifest Destiny and Mission in American History* (New York, 1963); Silbey, *The Shrine of Party*; Alexander, *Sectional Stress and Party Strength*; Major L. Wilson, "The Concept of Time and the Political Dialogue in the United States, 1828–1848," *American Quarterly* 19 (Winter 1967): 619–44.

2. *Democratic Review* 21 (Oct. 1847): 291–92; 17 (July–Aug. 1845): 5–10; 17 (Oct. 1845): 243–48.

3. JQA to Peter B. Porter, April 4, 1830. See also JQA to Alexander H. Everett, April 15, 1830; JQA to Samuel Southard, June 6, 1830; JQA to William Plumer, Sept. 24, 1830; JQA to Joseph Story, Oct. 23, 1830.

4. Of the literature on Indian removal, I have relied heavily on two excellent studies, although I have interpreted the facts somewhat differently: Parsons, "A Perpetual Harrow Upon My Feelings"; and Ronald N. Satz, *American Indian Policy in the Jacksonian Era* (Lincoln, Neb., 1975).

5. Satz, *American Indian Policy*, pp. 20–31; Dale Van Every, *The Disinherited: The Lost Birthright of the American Indian* (New York, 1966), pp. 113–32; Parsons, "A Perpetual Harrow Upon My Feelings," pp. 361–62.

6. *Register of Debates*, 22d Cong., 1st Sess. (1831–32), 2010–36 (March 10, 1832); JQA, *Memoirs*, 8, pp. 486–87, 491–92 (March 4, 5, 11, 1832).

7. Two Massachusetts Democrats, Nathaniel Borden and William Parmenter, also voted funds. JQA, *Memoirs*, 10, pp. 9–10 (June 4, 1838).

8. JQA, *Memoirs*, 10, pp. 233, 256, 333–35 (March 9, April 11, June

14–15, 1840); *Congressional Globe*, 26th Cong., 1st Sess. (1839–40), pp. 252, 527–28 (March 9, July 14, 1840).

9. M. M. Brooks to JQA, April 23, 1838; JQA to Robert Walsh, June 3, 1836, JQA to Dr. George Parkman, June 22, 1836, quoted in CFA, *Emancipation under Martial Law*, pp. 86ff.

10. JQA to Sherlock S. Gregory, Nov. 23, 1837; Big Kettle et al. to JQA, June 16, 1841; John Ross to JQA, June 16, 1841; JQA to John Ross, June 29, 1841; Seneca White et al. to JQA, June 18, 1841. See also JQA, *Memoirs*, 9, pp. 460, 536 (Dec. 29, 1837; May 21, 1838), 10, pp. 491–92 (June 30, 1841).

11. *Congressional Globe*, 24th Cong., 1st Sess. (1835–36), Appendix, 474–82 (June 27, 1836).

12. JQA, *Memoirs*, 9, pp. 299, 548 (June 27, 1836; May 30, 1838); JQA to Sherlock S. Gregory, Nov. 23, 1837.

13. JQA, *Memoirs*, 10, pp. 491–92 (June 30, 1841).

14. Of the vast literature on the acquisition of Texas, I have relied especially on Justin H. Smith, *The Annexation of Texas* (Corrected Edition; New York, 1941); and David M. Pletcher, *The Diplomacy of Annexation: Texas, Oregon and the Mexican War* (Columbia, Mo., 1973).

15. John M. Botts, *The Great Rebellion: Its Secret History, Rise, Progress, and Disastrous Failure* (New York, 1866), pp. 95–96.

16. "In Re That Aggressive Slavocracy," *Mississippi Valley Historical Review* 8 (June–Sept. 1921): 13–80.

17. CFA, *What Makes Slavery a Question of National Concern?* (Boston, 1855), p. 27; George W. Julian, "The Strength and Weakness of the Slave Power . . . ," in *Speeches on Political Questions* (New York, 1872), pp. 70ff.

18. JQA to Benjamin Lundy, May 12, 1836.

19. Marquis James, *The Raven* (New York, 1962), pp. 114–60; Richard R. Stenberg, "The Texas Schemes of Jackson and Houston, 1829–1836," *Southwestern Social Science Quarterly* 15 (Dec. 1934): 229–50; Llerena Friend, *Sam Houston: The Great Designer* (Austin, Texas, 1954), pp. 37–55.

20. Richard R. Stenberg, "Jackson's Neches Claim, 1829–1836," *Southwestern Historical Quarterly* 39 (April 1936): 255–74; James W. Silver, *Edmund Pendleton Gaines: Frontier General* (Baton Rouge, 1949), pp. 192ff.

21. JQA to Benjamin Lundy, May 12, 1836; JQA to CFA, May 24, 1836; JQA to William E. Channing, Nov. 21, 1837.

22. Lundy to JQA, May 9, 1836; JQA to Lundy, May 12, 1836.

23. For details on Lundy's life, see Merton L. Dillon, *Benjamin Lundy*

and the Struggle for Negro Freedom (Urbana, Ill., 1966); *The Life, Travels and Opinions of Benjamin Lundy . . . Compiled under the Direction and in Behalf of His Children* (Philadelphia, 1847). Most of the information Lundy provided Adams appeared later in pamphlet form. See [Benjamin Lundy], *The Origin and True Cause of the Texas Revolution . . .* (Philadelphia, 1836); [Benjamin Lundy], *The War in Texas . . .* (Second Edition, Revised and Enlarged; Philadelphia, 1837). See also Lundy to JQA, May 14, 19, 23–25, 1836.

24. *Ibid.* For more on the role of Texas speculators, see William M. Gouge, *The Fiscal History of Texas* (Philadelphia, 1852); Edward T. Miller, *A Financial History of Texas* (Austin, Texas, 1916); Elgin Williams, *The Animating Pursuits of Speculation: Land Traffic in the Annexation of Texas* (New York, 1949); Holman Hamilton, "Texas Bonds and Northern Profits," *Mississippi Valley Historical Review* 43 (March 1957): 579–94.

25. Lundy to JQA, May 14, 1836.

26. Lundy to JQA, May 14–June 27, 1836.

27. *Register of Debates*, 24th Cong., 1st Sess. (1835–36), 4046ff (May 25, 1836).

28. JQA, *Memoirs*, 9, p. 298 (June 19, 1836); CFA, "JQA and Martial Law," pp. 436–78.

29. Silver, *Gaines*, pp. 192–215; Stenberg, "Jackson's Neches Claim," pp. 255–74; Stenberg, "Texas Schemes of Jackson and Houston," pp. 229–50.

30. James C. Curtis, *The Fox at Bay: Martin Van Buren and the Presidency, 1837–1841* (Lexington, Ky., 1970), chap. 8.

31. *Congressional Globe*, 25th Cong., 1st Sess. (1837), 21, 24–26 (Sept. 12, 13, 1837).

32. American Anti-Slavery Society, *Fifth Annual Report*, p. 48. The actual petitions from the Plymouth district are in Record Group 233, Legislative Records, National Archives. The occupations of the male signers can be dug out of town directories, town tax assessment rolls, and town histories. Tracing females is usually much more difficult. For good examples of what has been done with antislavery petitions from other communities, see John B. Jentz, "The Antislavery Constituency in Jacksonian New York City," *Civil War History* 27 (June 1981): 101–22; and Edward Magdol, "A Window on the Abolitionist Constituency: Antislavery Petitions, 1836–1839," in Alan M. Kraut, ed., *Crusaders and Compromisers* (Westport, Conn., 1983), pp. 45–70.

33. *Speech of John Quincy Adams . . . Relating to the Annexation of Texas* (Washington, 1838).

34. Smith, *Annexation of Texas*, p. 65; Curtis, *The Fox at Bay*, chap. 8.
35. For further details on the British "plot," see Richards, *"Gentlemen of Property and Standing,"* pp. 65–71.
36. *National Intelligencer*, April 15, 1842.
37. *Niles' Register* 62 (April 30, 1842): 134–39.
38. JQA, *Memoirs*, 11, p. 252 (Sept. 17, 1842); Boston *Atlas*, Sept. 17, 1842; Hampshire *Gazette*, Nov. 1, 1842; *Address of John Quincy Adams to His Constituents . . . at Braintree, September 17th, 1842* (Boston, 1842).
39. Thomas W. Gilmer to the Editors of the *Baltimore Republican and Argus*, Jan. 10, 1843, as reprinted in *The Madisonian*, Jan. 23, 1843; Andrew Jackson to Aaron V. Brown, Feb. 9, 12, 1843, *Correspondence of Andrew Jackson* (ed. by John S. Bassett; 7 vols., Washington, 1926–35), 6, pp. 201–2.
40. *Congressional Globe*, 27th Cong., 3d Sess. (1842–43), *passim*; *National Intelligencer*, Feb.–May, 1843; Sydney Nathans, *Daniel Webster and Jacksonian Democracy* (Baltimore, 1973), pp. 206ff; *Writings and Speeches of Webster*, 16, pp. 418–26.
41. JQA, *Memoirs*, 11, p. 313 (Feb. 9, 1843); JQA and others, "Address to the People of the Free States of the Union, Washington, March 3, 1843," in *National Intelligencer*, May 4, 20, 1843; *Niles' Register* 64 (May 13, 1843): 173, 64 (July 1, 1843): 284.
42. "Address of the Hon. J. Q. Adams to His Constituents . . . at Dedham, October 21, 1843," Boston *Atlas*, Oct. 26, 1843.
43. Abel Upshur to William S. Murray, Aug. 8, 1843, *Senate Documents*, 28th Cong., 1st Sess. (1843–44), No. 341, 18–19; Duff Green to John Tyler, July 3, 1843, and Duff Green to Abel Upshur, Aug. 3, 1843, both in Frederick Merk, *Slavery and the Annexation of Texas* (New York, 1972), pp. 221–22, 224–25; Claude H. Hall, *Abel Parker Upshur, Conservative Virginian, 1790–1844* (Madison, Wisc., 1963), pp. 198–99.
44. JQA, "Lecture on the Chinese War," *Chinese Repository* 11 (1842): 274ff; JQA, *Memoirs*, 11, p. 31 (Dec. 3, 1841); JQA to Richard Rush, December 30, 1842.
45. JQA, *Memoirs*, 11, p. 380 (May 31, 1843).
46. Betty Fladeland, *Men and Brothers: Anglo-American Antislavery Cooperation* (Urbana, Ill., 1972), pp. 303–15; Wyatt-Brown, *Lewis Tappan*, pp. 248–64.
47. *The Madisonian*, Sept. 23–Nov. 7, 1843. See also the editorial in *The Madisonian*, Nov. 27, 1843.
48. For Whig support, see *National Intelligencer*, May 4, 20, 1843; *Niles' Register* 64 (May 13, July 1, 1843): 173–75, 284–85, and *passim*. For

the worries of the Van Burenites, see Van Buren Papers, Nov. 1843–April 1844, Library of Congress.

49. *The Madisonian*, Jan. 23, 1843, Sept. 1843–March 1844; Boston *Post*, Sept. 1843–March 1844.

50. Edwin A. Miles, " 'Fifty-four Forty or Fight'—An American Political Legend," *Mississippi Valley Historical Review* 44 (Sept. 1957): 291–309. See also Frederick Merk, *The Oregon Question* (Cambridge, Mass., 1967), pp. 189–233, 364–94, 409.

51. Cf. Frederick Merk, *Fruits of Propaganda in the Tyler Administration* (Cambridge, Mass., 1971), pp. 95–128; H. Donaldson Jordan, "A Politician of Expansion, Robert J. Walker," *Mississippi Valley Historical Review* 19 (Dec. 1932): 362–81; James C. N. Paul, *Rift in the Democracy* (Philadelphia, 1951), pp. 97–101; James P. Shenton, *Robert John Walker* (New York, 1961).

52. *Letter of Mr. Walker of Mississippi Relative to the Annexation of Texas* . . . (Washington, 1844). The letter was reprinted many times; for one facsimile see Merk, *Fruits of Propaganda*, pp. 221–52.

53. The most pertinent newspaper articles were reprinted in pamphlet form; see, e.g., *Thoughts of the Proposed Annexation of Texas to the United States* (New York, 1844) and *Texas and the Massachusetts Resolutions* (Boston, 1844).

54. Calhoun to Pakenham, April 18, 1844, *Senate Documents*, 28th Cong., 1st Sess. (1843–44), No. 341: 50–53.

55. Cf. Smith, *Annexation of Texas*, pp. 194–220; Wiltse, *Calhoun: Sectionalist*, 167–71; Jesse S. Reeves, *American Diplomacy under Tyler and Polk* (Baltimore, 1907), pp. 138–61; Charles G. Sellers, *James K. Polk: Continentalist, 1843–1846* (Princeton, 1966), pp. 58–60; Pletcher, *Diplomacy of Annexation*, pp. 143–44; Merk, *Slavery and Texas*, pp. 57–69; Sydney Nathans, "The Southern Connection: Slaveholders and Antebellum Expansion," *Reviews in American History* 1 (Sept. 1973): 389–95.

56. JQA, *Memoirs*, 12, pp. 21ff (May 1, 4, 1844).

57. JQA, *Memoirs*, 12, p. 34 (May 29, 1844).

58. JQA, *Memoirs*, 12, pp. 49–50 (June 10, 1844).

Chapter VII. Mr. Polk's War

1. JQA to Daniel L. Miller, Jr., Oct. 29, 1844.

2. Boston *Atlas*, Oct. 8–9.

3. Boston *Atlas*, Oct. 8–9, Nov. 2, 1844; *Niles' Register* 67 (Oct. 19,

Nov. 16, 1844): 105–11, 171; JQA, *Memoirs*, 12, pp. 84–102 (Oct. 7–Nov. 7, 1844).

4. For the closeness of the election, see Charles Sellers, "The Equilibrium Cycle in Two-Party Politics," *Public Opinion Quarterly* 29 (Spring 1965): 16–38; Sellers, *Polk: Continentalist*, chap. 4.

5. JQA, *Memoirs*, 12, p. 103 (Nov. 8, 1844). Adams undoubtedly knew that this was an oversimplification. See, e.g., *Memoirs*, 12, p. 110 (Nov. 25, 1844).

6. Quoted in Sellers, *Polk: Continentalist*, p. 159.

7. Computed from roll call votes, *Congressional Globe*, 24th Cong., 1st Sess. (1835–36), 406; 24th Cong., 2d Sess. (1836–37), 106; 25th Cong., 2d Sess. (1837–38), 47; 25th Cong., 3d Sess. (1838–39), 28; 26th Cong., 1st Sess. (1839–40), 150–51. Analysis of 1840 vote also found in *Emancipator*, Feb. 6, 27, 1840.

8. *Congressional Globe*, 28th Cong., 1st Sess. (1843–44), 317, Appendix, 28–32 (Feb. 24, Jan. 5, 1844).

9. *Congressional Globe*, 28th Cong., 1st Sess. (1843–44), Appendix, 113–14 (Jan. 11, 1844).

10. *Congressional Globe*, 28th Cong., 1st Sess. (1843–44), 173, Appendix, 40–41 (Feb. 1, Jan. 6, 1844); William Ernest Smith, *The Francis Preston Blair Family in Politics* (2 vols.; New York, 1933), 1, p. 157.

11. *Congressional Globe*, 28th Cong., 1st Sess. (1843–44), *passim*.

12. For the anger and fear of Van Buren's followers, see correspondence between May 1844 and Jan. 1845, in the Martin Van Buren Papers, Library of Congress; the Gideon Welles Papers, Library of Congress; and the Wright-Butler Letters, New York Public Library. See also Allan Nevins, ed., *The Diary of Philip Hone, 1828–1851* (New York, 1936), p. 722, and Paul, *Rift in the Democracy*.

13. Computed from vote, *Congressional Globe*, 28th Cong., 2d Sess. (1844–45), 7 (Dec. 3, 1844).

14. JQA, *Memoirs*, 12, pp. 115–16 (Dec. 3, 1844).

15. Richardson, *Messages and Papers of the Presidents*, 5, pp. 2196–97.

16. Sellers, *Polk: Continentalist*, p. 168; John N. Niles to Gideon Welles, Dec. 9, 1844, Jan. 24, 31, Feb. 9, 1845, Gideon Welles Papers; John Fairfield to Van Buren, Dec. 21, 1844, Van Buren Papers, Thomas Hart Benton, *Thirty Years View* (2 vols.; New York, 1856), 2, pp. 623, 631.

17. Sarah Elizabeth Lewis, "Digest of Congressional Action on the Annexation of Texas, December, 1844, to March, 1845," *Southwestern Historical Quarterly* 50 (Oct. 1946): 251–68; *Congressional Globe*, 28th Cong., 2d Sess. (1844–45), *passim*.

18. JQA, *Memoirs*, 12, pp. 118, 128, 133 (Dec. 9, 20, 28, 1844).
19. *Congressional Globe*, 28th Cong., 2d Sess. (1844–45), *passim*; Robert C. Winthrop, *Addresses and Speeches* (4 vols.; Boston, 1852–56), 1, pp. 441ff.
20. JQA, *Memoirs*, 12, pp. 150–53 (Jan. 22, 24, 25, 1845); *Congressional Globe*, 28th Cong., 2d Sess. (1844–45), 188–90.
21. Sellers, *Polk: Continentalist*, pp. 172–73; *House Journal*, 28th Cong., 2d Sess. (1844–45), p. 205 (Jan. 13, 1845).
22. Computed from vote, *Congressional Globe*, 28th Cong., 2d Sess. (1844–45), pp. 193–94.
23. *Massachusetts Acts and Resolves, 1845* (Boston, 1845), pp. 598–99; Boston, *Atlas*, Jan.–Feb. 1845.
24. JQA, *Memoirs*, 12, p. 171 (Feb. 19, 1845).
25. Sellers, *Polk: Continentalist*, pp. 185–208; Jordan, "A Politician of Expansion," pp. 362–81; Richard R. Stenberg, "President Polk and the Annexation of Texas," *Southwestern Social Science Quarterly* 14 (March 1934): 333–56; *Congressional Globe*, 28th Cong., 2d Sess. (1844–45), 359–62 (Feb. 27, 1845); JQA, *Memoirs*, 12, p. 173 (Feb. 27, 28, 1845).
26. Joshua Giddings and other antislavery Whigs made the same prediction.
27. *Congressional Globe*, 28th Cong., 2d Sess. (1844–45), pp. 197–209 (Jan. 27, 29, 1845).
28. *Congressional Globe*, 29th Cong., 1st Sess. (1845–46), pp. 338–42 (Feb. 9, 1846).
29. Richardson, *Messages and Papers of the Presidents*, 5, p. 2231. For background material on the Oregon question, I have followed Merk, *The Oregon Question*; Miles, " 'Fifty-four Forty or Fight'—An American Political Legend"; and Sellers, *Polk: Continentalist*, chap. 9 and *passim*.
30. JQA, *Memoirs*, 12, p. 221 (Dec. 14, 1845).
31. *Congressional Globe*, 29th Cong., 1st Sess. (1845–46), 338–42 (Feb. 9, 1846).
32. *Hansard's Parliamentary Debates*, Vol. 84, pp. 1321–22 (March 20, 1846); JQA, *Memoirs*, 12, p. 259 (April 27, 1846); Joseph Sturge to JQA, March 3, 1846; JQA to Sturge, April 1846.
33. For a brief summary of what historians have said about the Mexican war, see Seymour V. Connor, "Changing Interpretations of the Mexican War, 1846–1970," *Journal of the West* 11 (April 1972): 361–66.
34. Of the many fine books on Polk and the Mexican war, several are indispensable: Justin H. Smith, *The War with Mexico* (2 vols.; New

York, 1919); Frederick Merk, *Manifest Destiny and Mission in American History; A Reinterpretation* (New York, 1963); Sellers, *Polk: Continentalist*; Pletcher, *The Diplomacy of Annexation*.

35. The best discussion of the disputed Texas border is Frederick Merk, *The Monroe Doctrine and American Expansionism, 1843–1846* (New York, 1966), pp. 133–60.

36. For opposition to the war generally, see John H. Schroeder, *Mr. Polk's War: American Opposition and Dissent, 1846–1848* (Madison, Wisc., 1973); Schroeder, "Dilemmas of Dissent: Congress and Opposition to the Mexican War," *Capitol Studies*, 3 (Fall 1975): 15–30; Frederick Merk, "Dissent in the Mexican War," in Samuel Eliot Morison, Frederick Merk, and Frank Freidel, *Dissent in Three American Wars* (Cambridge, Mass., 1970), pp. 33–63; Ernest McPherson Lander, Jr., *Reluctant Imperialists: Calhoun, the South Carolinians, and the Mexican War* (Baton Rouge, 1980).

37. Don E. Fehrenbacher, *Chicago Giant: A Biography of "Long John" Wentworth* (Madison, Wisc., 1957), p. 64.

38. For both sides of the Slave Power controversy, compare Boston *Whig* with Boston *Atlas* and Boston *Advertiser*, May–Sept. 1846. For Whig opinion nationally, see *National Intelligencer*, which reprinted articles from Whig newspapers across the country.

39. See, e.g., Thomas Corwin to William Greene, June 16, 1846, in Belle L. Hamlin, ed., "Selections from the William Green Papers, I," *Quarterly Publication of the Historical and Philosophical Society of Ohio* 13 (1918): 3–38; Daniel Webster to Fletcher Webster, May 20, 1846, *Writings and Speeches of Webster*, 16, p. 450; Robert Winthrop to Edward Everett, June 7, 1846, Edward Everett Papers, Massachusetts Historical Society.

40. *Washington Union*, May 9, 1846; *Diary of James K. Polk during His Presidency, 1845–1849* (ed. by Milo Milton Quaife; 4 vols., Chicago, 1910), 1, pp. 384ff; *Congressional Globe*, 29th Cong., 1st Sess. (1845–46), 782–83, 791–804 (May 11, 12, 1846).

41. *Congressional Globe*, 29th Cong., 1st Sess. (1845–46), 791–95 (May 11, 1846).

42. Joshua Giddings to Joseph Addison Giddings, May 13, 1846, Giddings Papers, Ohio State Archaelogical and Historical Society (microfilm); Robert C. Winthrop to John Clifford, May 15, 1846, Winthrop Papers, Massachusetts Historical Society.

43. Joshua Giddings to Laura Waters Giddings, June 7, 1846, Giddings-Julian Mss., Library of Congress.

44. JQA, *Memoirs*, 12, pp. 268–69 (July 13, 15, 1846).

45. Joshua Giddings to Laura Waters Giddings, June 7, 1846, Giddings-

Julian Mss.; JQA to Charles Sumner, Aug. 29, 1846; JQA to CFA, June 29, 1846.

46. Boston *Whig*, June–July 1846; JQA to CFA, June 29, 1846.
47. For a thorough study of the controversy, see Frank Otto Gatell, "Palfrey's Vote, the Conscience Whigs, and the Election of Speaker Winthrop," *New England Quarterly* 31 (June 1958): 218–31.
48. Cf. Boston *Atlas* and Boston *Whig*, Dec. 1847–Jan. 1848; CFA to LCA, Dec. 22, 1847; LCA to CFA, Dec. 15, 1847; JQA to CFA, Dec. 20, 1847.
49. *Congressional Globe*, 29th Cong., 1st Sess. (1845–46), Appendix, 949; 29th Cong., 2d Sess. (1846–47), 143ff (Jan. 8, 1847) and *passim*.
50. JQA to Albert Gallatin, Dec. 26, 1847; *Congressional Globe*, 29th Cong., 2d Sess. (1846–47), 35–36 (Dec. 15, 1846), Appendix, 47ff (Dec. 15, 1846).
51. *Congressional Globe*, 30th Cong., 1st Sess. (1847–48), 93–94 (Jan. 3, 1848).
52. Martin Van Buren to George Bancroft, Feb. 15, 1845, in "Van Buren-Bancroft Correspondence, 1830–1845," *Massachusetts Historical Society Proceedings* 42 (June 1909): 439.
53. For Polk's troubles with northern Democrats, see especially Sellers, *Polk: Continentalist, passim*; Chaplain W. Morrison, *Democratic Politics and Sectionalism: The Wilmot Proviso Controversy* (Chapel Hill, 1967), pp. 3–20.
54. On the proviso generally, see Charles Buxton Going, *David Wilmot, Free Soiler* (New York, 1924); Morrison, *Democratic Politics and Sectionalism*; Eric Foner, "The Wilmot Proviso Revisited," *Journal of American History* 61 (Sept. 1969): 262–79.
55. JQA, *Memoirs*, 12, p. 270 (Aug. 10, 1846); *Congressional Globe*, 29th Cong., 1st Sess. (1845–46), 1210–17 (Aug. 8, 1846); Morrison, *Democratic Politics and Sectionalism*, pp. 17–19, 181 n.80.
56. *Congressional Globe*, 29th Cong., 1st Sess. (1845–46), 1215–16 (Aug. 8, 1846).
57. *House Journal*, 29th Cong., 1st Sess. (1845–46), 1285–87 (Aug. 8, 1846); *Congressional Globe*, 29th Cong., 1st Sess. (1845–46), 1217–18 (Aug. 8, 1846); 29th Cong., 2d Sess. (1846–47), 425, 573 (Feb. 15, March 3, 1847).
58. *Congressional Globe*, 29th Cong., 1st Sess. (1845–46), 1217–18 (Aug. 8, 1846).
59. *Congressional Globe*, 29th Cong., 1st Sess. (1845–46), 1220–23 (Aug. 10, 1846); A. R. McIlwain to Joshua Giddings, Aug. 9, 1846; J. M. Root to Giddings, Aug. 28, 1846, Giddings Papers; CFA, *Diary*, Aug. 15, 1846; Boston *Whig*, Aug. 16, 1846.

60. JQA, *Memoirs*, 12, p. 271 (Aug. 16, 1846).

61. JQA, *Memoirs*, 12, pp. 272–78 (Aug. 16–Nov. 12, 1846).

62. Statement, Dr. George Parkman, Dec. 24, 1846, Adams Papers; Last Will and Testament of John Quincy Adams, Jan. 18, 1847, Probate Office, Norfolk County, Massachusetts; JQA, *Memoirs*, 12, pp. 279–81 (March 14, 1847).

63. JQA, *Memoirs*, 12, pp. 279–81 (March 14, 1847); CFA, Diary, Feb. 7–12, 1847.

64. *Congressional Globe*, 29th Cong., 2d Sess. (1846–47), 166, 178–88 (Jan. 11, 14, 1847), Appendix, 116–19, 244–47.

65. *Congressional Globe*, 29th Cong., 2d Sess. (1846–47), 303, 352ff (Feb. 1, 8, 1847), Appendix, 314ff (Feb. 8, 1847); Going, *Wilmot*, pp. 159–81.

66. *Congressional Globe*, 29th Cong., 2d Sess. (1846–47), Appendix, 437–38 (March 2, 1847).

67. Computed from vote, *Congressional Globe*, 29th Cong., 2d Sess. (1846–47), 424–25 (Feb. 15, 1847); and *House Journal*, 29th Cong., 2d Sess. (1846–47), 349–50 (Feb. 15, 1847).

68. *Congressional Globe*, 29th Cong., 2d Sess. (1846–47), 453–55 (Feb. 19, 1847).

69. Computed from vote, *Congressional Globe*, 29th Cong., 2d Sess. (1846–47), 573 (March 3, 1847).

70. For full accounts of the various Whig divisions in Massachusetts, see David Donald, *Charles Sumner and the Coming of the Civil War* (New York, 1960), pp. 156ff, and Duberman, *Charles Francis Adams*, pp. 123ff.

71. Henry Adams, *Education of Henry Adams* (Boston, 1918), p. 14; JQA to Edward Everett, Sept. 10, 1847.

72. JQA to Julius Rockwell, June 13, 1847; JQA to Brantz Mayer, July 6, 1847.

73. LCA to Abigail B. Adams, Feb. 3, 1848; LCA to Harriet Boyd, Feb. 23, 1848.

74. JQA, Diary, Dec. 1, 1847; JQA to the Committee of the Washington Monument, Dec. 10, 1847.

75. *Congressional Globe*, 30th Cong., 1st Sess. (1847–48), 56–57 (Dec. 20, 1847).

76. *Congressional Globe*, 30th Cong., 1st Sess. (1847–48), 167–68 (Jan. 13, 1848).

77. Boston *Emancipator and Republican*, March 1, 1848; *National Intelligencer*, Feb. 22, 1848; Joshua Giddings to his daughter, Feb. 22, 1848, Giddings Papers; J. G. Palfrey to CFA, Feb. 21, 1848; LCA to Harriet Boyd, Feb. 23, 1848.

78. For a sample of these orations, etc., see *Token of a Nation's Sorrow: Addresses in the Congress of the United States and Funeral Solemnities on the Death of John Quincy Adams* . . . (Washington, 1848); *National Intelligencer*, Feb. 24–26, 1848; *The Adams Memorial* (Boston, 1848); *Testimonials of Respect to the Memory of John Quincy Adams by the Legislature of Massachusetts* (Boston, 1848).
79. *Louisville Journal*, March 11, 1848.

Index